WILD WEST SHOW!

WILD WEST SHOW!

EDITED BY THOMAS W. KNOWLES AND JOE R. LANSDALE

WINGS BOOKS

New York / Avenel, New Jersey

"The First Western," copyright © 1986 by Brian Garfield.

"The Western Pulps," copyright © 1986, 1990 by Bill Pronzini.

"The Cisco Kid" by Jose Salinas and Rod Reed. Copyright 1952,
King Features Syndicate, Inc. World rights reserved.

"Tumbleweeds" by T.K. Ryan. Copyright 1971, The Register
and Tribune Syndicate.

Cartoons copyright 1994 by Scott McKellar.

Excerpt from "The Pretender," a "Gunsmoke" script by
Calvin Clements, Jr., copyright © 1965 by CBS, Inc.

"The Attack on the Supply Wagon," by Frank McCarthy,
© Frank McCarthy. Reproduced with the permission of
The Greenwich Workshop, Inc. For information on Frank
McCarthy's limited edition fine art prints call 1-800-243-4246.

Published by Wings Books, distributed by
Random House Value Publishing, Inc.,
40 Engelhard Avenue, Avenel, New Jersey, 07001.

RANDOM HOUSE
New York • Toronto • London • Sydney • Auckland

Printed and bound in the United States of America

Library of Congress Cataloging-in-Publication Data

Wild West show! : how the myth of the West was made, from Buffalo
Bill to Lonesome Dove / contributions by Will Henry...[et al.] ; edited
by Thomas W. Knowles and Joe R. Lansdale.
      p. cm.
    Includes bibliographical references.
    ISBN 0-517-10186-6
    1. Popular culture—West (U.S.) 2. Popular culture—United
States. 3. West (U.S.)—In literature. 4. West (U.S.) in art. 5. West
(U.S.) in mass media. I. Henry, Will, 1912- . II. Knowles, Thomas W.
III. Lansdale, Joe R., 1951- .
F596.W5795 1994
978—dc20   94-13089
                                                CIP

Consulting Editors: Marc Jaffe and Vivienne Jaffe

Design Consultant: David Larkin

Designed by Catharyn Tivy

8 7 6 5 4 3 2 1

DEDICATION

Wild West Show! is dedicated to the memory of Ray Puechner, who brought up the idea in the first place; to Colonel William F. "Buffalo Bill" Cody for starting it all; to our absent and sorely missed *compadres,* Frank Fugate, Will Henry, Chad Oliver, and Thomas Thompson; to the chroniclers, journalists, photographers, and artists who recorded the West for those of us who came after; and to the composers, writers, directors, stunt players, and actors who have made the myth of the Wild West an integral part of our lives.

ACKNOWLEDGEMENTS

The editors would like to thank all the writers and artists whose contributions made this book possible. Special thanks go to Max Evans, Dale L. Walker, Loren D. Estleman, Abraham Hoffman, Joe Fenton, Cena Golder Richeson and Robert Conley for their hard work on short notice; to Scott McCullar and John Hagner for their artwork; to Troyce Wilson and Stephanie Perkins for their timely production assistance; and to Marc and Vivienne Jaffe and Catharyn Tivy, for riding this trail with us into the sunset.

   Our thanks also go to those who assisted us in gathering illustrations and permissions: Ellen Brown and Kent Keeth of the Baylor Texas Collection; Tom Burkes and Dan Agler of the Texas Ranger Hall of Fame Museum; Robert Easton of the Max Brand Estate; Bernice Green of CBS New York; Elizabeth Holmes of the Buffalo Bill Historical Center; Diane Keller of the Montana Historical Society; Susan Kowalczyk and Robyn G. Peterson of the Rockwell Museum, Corning, New York; Kevin McDonald of CBS California; Larry Mensching of the Joslyn Art Institute; Tim Novak of the Texas A&M University Memorial Student Center Forsythe Galleries; Beverly Rosenthal of the C.M. Russell Museum; Misty Skedgell of Turner/TNT; and Steve Smith of the Texas A&M University Special Collections and Archives.

CONTRIBUTORS

KRISTINE FREDRIKSSON

JEFF BANKS

BRIAN GARFIELD

BILL O'NEAL

ROBERT J. CONLEY

ED GORMAN

BILL PRONZINI

BILL CRIDER

JOHN HAGNER

JAMES M. REASONER

SCOTT CUPP

WILL HENRY

CENA GOLDER RICHESON

MARYLOIS DUNN

ABRAHAM HOFFMAN

LEE SCHULTZ

LOREN D. ESTLEMAN

THOMAS W. KNOWLES

THOMAS THOMPSON

MAX EVANS

SCOTT McCULLAR

DALE L. WALKER

JOE FENTON

L. J. WASHBURN

MICHAEL MARTIN MURPHEY

WILLIAM F. NOLAN

Photo and Illustration Credits: Archive Photos; Baylor Texas Collection; Blower Historical Collection, Edmonton, Canada; CBS Inc.; Chicago Tribune Syndicate; Denver Public Library; Max Evans; Dr. Kristine Fredriksson; Fox Broadcasting Company; Abraham Hoffman; Joslyn Art Institute, Omaha, Nebraska; Kansas State Historical Society, Topeka, Kansas; King Features Syndicate; Marvel Comics, Inc.; Michael Moorcock; Montana Historical Society; Scott McCullar; National Buffalo Association; National Stuntman Hall of Fame, Monument Valley, Utah; News America Syndicate and News Group; Paramount; the Professional Rodeo Cowboy Association; The Rockwell Museum, Corning, New York; Rodeo Historical Society, National Cowboy Hall of Fame; Lee Schultz; Texas A&M University Development Foundation, Bill and Irma Runyon Art Collections; Texas A&M University Special Collection and Archives; Texas Special Collections Film Archives; Texas Ranger Hall of Fame Museum; Turner Entertainment Co.; Turner/TNT Originals; United Media Syndicates; Warner Bros.; Wells Fargo History Room, San Francisco.

TABLE OF CONTENTS

THE OVERTURE

THE INTRODUCTION

ACT I: ROPE, GUNSMOKE, AND GREASEPAINT

From the apocryphal life of William F. Cody, the man who created the mythical West and introduced it to the rest of the world, to the rodeo as the Wild West's spiritual successor. How the modern rodeo cowboys and cowgirls are the survivors of the Old West.

ACT II: DREAMERS, LIARS, AND POETS

The chroniclers of the West—the journalists, dime novelists, poets, and pulp writers from Ned Buntline to Owen Wister to Max Brand.

ACT III: THE ARTISTS' EYE

The Wild West from the perspective of men who dared to capture it on sketch pad and canvas.

ACT IV: LARGER THAN LIFE

The Western film, with its cast of thousands—from Tom Mix and the Duke to Randolph Scott and Clint Eastwood, from John Ford to Sam Peckinpah, with sidekicks and scumbags, villains and stuntmen.

PLAYERS ON HORSEBACK

SUNSET WARRIORS

THE DIRECTORS

ACT V: THE BIG SKY ON THE SMALL SCREEN

Sizing down the Western myth for the stage, the theatre of the mind and the 12-inch screen, with musical accompaniment and TV trivia.

THE CURTAIN

THE OVERTURE

WELCOME TO THE WILD WEST SHOW!

STEP RIGHT ON UP AND RIGHT ON IN, BUCKAROOS! GET YOUR TICKETS here for our One and Only Great Wild West Show and Congress of Rough Riders! Concession stand to your right, sideshows to your left.

All the West's our stage, the arena of our dreams! Grab your ticket, hold on tight and dream along with us. Breathe in the smell of sawdust and ink and gunsmoke and popcorn, listen well for the thunder of hooves and the clatter of typewriter keys and the bloodcurdling war-cries of a thousand extras. Look over here, where William S. Hart and the cowboy stars of yesteryear flicker to life in hand-cranked film projected onto a silver screen. Look over there, where James Arness survives the thousandth rerun of his high-noon gunfight in the opening credits of *Gunsmoke...*

...so welcome to *Wild West Show!,* where the glorious myth of the Wild West lives on in radio static, technicolor and television, purple prose and comic strips and classic novels, where it's blazed in living color on canvas and frozen into curves in bronze, and where it fills arenas dusty with the bravery of rodeo clowns and trick-riding cowgirls...

...and as our band strikes up Aaron Copland's *Rodeo,* out rides our ringmaster on a prancing, cloud-white stallion. It's the great Buffalo Bill, Col. William F. Cody himself. And who better, for it was ol' Bill that gave the legend life, wove it together like a magic Navajo blanket out of tall tales and rumors and half-truths and grand dreams. He leads off our mythmakers' parade, a glittering stream of writers and performers, artists and fakers, directors and stuntmen, bull riders and sidekicks, composers and poets and...

...in rides our own New Congress of Rough Writers, the authors and artists who've joined us here to follow the trail blazed by Owen Wister and Charlie Russell. They've had a long rehearsal for this performance, for *Wild West Show!* has been eight years in the making. Most of them are members of the Western Writers of America, but all of them are fine storytellers, and they're here because they believe in the dream of the Wild West.

You'll see that we've capitalized the word "West" and "Wild West" in this book except when it describes a simple direction. We've made "West!" our war cry, our Rebel yell, because it helps us to remember when the West was Wild—in our dreams, anyway. *Wild West Show!* is our illustrated scrapbook of those dreams, filled with bits of humor, childhood memories, and secret pleasures from the imaginary West as we experienced it in print and film, music, television and art.

Because we're storytellers at heart, we've concentrated on what our favorite stories meant to each of us. Each of our Rough Riders has translated a part of the myth of the Wild West through his or her own unique perspective. *Wild West Show!* is a book of little dreams and big ones, of what the West might have been, never was, and perhaps should have been. For us, it's a journey of the heart.

So ride along with us as...

...Cody's horse rears, the Colonel gives a shout and waves his *sombrero,* and the curtain goes up. The Deadwood stage thunders by, chased hell-bent for leather by a horde of shooting, screaming bandits, *federales,* Comancheros and Apaches on the warpath. The Ringo Kid aims his ring-levered Winchester and shoots from the roof of the stage while the Virginian and Trampas duke it out over the dead driver's reins. Over in the bandbox, Sitting Bull stands calm, chatting with Annie Oakley, Sam Peckinpah and Tonto—they've seen it all before—while Remington and Russell slap paint to canvas and Ned Buntline scribbles furiously.

It looks bad for our heroes, but look there! It's the Cisco Kid, Hopalong and the Lone Ranger riding to the rescue. A trumpet call floats in from the West—it's John Ford and Sergeant Rutledge charging in at the head of a troop of U.S. Cavalry. The Man With No Name smirks at Ringo's girl, Dallas, then lights his cigar and leans out the stage window to take careful aim. Destry leaps onto the harness tree, trying to turn the maddened horses of the stage team from their headlong rush toward the canyon rim...

...so hold on tight, *amigos,* and enjoy the ride.

Thomas W. Knowles and Joe R. Lansdale

THE WILD WEST SHOW!

A SONG BY MICHAEL MARTIN MURPHEY

War paint and feathers, ice cream and cake,
 Navajo blankets and a poisonous snake;
Sharpshootin' cowgirls on a trick-ridin' spree;
 it's the goldangdest thing that you ever did see!

Now all the kids holler (Hear them holler!),
 up on the bandstand,
For an autographed picture
 of a medicine man,
When out comes Annie Oakley
 with a pearl-handled gun,
Says she can outshoot anyone!

It's the Wild West Show!
 It's the Wild West Show!
It's the Wild West Show!
 Everybody goes to the Wild West Show!

Cowboys and Injuns must be makin' the news;
 they're printing up a lot of tickets;
Lord, they're writing reviews;
 they're makin' a million dollars,
But there ain't no one to blame;
 critics don't like it,
So everyone came!

They say in the paper
 that they've got Sittin' Bull;
Now there just ain't no tellin' what

that Injun might pull!
So save up your money, boys,
 and maybe we'll go;
Maybe we'll stay for the whole damn show!

It's the Wild West Show!
 It's the Wild West Show!
It's the Wild West Show!
 There's gotta be buffalo at the Wild West Show!

Buffalo Bill comes out
 in real buckskin pants;
He rides a white stallion
 while the Indians dance;
And they whoop and they holler
 and they shoot off their blanks;
Ol' Bill must be laughin' all the way to the bank!

You know it's just like the real thing,
 although it ain't real (It ain't real!).
Them Indians play dead, it's part of the deal;
 the spectators ogle, and they stare goggle-eyed.
God, it's sweeping the country,
 it's gone nation-wide!

It's the Wild West Show! (Everybody go!)
 It's the Wild West Show!
It's the Wild West Show!
 Genuine buffalo at the Wild West Show!

The Introduction

Dreams West

by Thomas W. Knowles

THE WILD WEST IS BACK. IT'S BACK IN BOOKS, ON TELEVISION, AND IN the movies. Some of us always knew it would return because the legendary, mythical West is just too strong to remain dormant forever. Just what is this legendary power, the "myth of the Wild West," and where does it get its strength?

A myth is a symbol so powerful that it takes on a cultural significance beyond its historical roots. When we think of the "Wild West," the first image that comes to mind is that of the American cowboy. He's the ultimate rugged individualist, a man who lives on his own terms; he's the Code of the West personified.

And even though that symbolic cowboy bears little resemblance to the real-life cowboys of the historical West, he's no less important. Myths grow out of the need for heroes, and human beings are too imperfect to fit that need until time and wishful thinking transform them into symbols.

The 19th-century "settling of the West" implanted in the American psyche a tradition of heroic myth complete with figures equal to the gods and heroes of ancient Greece. A century later, that mythology still pervades American attitudes and popular culture, from firearms to cowboy clothing, from folklore to literature, from pop art to fine art, music, literature and film. In a sense, it defines America.

The most pervasive and prolific modern purveyor of mythic Western images is the motion picture, and it's from the filmed Western that we get most of the standard myths: the strong, silent cowboy hero, the renegade Indian and the noble redman, the rancher's spirited daughter and the gold-hearted dance hall girl, the loyal but foolish sidekick and the cowardly but clever bad guy, the high-noon gunfight and the barroom brawl. Those are only some of the standards, and they're historically inaccurate, stereotypical and contradictory even in films.

So how do we define the mythological West without slipping into movie stereotypes?

If we begin with the mythological West as we know it in the present day, we might as well try to define the edges of a dream. Academics and sociologists study it, critics and historians dissect and dismiss it, and Hollywood uses and abuses it, but their definitions are arbitrary and based on their own needs. As writers and artists, we translate our daydreams about the West into words and images, and in doing so, we shape the myth to fit our individual visions. Despite our best efforts, we almost always fall short of the mark. Perhaps that's because the mythical Wild West lies in the undiscovered country of the imagination, and so defies any human boundaries.

Our other choice is to begin with the past and move forward. What's the relationship between myth and reality?

As a writer and a Texan, I find that my own perception of the mythical Wild West has its roots in what survives of the Old West. For me, the West begins at Fort Worth and stretches forever into the sunset, and when I drive the winding Hill Country roads or cross the sea of grass that's the Texas Panhandle, I can still catch a glimpse of the Old West's shadow from the corner of my eye. Like Palo Duro Canyon, it lies in ambush just over the next hill, ready to magically appear and blind me with a blaze of colors brilliant in the setting sun.

I grew up with the remainders and reminders of the Old West: a chunk of limestone I overturned to expose a "1540 A.D." carefully scratched there by a passing *conquistador;* a translucent white stone arrow point washed out of a river sandbar; an ancient Indian burial site I found in a river cave; a local rancher's carefully preserved buffalo herd. My grandparents told me stories about *their* grandparents, who settled in Texas in the early days of the Republic—tales of Texas Rangers, bandits, Mexican lions, floods and Comanches. Those stories led me to research the history of the conflict between my Native American and European ancestors, and so sparked my interest in the West and its legends.

If our imaginary vision of the Wild West is rooted in the history of the Old West, when did the reality begin to evolve into legend?

The mythology of the Wild West bloomed even as the first of the European immigrants turned toward the sunrise; not only that, it was a driving force in the exploration and settlement of the West. The legends sprang from true stories, exaggerations and tall tales. Just as the stories I heard as a child drew me to the history of the West, so did

Tom Knowles in his official Roy Rogers outfit, December 1957

OPPOSITE:
Detail from *A Bucking Bronco,* Frederic Remington (*Harper's New Monthly*) (courtesy of Texas A&M University Special Collections and Archives)

> "Persons attempting to find a motive in this narrative will be prosecuted; persons attempting to find a moral in it will be banished; persons attempting to find a plot in it will be shot."
>
> MARK TWAIN "BY ORDER OF THE AUTHOR" (1884) PREFACE TO *THE ADVENTURES OF HUCKLEBERRY FINN*

stories about the West influence its history.

It was the Indian legend of *Cibola,* "the Seven Cities of Gold," that lured Francisco Vasquez de Coronado and his *conquistadores* out into that vast unknown, the staked plains of the Southwest. The great explorers, Lewis and Clark, brought back journals filled with new information, drawings and maps of a world unknown, full of promise and wonder for a new and expanding nation. The fur trappers and the mountain men came in from the wild as changed men, living narratives of the adventure of the West, and the stories they told at river ports and trading towns sparked the imaginations of the adventurous and the greedy alike.

That's where the legend is born and the myth starts — with stories. The stories of the wild and the unknown, truth and fiction, are what drew people to the West then, and they're what draw us to it now.

The stories grew simultaneously with the history of the West, and what began with a simple oral tradition evolved into a complex and diverse mythology in many forms — music, literature, art and theatre.

Music

The cowboy songs and popular songs of the Old West made up a powerful component of the West's imaginary landscape, and that's because they told stories in words and music that came from the heart. Even most modern Americans know at least the tunes and some of the words to "The Streets of Laredo," "The Yellow Rose of Texas," "Oh, Bury Me Not On the Lone Prairie" and other cowboy songs. We've heard their influence on 20th century popular culture, from singing cowboys to Country-Western music, in Frankie Laine's vocals and Dimitri Tiomkin's expressive motion picture scores.

But the West's influence on music extends beyond popular culture. When the great Czech classical composer, Antonin Dvorak, came to America in the 1880s, he found the rhythms of cowboy songs, Negro spirituals and Indian chants so evocative of the country he saw that he incorporated them in his "New World Symphony." The tradition of the cowboy song shaped Aaron Copland's folk ballets (*Billy the Kid* and *Rodeo*) and musicals like *Oklahoma!* and *Annie Get Your Gun.*

Literature

Journalists and explorers transformed the oral tradition of storytelling into print by recording and publishing accounts of their experiences. Francis Parkman's travelogue about his journey to the West in the 1840s, *The Overland Trail,* is an accurate description of a frontier on the verge of giving way to onrushing civilization. He wrote with the exuberance of a young man who experienced the extraordinary, who was befriended by and lived with the Dakota Sioux, then at the height of their culture. Parkman observed limitless herds of buffalo, trapped with the mountain men, weathered thunderstorms in the sacred Black Hills, suffered through incredible hardships, and found beauty in the wilderness. He colored his travelogue with the power of his vision of the West and the personal effect it had on him.

Other writers followed Parkman—Andy Adams, Jack London, Bret Harte, Mark Twain, Robert Service—as they wrote from their experiences in the West. Some of them wrote verse, some fiction, but they only wrote about the West after they had lived in it.

The tradition of the tall tale found its way into journalism and print, from the rather fictionalized memoirs of real-life Westerner William F. Cody to the outrageous pulp fables of Ned Buntline, the man who made Billy the Kid a media hero. "Penny dreadfuls" and dime novels deserved their name, but they were the forerunners of a new genre of literature, the Western novel. It's not that great a leap from tall tale and pulp heroes to the archetypical stoic Westerner of the novels. He endures, from the strong and silent hero of Owen Wister's landmark *The Virginian,* to the mysterious gunfighter of Jack Schaefer's *Shane,* to the incredibly self-contained former Texas Ranger, Captain Woodrow Call of Larry Mc-Murtry's *Lonesome Dove.*

Setting Traps for Beaver, **Alfred Jacob Miller (courtesy of InterNorth Art Foundation/Joslyn Art Museum, Omaha, NE)**

Art

Some stories work best as images. The artists who went West with the explorers and mountain men found a land of such indescribable grandeur that they were forced to exaggerate what they saw in order to transfer its emotional impact on canvas. They stretched the West's "big sky" to enormous, Olympian lengths, painted the endless prairies in vivid colors and sensual shapes, and sharpened the angles of the land into jumbled crags that reached almost to heaven and canyon abysses that reached almost to hell.

George Catlin painted the Indians with rapid brush strokes, but somehow his brush captured their souls on canvas even as his open nature earned him their friendship. Karl Bodmer spread out the mighty rivers until they became oceans, and he saw majestic castles in the rocky cliffs that lined them. Though he depicted the Indians with a draftsman's eye for accuracy, he bestowed upon them the magnificent patina of a fairy tale, and they became bold knights of the plains dressed in brilliant robes of feathers and furs and skins. Alfred Jacob Miller's robust mountain men embodied the spirit of adventure and wild freedom.

Later artists like Albert Bierstadt and Thomas Moran also drew on the West's visceral appeal in order to express its true nature, and their idealized landscapes reflected and reinforced the already growing influence of the Western myth. Even as Charles Russell and Frederic Remington emphasized realism and accuracy in their illustrations, paintings, and sculptures, they used those visual images to convey narratives of their characters' lives. They each picked their favorite inhabitants of the Wild West (Indians for Russell, cavalrymen and cowboys for Remington) and imbued them with heroic, mythical qualities. They reached beyond literal details to find the essence of the West; they mixed it like an extra pigment in their paints to capture the action, the drama and the *feel* of the West.

Wild West Shows

Even before the last days of the frontier, Buffalo Bill Cody almost single-handedly created the legendary Wild West and introduced it to the world with his Wild West and Congress of Rough Riders. As a true hero of the historical West, Cody crossed the border between reality and myth. He and his many imitators and inheritors—Pawnee Bill, the Miller Brothers' 101 Ranch, Tom Mix and others—began to sell the legend of the Wild West as show business.

Cody's first step out into the arena was the moment when the legends, the tall tales and the stories took on the aspect of heroic mythology.

THE WILD WEST ENDURES TODAY IN CHAMPIONSHIP RODEOS, IN MODern Western novels and modern Western art, on television and in motion pictures. And so it continues, from *Cibola* to the Yukon, from Buffalo Bill to the Duke to Clint Eastwood, from Wister to Grey to McMurtry—the myth and the legend of the Wild West. It has a life of its own.

And as the journalist said at the end of *The Man Who Shot Liberty Valance,* "This is the West, sir. When the legend becomes fact, print the legend."

The legend follows.

A Chronology of the West In Art, Literature, Music and Film

1796

George Catlin is born July 26 in Wilkes-Barre, Pennsylvania.

1810

Alfred Jacob Miller is born January 10 in Baltimore, Maryland.

1823

Ned Buntline is born Edward Zane Carroll Judson in Stamford, New York.

James Fenimore Cooper publishes *The Pioneers,* the first of his "Leatherstocking Tales" starring Natty Bumppo; he follows it with *The Last of the Mohicans* (1826), *The Prairie* (1827), the *Pathfinder* (1840) and *The Deerslayer* (1841).

1830

Artist George Catlin arrives in St. Louis to preserve images of the Plains Indians before they are driven farther west under terms of the Indian Removal Act.

1833

Swiss artist Karl Edward Bodmer and German Prince Maximilian arrive at St. Louis in March, there to begin an expedition up the Missouri River.

1835

Samuel Langhorne Clemens (Mark Twain) is born November 30 in Florida, Missouri.

1836

Francis Bret Hart (Bret Harte) is born in Albany, New York, on August 25.

1837

Artist Alfred Jacob Miller joins Scots nobleman and mountain man William Drummond Stewart in St. Louis for an expedition beyond the north fork of the Platte River.

Thomas Moran is born January 12 in Bolton Lancashire, England.

1839

Alfred Jacob Miller exhibits his work at the Apollo Gallery in New York.

1842

In Nashville, Tennessee, Ned Buntline shoots Robert Porterfield and narrowly escapes death by lynching.

1844

Charles King is born on October 12 in Albany, New York.

1846

William F. Cody (Buffalo Bill) is born February 26 in Scott County, Iowa.

Francis Parkman boards the steamboat *Radnor* at St. Louis, Missouri, on April 28, and begins his trek to the Rocky Mountains. Upon his return, he publishes his experiences in *The Oregon Trail; or a Summer's Journey Out of Bounds.*

1854

Bret Harte arrives in San Francisco aboard the steamer *Brother Johnathan* on March 26.

1860

Phoebe (Annie Oakley) Moses, "Little Sure Shot," is born August 13 in Darke County, Ohio.

1861

Mark Twain and his brother, Orion Clemens, arrive in Carson City, Nevada, on August 14.

Frederic S. Remington is born October 4 in Canton, New York.

1862

In September, Mark Twain signs on as a reporter for the *Territorial Enterprise* in Virginia City, Nevada.

1863

Frank E. Butler, future sharpshooter and husband of Annie Oakley, is born in Ireland.

Mark Twain, 1864 (courtesy of History Room, Wells Fargo Bank, San Francisco, CA)

1864

Charles M. Russell is born March 19 in St. Louis, Missouri.

1867

Mark Twain's "The Celebrated Jumping Frog of Calaveras County" appears in the last issue of *The Saturday Press.*

1868

Bookseller Anton Roman convinces Bret Harte to take the editor's position for his new magazine, *Overland Monthly.* On July 1, Harte publishes his short story, "The Luck of Roaring Camp," in the first issue.

1869

Bret Harte publishes "The Outcasts of Poker Flat" in the January issue of *Overland Monthly.*

1870

Horace Greeley of the *New York Daily Tribune* is incorrectly credited with the quote, "Go West, young man!"

William S. Hart is born in Newburgh, New York, on December 6.

Jack London (courtesy of History Room, Wells Fargo Bank, San Francisco, CA)

1871

In July, artist Thomas Moran joins the Hayden Geological Survey expedition in Virginia City, Montana; they travel to the Yellowstone country.

1872

Buffalo Bill Cody and Ned Buntline open their play, *The Scouts of the Plains,* in Chicago; critics hate it, but Cody plays to a packed house.

Zane Grey is born Pearl Zane Gray in Zanesville, Ohio, on December 31.

Thomas Moran's illustrations of the Yellowstone region for Dr. Ferdinand V. Hayden's article in the February issue of *Scribner's* have a profound influence in the decision to preserve the area as a national park. Moran travels to the Yosemite, Utah and Arizona, and the Hayden Survey names a peak in the Grand Teton Range in his honor.

George Catlin dies on December 23.

1873

Buffalo Bill Cody gets Wild Bill Hickok to join the cast of *The Scouts of the Plains;* Hickok leaves after five months.

1874

Robert Service is born in Preston, Lancashire, England, on January 16.

Mark Twain publishes *Roughing It,*

about his experiences in the West.

Alfred Jacob Miller dies in Baltimore, Maryland.

1875

David Wark Griffith is born in Kentucky on January 23.

1876

Jack London is born in San Francisco on January 12.

According to his own controversial autobiography, Buffalo Bill Cody meets Cheyenne Chief Yellow Hand in single combat near the Little Big Horn on July 17, kills him and scalps him.

Jack McCall shoots and kills Wild Bill Hickok on August 2 in Deadwood, Dakota Territory.

Thomas Moran's large oil painting of *The Chasm of the Colorado* is purchased by the U.S. Congress.

1878

Edward L. Wheeler introduces Hurricane Nell to the pulps in *Bob Woolf, the Border Ruffian; or, The Girl Dead-Shot.*

1879

William F. Cody publishes his autobiography, *The Life of Buffalo Bill.*

Thomas Moran accompanies a military expedition to the Grand Teton Range.

1880

Tom Mix is born on January 6 in Mix Run, Pennsylvania.

Annie Oakley marries Frank Butler and he becomes her manager.

Charlie Russell goes west to herd sheep in the Judith Basin in Montana.

1882

Oscar Wilde tours the West.

While in America as director of the National Conservatory of New York, Czech composer Antonin Dvorak is inspired by folk music and the countryside he observes in his travels in the New World to compose his "Te Deum" (Op. 103) and his "New World Symphony" in E Minor (Op. 95).

Bronco Billy Anderson is born Max Aronson in Little Rock, Arkansas.

The J. B. Lippincott Company of Philadelphia publishes Capt. Charles King's novel, *The Colonel's Daughter; Or, Winning His Spurs.*

Andy Adams begins ten years as a working cowboy by signing on for a

A turn of the century poster featuring the cowgirls of Pawnee Bill's (Gordon Lillie's) Historic Wild West (courtesy of Denver Public Library)

trail drive with the Circle Dot outfit of South Texas.

1883

The first public rodeo to offer prizes for events is held in Pecos, Texas, on July 4.

Buffalo Bill Cody forms his Wild West and Congress of Rough Riders and takes the show on the road.

1884

Showman Alvaren Allen persuades Sioux medicine chief Sitting Bull to tour 15 American cities, billing him incorrectly as "The Slayer of Custer."

Frederic Remington marries Eva Clayton in Gloversville, New York, on October 1.

1885

Sitting Bull joins Buffalo Bill Cody's Wild West for a year; the former scout and the former medicine chief become close friends.

Annie Oakley and Frank Butler join Buffalo Bill Cody's Wild West, and Annie quickly becomes Cody's star performer; Sitting Bull tags her with the sobriquet, "Little Sure Shot."

1886

Frederic Remington publishes a full-page illustration in the January 6 issue of *Harper's Weekly,* thus beginning his long career as an illustrator and correspondent for the magazine.

Ned Buntline dies at Stamford, New York.

1887

Buffalo Bill Cody's Wild West travels to London for Queen Victoria's Golden Jubilee.

Charlie Russell draws, "Waiting for a Chinook," to illustrate the devastation done by the winter of 1886-87 to the cattle herds in Montana.

1888

The first rodeo to charge admission as well as awarding prizes to the winners is held at Prescott, Arizona Territory, on July 4.

1890

General Nelson Miles sends Buffalo

Bill Cody to the Standing Rock Reservation in South Dakota, hoping he can persuade Sitting Bull not to get involved in the troubles caused by the Ghost Dance; the reservation officials block Cody; Indian police shoot and kill Sitting Bull on December 15; his trained show horse, a present from Cody, bows at the sound of the shots.

1891

Tim McCoy is born in Saginaw, Michigan, on April 10.

Buck Jones is born Charles Frederick Gebhard in Vincennes, Indiana, on December 12.

1892

Frederick Faust (Max Brand) is born in Seattle, Washington.

Edward "Hoot" Gibson is born in Tekamah, Nebraska, on August 6.

1893

Frederic Remington's first major one-man show is a critical and financial success in New York.

1895

In February, essayist William Cowper Brann publishes the first issue of his *Iconoclast* magazine (motto—"It Strikes to Kill!) in Waco, Texas.

Ken Maynard is born in Vevay, Indiana, on July 21.

1896

Bret Harte collects his work into the 20-volume work, *The Writings of Bret Harte.*

Enos Edward "Yakima" Canutt is born November 29 in Colfax, Washington.

1897

Jack London departs San Francisco for the Yukon on the steamship *Umatilla* on July 25 and arrives in Juneau on August 2; his first short story to appear in a magazine is published in the September issue of *The Owl.*

1898

Iconoclast publisher William Cowper Brann is fatally wounded in a gunfight with Tom E. Davis in Waco, Texas, on April 1; he dies April 2 and is mourned with a huge, elaborate funer-

al procession.

1900

On a canoeing trip on the Lackawaxen River in August, Zane Grey meets Lina Roth, whom he later marries.

Aaron Copland is born in Brooklyn (Billy the Kid's birthplace) on November 14.

Detail from "End of the Fight," Frederic Remington (Harper's New Monthly) *(courtesy of Texas A&M University Special Collections and Archives)*

1901

Gary Cooper is born in Montana as Frank James Cooper.

Rancher's daughter Prairie Rose Henderson competes as a bronc rider in the Cheyenne Frontier Days rodeo.

1902

Owen Wister publishes his landmark Western novel, *The Virginian.*

Bret Harte dies in England on May 5.

1903

Edwin S. Porter and Thomas A. Edison film the seminal silent Western, *The Great Train Robbery,* near Dover, New Jersey; Bronco Billy Anderson plays a small part.

The Macmillan Co. publishes Jack

London's novel, *The Call of the Wild.*

Randolph Scott is born in Orange, Virginia.

1904

The Macmillan Co. publishes Jack London's novel, *The Sea Wolf.*

Bronco Billy Anderson moves from acting at Edison studios to directing at Vitagraph.

1905

The Macmillan Co. publishes Jack London's novel, *White Fang.*

Tom Mix joins the Miller Brothers' 101 Ranch Wild West Show in Oklahoma.

1906

Zane Grey publishes his first commercial novel, *The Spirit of the Border.*

John Huston is born in Nevada, Missouri, on August 5.

1907

John Wayne, "the Duke," is born Marion Robert Morrison May 26 in Winterset, Iowa.

Gene Autry is born in Tioga, Texas.

Clarence Edward Mulford's Hopalong Cassidy stories are published in a single volume, *Bar-20,* by Doubleday.

Producer William Selig and director Francis Boggs set up shop in Los Angeles; they quickly turn out a number of silent Westerns, including *The Bandit King* and *The Girl from Montana.*

1908

Former bandit Al Jennings and Bill Tilghman, the lawman who captured him, form the Oklahoma Mutocene Company to produce the realistic Western film, *The Bank Robbery.*

Louis L'Amour is born Louis Dearborn LaMoore March 22 in Jamestown, North Dakota.

Bronco Billy Anderson makes the one-reeler, *Bronco Billy and the Baby,* the first version of *The Three Godfathers.*

1909

Frederic Remington dies on December 26 at the age of 48, of complications after an appendectomy.

1910

Mark Twain dies on April 10 in Redding, Connecticut.

1911

Charlie Russell's art exhibition in the Folsom Galleries in New York gain him worldwide recognition.

1912

Buffalo Bill Cody's Wild West makes its farewell tour.

D.W. Griffith produces the two-reeler Western, *The Massacre.*

1913

D.W. Griffith produces the two-reeler Western, *The Battle of Elderbush Gulch.*

1914

C.B. DeMille produces his first feature Western, *The Squaw Man,* at a rented barn near the small town of Hollywood, California; he follows it up with the first film version of *The Virginian;* both films star Dustin Farnum.

Buffalo Bill Cody films a reenactment of the Indian Wars, with a script by novelist Charles King; no prints of the film still exist.

1916

Jack London slips into a coma and dies at age forty of complications from kidney disease on November 22 at Wolf House, on his ranch near Glen Ellen, California.

1917

Buffalo Bill Cody dies January 10 and is buried on Lookout Mountain near Denver, Colorado.

The first indoor rodeo is held in Ft. Worth, Texas, at the Stockyard Coliseum.

Max Brand's first short Western, "The Adopted Son," appears in *All-Story Weekly* in October.

1918

In December, the William S. Hart Company begins filming silent pictures in the studio owned by Mack Sennett on the Famous Players-Lasky (Paramount Studios) lot.

1919

Jay Silverheels is born on the Six Nations Indian Reserve in Ontario, Canada.

Max Brand publishes first major pulp novel, *The Untamed.*

1924

Audie Murphy is born in Hunt County, Texas, on June 20.

1925

William S. Hart stars in his final epic Western, *Tumbleweeds.*

1926

Thomas Moran dies August 25 at age ninety.

In October, Charles M. Russell suffers a fatal heart attack at his home in Great Falls, Montana.

Annie Oakley dies November 2, in Dayton, Ohio; Frank Butler dies November 22.

Colonel Tim McCoy releases his first motion picture, *War Paint.*

1929

As the Cisco Kid in *In Old Arizona* (Fox), the first major sound Western, Warner Baxter wins the Oscar for best actor; Raoul Walsh directs.

Gary Cooper stars as *The Virginian* in the Paramount version of Owen Wister's novel, directed by Victor Fleming; Walter Huston plays Trampas and a young Randolph Scott has a small part.

Tom Mix tours with John Ringling's Sells-Floto Circus as the show's star attraction.

1930

A young John Wayne gets his first big break in *The Big Trail,* a wagon train epic directed by Raoul Walsh for Fox.

Hoot Gibson makes *The Concentratin' Kid,* his final picture for Universal.

Clint Eastwood is born in San Francisco, California, on May 30

1931

Cimarron, directed by Wesley Ruggles for RKO, wins the Oscar for best

Gary Cooper talks over good and evil with Richard Arlen in Paramount's 1929 version of The Virginian.

picture.

Stuart N. Lake publishes a biography, *Wyatt Earp, Frontier Marshal,* and in it creates the myth of the "Buntline Special."

1932

Tom Mix makes his first sound picture, Universal's *Destry Rides Again,* based on Max Brand's novel.

1933

In January, "The Lone Ranger" radio series is first broadcast from WXYZ in Detroit on the Michigan State Network.

Novelist Charles King dies at the age of eighty-eight on March 17.

1934

Gene Autry rides into the movies in the Ken Maynard Western, *In Old Santa Fe.*

Paramount hires William Boyd to play Hopalong Cassidy in the first of a series of films.

1935

RKO's *Annie Oakley* stars Barbara Stanwyck and Preston Foster.

Mascot's serial, *The Phantom Empire,* mixes the Western with lost-world science fiction and gives Gene Autry's career a big boost.

True Gang Life magazine publishes Louis L'Amour's first short story sale, "Anything for a Pal," in the October issue.

1936

Randolph Scott stars as Hawkeye in one of the best versions of *The Last of the Mohicans,* from United Artists.

1937

Buck Jones plays himself in his short-lived radio show, "Hoofbeats."

1938

Aaron Copland incorporates melodies from traditional cowboy songs ("The Streets of Laredo," "The Old Chisholm Trail," etc.) in his score for his first folk ballet, *Billy the Kid.*

1939

John Ford directs John Wayne and Claire Trevor in *Stagecoach,* the picture that pulls the Duke's career out of the B Westerns; it garners Oscar nominations for best picture, best director, and black and white cinematography, while Thomas Mitchell (the drunken doctor) wins as best supporting actor.

Zane Grey dies at age 67 in Altadena, California.

1940

Gene Autry launches his half-hour musical adventure radio show.

Tom Mix is killed in a car crash near Florence, Arizona, on October 12.

1942

On commission from the Ballet Russe de Monte Carlo, Aaron Copland composes his second folk ballet with a cowboy theme, *Rodeo,* between May and September.

Buck Jones dies on November 30 from injuries he suffered in the infamous fire at the Coconut Grove nightclub.

CBS premiers the first Western continuing series on radio, "The Adventures of Bobby Benson."

Roy Rogers begins his radio show on the Mutual Network.

1943

The Rodgers and Hammerstein musical, *Oklahoma!,* opens at the St. James Theatre in New York in March.

1944

Frederick Faust (Max Brand) is killed in action on the Italian front in May.

1946

Henry Fonda, Victor Mature and Walter Brennan star in Fox's classic black and white version of the gunfight at the O.K. Corral, *My Darling Clementine,* directed by John Ford.

William S. Hart dies at age seventy-three on June 23.

"Death Valley Days," the first of the radio Western anthologies, leaves the air.

1948

Howard Hawks directs the great trail drive epic, *Red River,* based on the Borden Chase novel; John Wayne stars as the driven rancher Thomas Dunstan in a role that should have netted him an Academy Award; Montgomery Clift makes his screen debut as Dunstan's adopted son.

John Huston directs Humphrey Bogart in *The Treasure of the Sierra Madre,* which sweeps the Oscars.

John Ford (courtesy of CBS)

1949

"The Lone Ranger" television series airs on ABC and CBS through 1957.

1950

Annie Get Your Gun made by MGM stars Betty Hutton (rather than Judy Garland, as originally planned) as Little Sure Shot and Howard Keel; the score gets an Oscar nomination.

"The Cisco Kid" television series airs in syndication and "The Gene Autry Show" airs on CBS, both through 1956.

1951

"The Tim McCoy Show" airs for one season in syndication on television; "Wild Bill Hickok" airs on NBC and CBS through 1958; "The Roy Rogers Show" airs on NBC and CBS through 1962.

1952

It's a *High Noon* best actor Oscar for Gary Cooper's performance as Marshal Will Kane, with Grace Kelly as his Quaker bride, Lloyd Bridges as his reluctant deputy and the marvelous Katy Jurado as his old flame; Fred Zinneman directs for United Artists; Dimitri Tiomkin writes the Oscar-winning musical score, Ned Washington writes the lyrics to "Do Not Forsake Me Oh My Darling," and Tex Ritter sings it (not Frankie Laine, who later recorded a cover version).

"Gunsmoke" begins its nine-year run on CBS radio.

"The Adventures of Rin-Tin-Tin" begins on television and airs on ABC and CBS through 1955.

1953

Alan Ladd stars as the mysterious and mythic *Shane* (Paramount) in a film based on the novel by Jack Schaefer; Jean Arthur co-stars as the farm wife with divided loyalties, with Van Heflin as her husband and Brandon De Wilde as the hero-worshiping farmboy, while Jack Palance plays the hired gun as menace incarnate, with Elisha Cook as his doomed victim; a young Ben Johnson stands out; the picture gets four Oscar nominations.

1954

MGM films *Seven Brides for Seven Brothers,* perhaps the best-ever Western musical, with Howard Keel, Jane Powell and Russ Tamblyn dancing and singing their way through a barn raising and a multiple kidnapping.

"Annie Oakley" airs on television on ABC through 1959.

1955

"Gunsmoke" begins its long television ride on CBS, to run through to 1975.

Gordon McCrae and Shirley Jones star in the film version of *Oklahoma,* which wins the Oscar for the best score; Gloria Grahame shines as the girl who "just cain't say no."

1956

"Red Ryder" airs through 1957 in television syndication.

John Ford directs his masterpiece about frontier vengeance, obsession and hatred based on an Alan Le May novel, *The Searchers* (Warner Brothers). John Wayne turns in perhaps his best performance as the embittered Ethan Edwards. Jeff Hunter, Natalie Wood, Vera Miles, Ward Bond, Ken Curtis and Monument Valley, Utah, co-star.

1957

Richard Boone stars as the stylish "soldier of fortune," Paladin, in "Have Gun, Will Travel" on CBS television through 1963; "Zorro" airs on ABC through 1959, "Maverick" on ABC through 1962, and "Wagon Train" on NBC and ABC through 1965.

Burt Lancaster stars as Wyatt Earp and Kirk Douglas as Doc Holliday in Paramount's *Gunfight at the O.K. Corral,* directed by John Sturges and produced by Hal B. Wallis.

1958

"Bat Masterson" airs on NBC television through 1961.

Hopalong Cassidy author Clarence Edward Mulford dies.

Robert Service dies of a heart attack in Lancieux, Brittany, on September 11.

Alan Ladd as Jack Schaefer's mysterious stranger, Shane (1953 Paramount), with Jean Arthur and Van Heflin.

1959

Director Howard Hawks makes his antithesis to *High Noon* in *Rio Bravo,* scripted by Leigh Brackett and starring John Wayne, Dean Martin, Angie Dickinson, Rick Nelson, Walter Brennan and Claude Akins.

The quintessential trail-drive drama, "Rawhide," airs on CBS television and runs through 1966; Eric Fleming plays trail boss Gil Favor and Clint Eastwood plays ramrod Rowdy Yates to music by Dimitri Tiomkin, lyrics by Ned Washington and vocals by Frankie Laine.

"Bonanza" airs on NBC television; the Cartwright clan hangs around Virgina City through 1973.

Robert Mitchum stars in *The Wonderful Country,* based on the Tom Lea novel; not only Mitchum's best Western film, but also produced by Mitchum's own company.

1960

Hollywood and director John Sturges remake Akira Kurosawa's classic *Seven Samurai* (1952) as *The Magnificent Seven,* with Yul Brynner, Steve McQueen, James Coburn, Charles Bronson, Robert Vaughn and Brad Dexter as aging gunfighters in place of Kurosawa's lost *samurai,* Eli Wallach as the bandit chieftain, and Horst Bucholz as the young farmer turned wannabe *pistolero;* Elmer Bernstein scores the theme music, which becomes an instant classic.

John Wayne produces, directs (with some help from John Ford) and stars as Davy Crockett in *The Alamo,* for which he built a complete reproduction of the mission fort and old San Antonio at Brackettville, Texas; Oscar nominations include best picture, color cinematography, sound, and best supporting actor (Chill Wills); co-stars include Richard Widmark, Laurence Harvey, Frankie Avalon, Linda Cristal and Richard Boone; Dimitri Tiomkin composes the score and conducts the orchestra.

John Huston directs Burt Lancaster, Audrey Hepburn, Audie Murphy and Lillian Gish in *The Unforgiven* (United Artists), based (like *The Searchers*) on a novel by Alan Le May.

Sam Peckinpah's series, "The West-

Ronald Reagan was U.S. Marshal in "Law and Order" (1953)

erner," airs on NBC television for one season.

1961

Though terminally ill with cancer, Gary Cooper narrates the NBC television documentary, "The Real West."

Jimmy Stewart and Richard Widmark team up in *Two Rode Together,* directed by John Ford (Ford/Columbia).

1962

Hoot Gibson dies of cancer.

John Wayne, Jimmy Stewart, Lee Marvin, Vera Miles, Edmond O'Brien, Andy Devine and Woody Strode star in John Ford's classic film-noir Western, *The Man Who Shot Liberty Valance* (Ford/Paramount).

1963

John Wayne and Maureen O'Hara battle it out in *McLintock!* (United Artists/Batjac), a comic Western version of *The Taming of the Shrew.*

1964

Clint Eastwood leaves "Rawhide" to don the poncho of the "Man With No Name" in Sergio Leone's *A Fistful of Dollars,* the first of the Italian "spaghetti Westerns," a retelling of Japanese director Akira Kurosawa's *Yojimbo* (1961).

1965

Lee Marvin wins the best actor Oscar as has-been gunfighter Kid Sheleen in *Cat Ballou,* though his drunken horse and a *Life* magazine photo deserved at least some of the credit; Nat King Cole, in his last screen appearance, sings (with Stubby Kaye) "The Ballad of Cat Ballou."

John Wayne returns from his first bout with cancer to ride with Dean Martin, Earl Holliman and Michael Anderson, Jr. as *The Sons of Katie Elder;* James Gregory and Dennis Hopper play the bad guys.

Thomas Berger publishes his revisionist novel, *Little Big Man.*

1966

Lee Marvin, Burt Lancaster, Woody Strode and Robert Ryan are *The Professionals* (Columbia), in an excellent action film made more complex by setting it during the final days of the Wild West; Jack Palance, Claudia Cardinale and Ralph Bellamy co-star.

1967

Clint Eastwood breaks out of spaghetti Westerns and back into Hollywood with *Hang 'Em High,* in which he stars and co-directs with Ted Post at the same time as he first forms his Malpaso film company.

Howard Hawks directs *El Dorado* (again scripted by Leigh Brackett), a John Wayne star vehicle from Laurel Films, basically a remake of 1959's *Rio Bravo* with new actors in the secondary roles.

Charlton Heston gives his best performance as a lonely, aging cowboy in *Will Penny,* directed by Tom Gries for Paramount.

1968

Paramount releases *Villa Rides,* written by Sam Peckinpah and Robert Towne; Yul Brynner stars in the title

Cogburn in *True Grit,* adapted from the Charles Portis novel.

Paul Newman, Robert Redford and Katharine Ross star as heroic outlaws in *Butch Cassidy and the Sundance Kid,* directed by George Roy Hill; Oscars go to William Goldman for his screenplay, Conrad Hall for cinematography, Burt Bacharach and Hal David for best score and song.

1970

Sam Peckinpah breaks his own tradition to make the gentle comic Western, *The Ballad of Cable Hogue;* Jas-

1971

Bronco Billy Anderson dies at age eighty-nine.

With some help from Roscoe Lee Brown, John Wayne trains a whole new generation of frontiersmen in *The Cowboys;* Bruce Dern does the psychopathic villain to a turn.

Robert Duvall plays a mad Jesse James to Cliff Robertson's folksy, rather heroic Cole Younger in *The Great Northfield Minnesota Raid,* which paints a sometimes humorous, sometimes grim picture of the James-Younger gang's Waterloo.

Peter Fonda takes his directorial bow and stars in *The Hired Hand,* a gritty Western that conveys a realistic feeling of the frontier; Verna Bloom is excellent as Fonda's abandoned wife; Warren Oates does well as his saddle buddy.

Audie Murphy dies in a plane crash near Roanoke, Virginia, on May 28, Memorial Day weekend.

1972

Clint Eastwood directs and stars in his homage to Sergio Leone, *High Plains Drifter,* successfully blending the supernatural with the Western.

In *Jeremiah Johnson,* Robert Redford plays a somewhat kinder, gentler version of historical mountain man Joe Johnston (the Crow Killer), backed by beautiful cinematography; Will Geer steals scenes as Bearclaw Grizzlap, Johnson's tutor in the ways of the mountains.

Steve McQueen, Robert Preston and Ben Johnson play rodeo cowboys at the end of the trail in Sam Peckinpah's modern Western, *Junior Bonner.*

1973

In the Motion Picture Country home, Ken Maynard dies of stomach cancer on March 23.

James Coburn and Kris Kristofferson star as Sam Peckinpah's *Pat Garrett and Billy the Kid* (MGM), with an appearance and music by Bob Dylan; Katy Jurado and Slim Pickens stand out in one scene played to Dylan's "Knockin' on Heaven's Door."

Members of the crew look on as Santa Anna's troops take the barricade at "The Alamo" (1960 Batjac Productions)

role, backed by Robert Mitchum and Charles Bronson.

Sergio Leone writes and directs the ultimate spaghetti Western (168 minutes of it), *Once Upon a Time in the West;* the cast includes Henry Fonda, Charles Bronson, Jason Robards, Claudia Cardinale, Woody Strode and Jack Elam.

1969

Sam Peckinpah directs *The Wild Bunch* (Warner Brothers), his bloody eulogy to the fading of the Wild West, with stars William Holden, Robert Ryan, Ernest Borgnine, Ben Johnson, Warren Oates, Edmond O'Brien, Emilio Fernandez, L. Q. Jones, Jaime Sanchez and Strother Martin.

John Wayne turns in an Oscar-winning performance as Marshal Rooster

on Robards stars in the title role, supported by Stella Stevens, David Warner, Slim Pickens and Max Evans, and with Strother Martin and L.Q. Jones at their best (or worst) as two sidewinding villains.

In *Little Big Man,* Dustin Hoffman ages from childhood to 121 to tell the story of the Sioux, Custer and the Battle of the Little Big Horn from the Indian's perspective; Chief Dan George steals the show as Old Lodge Skins.

Lee Marvin and Jack Palance look as if they'd just stepped out of a Russell or Remington painting in *Monte Walsh,* a tale of the end of the trail for the independent cowboy.

Burt Lancaster stars in *Valdez is Coming,* an excellent film version of Elmore Leonard's novel.

1974

The Rodeo Cowboys Association becomes the Professional Rodeo Cowboys Association (PRCA).

"Little House on the Prairie," a family Western based on the Laura Ingalls Wilder novels, airs on NBC television through 1983.

1975

"Gunsmoke," the longest-running television Western series, goes off the air.

1976

Clint Eastwood directs and stars in *The Outlaw Josey Wales,* based on the Forrest Carter novel; it has the look and feel of historical accuracy, and real Indians Chief Dan George and Will Sampson get to play real Indians.

John Wayne stars in *The Shootist* (De Laurentis), his last film, the story of dying gunfighter J.B. Books. It's not only an elegy for the passing of the Old West but a personal elegy for the Duke, excellently directed by Don Siegel. The cast includes Lauren Bacall, James Stewart, Harry Morgan, Richard Boone and Hugh O'Brian.

1977

In "The Life and Times of Grizzly Adams" on NBC, Dan Haggerty, Denver

Paul Newman in "Hombre" (1967 Fox)

Pyle and a bear hide out in the mountains for two seasons.

1978

ABC's "How the West Was Won" all too briefly brings James Arness (age only makes him look even more like a force of nature) back to television as mountain man Zeb McCahan.

1979

John Wayne dies on June 13.

"The Sacketts," based on the Louis L'Amour novels *The Daybreakers* and *Sackett,* premieres as a television miniseries; Sam Elliot, Tom Selleck and Jeff Osterhage star as the Sackett brothers.

1980

Steve McQueen co-stars with Linda Evans, Richard Farnsworth, Slim Pickens and Elisha Cook in *Tom Horn,* a historically realistic Western that's a few years too far ahead of Clint Eastwood's *Unforgiven* to be accepted.

Walter Hill casts brothers as brothers in *The Long Riders,* a stylish version of the James Gang's story; James and Stacey Keach play Frank and Jesse James; David, Robert and Keith Carradine play the Youngers; Randy and Dennis Quaid play the Millers.

Jay Silverheels dies.

1981

Producer William Fraker almost erases the triumph of his earlier *Monte Walsh* (1970) with the big-budget disaster of *The Legend of the Lone Ranger,* though Michael Horse stands out as Tonto.

1982

Chief Dan George dies at age eighty-two.

Three surprisingly realistic Western movies come from quirky, small-budget sources:

Barbarosa (Wittliff, Nelson, Busey/ ITC), with Willie Nelson, Gary Busey and Gilbert Roland, filmed in Texas but directed by an Australian.

Francis Ford Coppola suggests former stuntman Richard Farnsworth for the role of Bill Miner, *The Grey Fox* (Mercury Pictures/Canada), a former stage-

coach robber released from prison at the turn of the century.

In *Harry Tracy* (Guardian Trust Co./ Canada), a film made in Canada, Bruce Dern plays the title role as a calm, dignified gentleman bandit, a former member of Cassidy's Hole in the Wall Gang; Canadian folksinger Gordon Lightfoot plays the lawman who pursues him.

John Wayne as J.B. Books in "The Shootist" (1976 De Laurentis)

Sam Elliot, Tom Selleck and Jeff Osterhage team up again to play another set of brothers in a television adaptation of another L'Amour novel, *The Shadow Riders;* Katharine Ross, Ben Johnson and Geoffrey Lewis co-star.

1983

"The Yellow Rose," a modern Western with Sam Elliot, Cybill Shepherd and Chuck Connors, airs on NBC through 1984.

1984

Evan S. Connell publishes *Son of the Morning Star,* a novel about the life of George Armstrong Custer and the events leading up to the Battle of the Little Big Horn.

1985

Larry McMurtry publishes *Lonesome Dove,* which he originally planned as a screenplay with Jimmy Stewart, Henry Fonda and John Wayne in mind. The novel becomes a best-seller and does much to revive interest in the West and the Western.

Director/screenwriter Lawrence Kasdan's big-budget ensemble Western, *Silverado* (Columbia), uses almost all of the cliches of the Old Western movie, but does it with a smile and excellent scenic visuals. Though he doesn't quite resurrect the Western, Kasdan gives Kevin Costner a chance to stand out as Scott Glenn's fast-gun kid brother in a cast that includes Kevin Kline, Rosanna Arquette, Danny Glover, Brian Dennehy, Linda Hunt, John Cleese and Jeff Goldblum.

Robert Duvall and Anjelica Huston star in "Lonesome Dove" (courtesy of CBS)

Clint Eastwood plays the spectral avenger of *Pale Rider* (Malpaso).

1986

Stuntman Yakima Canutt, last of the old Gower Gulch Gang, dies May 24.

Willie Nelson stars as a preacher turned gunfighter in another Texas Western film, this one titled for his song, *The Red-Headed Stranger;* Katharine Ross and Morgan Fairchild co-star.

1987

Will Sampson dies of a heart attack.

John Huston dies at age eighty-one.

NBC airs "The Alamo: Thirteen Days to Glory," based on Lon Tinkle's classic book, and filmed at Alamo Village at Brackettville, Texas, with James Arness as Bowie, Brian Keith as Crockett, Alec Baldwin as Travis, and Raul Julia as Santa Anna.

CBS reunites James Arness and Amanda Blake for a "Gunsmoke" television movie, *Return to Dodge.*

HBO airs "The Quick and the Dead," based on the Louis L'Amour novel, with Sam Elliot, Tom Conti and Kate Capshaw.

1988

Louis L'Amour dies June 10.

Michael Blake publishes his novel, *Dances With Wolves.*

CBS airs its miniseries of "Lonesome Dove," based on the Larry McMurtry novel, starring Robert Duvall, Tommy Lee Jones, Danny Glover, Robert Urich, Rick Schroder, Anjelica Huston, Diane Lane and Frederic Forrest. It does much to revive interest in the Western film.

1989

Shades of *The Left-Handed Gun* (Paul Newman, 1958 Warner Brothers), Turner Originals remakes Gore Vidal's version of *Billy the Kid* with Val Kilmer as the Kid and Duncan Regehr as Pat Garrett.

1990

Kevin Costner directs *Dances With Wolves* (Tig/Orion)and stars as John Dunbar, the hero of the three-hour epic; it takes Oscars for best picture, cinematography, original score, sound and also best film editing; Costner takes the Oscar as best director, Michael Blake wins for best screenplay, which he adapted from his novel.

A retired Matt Dillon discovers he has a daughter in the CBS "Gunsmoke" television movie, *The Last Apache.*

1991

James Arness stars with veteran character actor Pat Hingle in the CBS "Gunsmoke" television movie, *To the Last Man.*

1992

Clint Eastwood wins Oscars as the director and the star of *Unforgiven,* his revisionist historical Western, and in doing so sets everyone in Hollywood scrambling to make Westerns; Gene Hackman also takes an Oscar for his magnificent performance as Little Bill.

20th Century Fox and Michael Mann revise James Fenimore Cooper's *The*

Last of the Mohicans, with Daniel Day-Lewis as Hawkeye (they don't call him Bumppo), Madeline Stowe as Cora, Russell Means as Chingachgook and Wes Studi as Magua.

1993

Jane Seymour stars as "Dr. Quinn, Medicine Woman," which premieres in January on CBS.

James Arness makes *The Long Ride* with James Brolin and Ali McGraw in a CBS "Gunsmoke" television movie.

CBS airs its sequel miniseries, "Return to Lonesome Dove," with John Voight and Barbara Hershey in the roles originally played by Tommy Lee Jones and Anjelica Huston; Rick Schroder returns as Newt, with a cast that includes Oliver Reed, Louis Gossett, Jr., and William Peterson.

Joseph Running Fox stars as *Geronimo,* with Nick Ramus as Mangus Coloradus in a TNT Original television film.

Walter Hill produces *Geronimo, An American Legend* for Columbia; Wes Studi plays the Apache war chief; Jason Patric, Robert Duvall and Gene Hackman play the white-eyes.

1994

TNT airs its new version of the story of O. Henry's "Robin Hood of the Old West," *The Cisco Kid,* a Turner Original movie with Jimmy Smits and Cheech Marin as Cisco and Pancho.

James Arness and Bruce Boxleitner star in a CBS "Gunsmoke" television movie, *One Man's Justice.*

Kurt Russell, Val Kilmer, Sam Elliot and Bill Paxton lead the way back to the O.K. Corral in *Tombstone* (Hollywood Pictures); Robert Mitchum does a voiceover.

Maverick shifts its particular brand of Western levity to the big screen in a Warner film directed by Richard Donner; Mel Gibson plays the title role, but original Maverick James Garner backs him up, along with Jody Foster, James Coburn and Graham Greene.

ACT I: ROPE, GUNSMOKE, AND GREASEPAINT

THE WILD WEST'S RINGMASTER: BUFFALO BILL, 1846-1917

BY LOREN D. ESTLEMAN

HIS LIFE SPANNED THE FRONTIER'S GOLDEN AGE, BOUNDED BY THE Gold Rush and *The Great Train Robbery*. He shook hands with Kit Carson and William S. Hart, scalped a Cheyenne war chief, and took tea with Queen Victoria. When he was approaching the end of a career in which he introduced Sioux braves to the Vatican and Wild Bill Hickok to Broadway, he was asked how he wished to be remembered and replied that it was as a Wyoming rancher. Christened William Frederick Cody, he was the last and most famous in a long line of frontiersmen to bear the nickname "Buffalo Bill."

It is not enough to say that Buffalo Bill is to the West what Homer is to Ilium. The ruins of Troy and the bones of Hector and Achilles were already there when the blind poet sang of them, and they remained unchanged by his death. Buffalo Bill invented the Wild West out of whole cloth and buckskin. What shape the history of the trans-Mississippi expansion might have assumed without him is impossible to feature. He blew it up, painted it with primary colors, peopled it with angels and devils, and put it under canvas and on wheels for the world to see. Three generations came to maturity cheering the rescuers of the Deadwood

This Winchester Express .50–.95 caliber model 1876 rifle is engraved "Presented to Col. W.F. Cody, "Buffalo Bill," by the members of his Wild West, London Engagement 1887." This was the occasion of the Wild West's first performance before Queen Victoria. The glass target balls are very rare survivors from the actual Wild West's stock. (courtesy of Texas Ranger Hall of Fame Museum, Waco, Texas)

Stage and pounding the bleachers for a triumphant Cody as he waved the moldy scalp and headdress of Chief Yellow Hand. Some of them later acted as midwives to the squalling infant motion-picture industry, and set down those images, first on jumpy black-and-white frames hand cranked in corner candy stores, then half a century later in blazing Technicolor on drive-in screens two stories high and a hundred feet wide. Buffalo Bill would have embraced Technicolor and Cinemascope. The only mythology in world history directly traceable to one man is Cody's own.

He had help. Legend tells us that a paunchy fortyish alcoholic drifter named Edward Zane Carroll Judson discovered the twenty-three-year-old scout snoozing under a wagon in Nebraska and pulled him from its shade into the glare of history. History itself demurs, describing a more conventional indoor meeting. No matter. The important thing is that young Will Cody fell into the clutches of Ned Buntline, the pseudonym by which Judson, the inventor of the dime novel, is popularly known. From his prolix pen came the first of thousands of blood-and-thunder fictions about his charge, laden with Indian atrocities, platonic romances, and lectures on temperance. They were the first such items ever to sell in the millions, and their popularity inspired Buntline to invite Cody to Chicago to star in a theatrical production entitled, *Scouts of the Plains*.

The play should have been a disaster. In his excitement, Cody

brought in his scout friend, Texas Jack Omohundro, but neglected to bring in the Indians he had promised Buntline. Buntline hired the theater, but put off writing the play until the weekend before rehearsals were scheduled to begin, then got drunk and threw it together in four hours in his room in the Palmer House. He cast vagrant actors as Indians, an Italian actress as a Cheyenne princess, and himself as Cale Durg, Cody's and Omohundro's fictional fellow scout. When Cody forgot his lines on opening night, Omohundro improvised, feeding Cody questions about his frontier experiences, to which Cody responded for the rest of the performance. Each act closed with the "Indians" thundering onstage to fall in a body whenever a blank shot was fired. Bound and prepared for burning at the stake at the end of the second act, Buntline attempted to prolong the suspense by launching into a tirade against the evils of rum, whereupon the audience began calling for his immediate incineration. The play was noisy and confused, and drew savage notices and record-breaking attendances throughout its run. It was the first time that gunfire had been heard on a civilized stage, the first time that an authentic American hero had been cast as himself, and it represented the personification of the florid and incarnadine prose of the dime press. *Scouts of the Plains* earned as much as *East Lynne* did during the latter's American tour.

When legal problems forced Buntline to pull out of the road production, Cody replaced him with his old friend James Butler Hickok. That "Wild Bill" of the boomtowns and cattle camps signified his arrival in New York City by knocking down his hansom cab driver for charging too much. The first time a harsh acetylene spotlight was trained on him, Hickok, whose eyes bothered him, shattered it with his prop pistol, which he'd loaded with live ammunition. In the middle of a campfire scene, he hurled away a whiskey bottle filled with cold tea and demanded the real article, then had too much of that and played his love scene with the Italian Indian princess more energetically than either the script or the actress intended. He frightened the extras by firing at their feet during slow moments onstage; he cleaned out a saloon full of oilfield roughnecks with a chair during a layover in Titusville, Pennsylvania. He eventually left the show after buttonholing a stagehand and instructing him to "tell that long-haired son of a bitch I am through with him and show business." Months later he was shot in the back of the head while playing poker in Deadwood, Dakota Territory, having graced the eastern theater circuit with his legend.

Undaunted by this experience, in 1883 Cody expunged his company of actors, replaced them with real frontiersmen, and took the show outdoors to invent the Wild West exhibition, complete with galloping

Hon. W.F. Cody saddle c.1895, Collins & Morrison, makers, Omaha. Personally owned and used by Buffalo Bill (courtesy of Buffalo Bill Historical Center, Cody, WY)

horses and colorful costumes and feats of marksmanship. Annie Oakley, who with her husband, Frank Butler, provided many of the last, quickly became as big a star as Cody himself, and remained with the show for many years. In her sixties she was still shattering her old records, and today her name is synonymous with sharpshooting skill. Sitting Bull, Custer's Sioux conqueror, left after one season with Cody, but added immeasurably to the exhibition's fame.

Cody's Wild West toured Europe, and while they were in England, Queen Victoria came out of mourning to attend. She developed a crush on Buffalo Bill that his shrewish wife later tried to blow up into a charge of adultery. The attendance outstripped that at the 1893 World's Columbian Exposition in Chicago where the show pitched its tents opposite the entrance and thus planted the seeds for a worldwide fascination with the American frontier that continues today. Buffalo Bill was then, and remains, the most famous American of the nineteenth century.

"I am sorry to have to lie so outrageously in this yarn. My hero has killed more Indians on one war trail than I have killed in all my life...if you think the revolver and bowie knife are used too freely, you may cut out a fatal shot or stab wherever you think wise."

BUFFALO BILL CODY TO HIS EDITORS, 1875

THERE WAS LITTLE ENOUGH PROMISE OF THAT IN THE EIGHT-year-old boy who saw his father stabbed at the Salt Creek trading post in 1854 for speaking out against the spread of slavery into Kansas. Isaac Cody never fully recovered from the wound or the subsequent stigma of a hated abolitionist, and he died three years later, leaving young Will to support his mother, his sisters, and his sickly younger brother. His mother persuaded the stern, God-fearing Alexander Majors, of the freighting firm of Majors & Waddell, to take Will on as an extra hand with a wagon train to Nebraska. The first of the many legends that are inseparable from Cody's life story is assigned to that expedition, when he is said to have shot his first Indian, on the banks of the Platte. On his second trip he made the acquaintance of Hickok, a bullwhacker with the party, with whom he was forced to hike back to Kansas when Mormons hijacked the train. During that trek the two formed a friendship that would continue until Hickok broke his contract with Cody's theatrical troupe.

The importance of this association for Cody's future cannot be overstated. In addition to his considerable skill as a gunman, Hickok was a born liar, given to exaggerating his adventures for the benefit of greenhorns and eastern journalists, and it is probably from him that Cody learned the rudiments of applied prevarication. Buntline supplied refinements, and Arizona John Burke, publicist for Cody's Wild West, smeared the tall tales across barn-size posters, and through thousands of pages of souvenir pamphlets written by Prentiss Ingraham, one of the most prolific writers in American history. By the time Jim Bailey bought into the show, there was nothing that P. T. Barnum's old partner could teach

Ned Buntline, Buffalo Bill, Mlle Morlac-
chi and Texas Jack Omohundro c. 1870
(courtesy of Buffalo Bill Historical Center, Cody, WY)

Buffalo Bill about the politics of self-aggrandizement.

A brief sojourn with the Pony Express followed the wagon-train experience, then Civil War service, the latter apparently of a sufficiently undistinguished nature to escape mention in existing records of that four-year conflict. Later in life, Cody colored it with harrowing tales of infiltration behind Confederate lines, and an anecdote about awakening from a drunken revel to find himself enlisted. After Appomattox he met and proposed to Louisa Frederici, a St. Louis belle, and began a stormy marriage rocked by frequent desertions, affairs, a sensational divorce trial, and the early deaths of three of their four children.

In his early twenties, while engaged in providing meat for the track gangs laying the Kansas Pacific Railroad, Cody competed with Billy Comstock for the right to bear the sobriquet of Buffalo Bill. At the end of an eight-hour contest witnessed by soldiers from Fort Hayes and Fort Wallace, as well as by journalists and tourists from St. Louis, he had slaughtered sixty-nine buffalo to Comstock's forty-six.

731. WILD WEST.

Buffalo Bill

Buffalo Bill on horseback c. 1887, stereocard (courtesy of Buffalo Bill Historical Center, Cody, WY)

After this, Cody became a scout under the command of Major Frank North with General E. A. Carr's Fifth Cavalry at Fort McPherson, Nebraska. During an attack on a Cheyenne camp at Summit Springs in Colorado Territory, the chief—Tall Bull—was slain. Because Cody was seen leading the chief's horse after the skirmish, he was credited with the kill. It is one of history's sardonic twists that Major North, who was widely believed to have been the man actually responsible for Tall Bull's death, was killed many years later in a fall from a horse while in the employ of Cody's Wild West.

Russia's Grand Duke Alexis came to the United States in 1872 to hunt buffalo. Escorted by cavalry led by General Philip Sheridan and Lieutenant George Armstrong Custer, guided by Cody, the Russian delegation brought down an impressive number of the beasts despite the Grand Duke's notoriously poor marksmanship. Upon returning home, the Russians sent Cody a stickpin fashioned in the shape of a buffalo with diamonds for eyes. The expedition was heavily publicized and added to Cody's legend.

In 1876, Kit Carson Cody, Cody's four-year-old son, died. To assuage his grief, Cody reported for scout duty in the summer campaign against the High Plains Indians. The 5th Cavalry was on the march when word came in of the defeat of Custer's detachment of the 7th Cavalry at the Little Big Horn in Montana. Witnesses to the subsequent engagement reported that Cody was still wearing his eastern theatrical costume when he killed the Cheyenne chieftain, Yellow Hand, and took the celebrated "first scalp for Custer."

It was his last campaign until 1890, when his friend, General Nelson A. Miles, asked him to take Sitting Bull into custody on South Dakota's Standing Rock Sioux Indian reservation at the height of the Ghost Dance scare. Reservation officials deliberately misdirected him until President Harrison could countermand Miles's order. Shortly thereafter, Sitting Bull was killed by reservation police in an attempt to arrest him, and the Ghost Dance movement ended in the tragedy of Wounded Knee.

Cody's infatuation with Katherine Clemmons, an English actress, prompted him to invest thousands of dollars in productions centered around her modest talent, and to sue his wife for divorce in 1904. The sordid proceedings brought to light a naive attempt by Louisa Cody to cure her husband's alcoholism by spiking his coffee with a concoction called Dragon's Blood, for which he accused her of trying to poison him. It also revealed his affair with Clemmons and Louisa's paranoia about his relationship with Queen Victoria. Louisa, who had accepted title to Welcome Wigwam, Cody's beloved home in North Platte, Nebraska, in return for agreeing to the divorce—only to contest it after she had taken possession—also testified that his actions were to blame for the sudden death of their oldest daughter, Arta. The court refused to grant Cody the divorce and ordered him to pay his wife's legal expenses.

This last was more than just an annoyance. Although Cody's Wild West made him millions, he threw most of it away on bad investments and gave away the rest. He spent many thousands expanding, irrigating, transplanting trees, and building on his sprawling Scout's Rest Ranch in North Platte. He personally financed a water pipeline to Cody, the town he founded in Wyoming, that proved unworkable and had to be taken out of his hands. He supported his sisters, surviving daughters, and in-laws in one failed business venture after another, and he was always generous when his friends came to him down on their luck. Those friends were absent when the Wild West defaulted on a whopping printer's bill and went on the sheriff's block in Denver in 1913.

Cody's Wild West had, like its founder, succumbed to its own legend. When it could no longer compete with the less-limited potential of motion pictures, Cody tried his hand at that medium, hauling his paunchy rheumatic frame into the saddle for the benefit of hand-cranked cameras under the direction of G. M. "Bronco Billy" Anderson. Cody suffered the temperament of General Nelson A. Miles, who refused to portray himself unless all eleven thousand troops he commanded at Wounded Knee were represented on film during the re-creation, a problem Cody solved by marching three hundred soldiers on loan from the U.S. Army past an

Buffalo Bill and Sitting Bull c. 1885 (courtesy of Buffalo Bill Historical Center, Cody, WY)

Joel McCrea as "Buffalo Bill" (1944 Fox) with Maureen O'Hara

The origin of ticket-scalping

empty camera forty times. He also had to negotiate with disgruntled Indian extras who threatened to use live ammunition during the battle scenes. But the work was too energetic and the silent screen too full of William S. Hart and Mary Pickford to leave room for a nineteenth-century relic reliving his glorious past. The film was not a success.

Cody had by that time fallen in with Harry H. Tammen, the crass and grasping owner of the *Denver Post* and the Sells-Floto Circus. Tammen in effect owned Buffalo Bill and forced him to continue his frontier play-acting as an employee of, and a sideshow attraction to, the circus. In his late sixties, Cody was suffering from the effects of a lifetime of hard drinking and from the prostate problems that would eventually kill him. He had to be helped onto his horse before each performance. He confided to intimates that his greatest fear was of "dying out there in front of all those people." Finally, he could no longer ride; he had to make his triumphant circuit of the arena at the reins of a horsedrawn phaeton. Unable to endure the humiliation of delivering the same eloquent farewell speech he had been giving since 1910, he eventually summoned Tammen into his dressing tent and threatened to shoot him with his matched gold-and-silver-plated Colt Peacemakers unless the entrepreneur freed him from his contract. Tammen complied.

Cody's life ended on January 10, 1917, at his sister May's home. He was sixty-nine when he died, but his death was not the end of him as a spectacle. Tammen offered to pay for his funeral in return for a free hand in the arrangements. A financially strapped Louisa Cody agreed. Under the exclusive coverage of Tammen's *Post* and in spite of the deceased's request to be buried near Cody, Wyoming, a procession of circus wagons, wheezing motorcars, veterans of the Civil and Spanish-American wars, Elks, and Boy Scouts wearing the yellow neckerchief inspired by Buffalo Bill accompanied the horsedrawn hearse to the top of Lookout Mountain west of Denver in July. Cody's body had been kept in cold storage for six months while a work crew wedged a steel crypt designed to discourage grave robbers into the mountain. Six of Cody's old girlfriends wept while a brass band played, "Tenting Tonight," and eulogies were read. The *Post* continued the festival atmosphere for weeks afterward, soliciting readers' opinions on what sort of inscription should be placed on the monument. The old showman would have loved it.

"Buffalo Bill's defunct," wrote e.e. cummings. And yet his image remains, rifle-backed in the saddle, wearing buckskins and a white sombrero, with his snowy whiskers and his hair to his shoulders, as potent as gunfire on a dusty street and bugles catching fire in the sun. William Frederick Cody is far less easy to pin down, just as is the West that Buffalo Bill did so much to obscure under flags and bunting. ■

ANNIE AND FRANK

BY MARYLOIS DUNN

THERE ARE ALMOST AS MANY LEGENDS ABOUT ANNIE OAKLEY AND Frank Butler as there are about their mentor, Buffalo Bill. And why not? The legends came from the same publicity mill, Buffalo Bill Cody's Wild West. The truth, however much simpler, is more charming.

Phoebe Anne Oakley Moses, or Mozee (take your pick), was one of six children born to a Quaker family. Before her father was killed, they lived in a tiny cabin far back in the woods of Darke County, Ohio. Her birth date was recorded in the family Bible as August 13, 1860. As a toddler, Annie was fascinated by her father's Kentucky long rifle, which hung over the cabin fireplace. By the time she was ten years old, she was polishing the gun like her daddy used to do to keep it shiny and ready to shoot. She told the story of how a neighbor showed her how to measure the powder, center the patch over the muzzle, tap in the ball and ram it home before she seated the percussion cap in place.

Annie was one of those people who knew where the ball would go before she aimed the gun. Some people seem to be born with a sense of the Coriolis effect of the earth's rotation—that tendency of projected objects to turn slightly to the right in the Northern Hemisphere, to the left in the Southern Hemisphere. Most of us are unaware of the effect, but the great baseball pitchers, riflemen and artillery men are, and they use it. Some of them use the Coriolis effect without ever having heard of it, and Annie was one of those. She shot very few practice shots before she gained the reputation of never missing the mark.

She put meat on the family table and earned hard cash by shooting quail, rabbits and other game birds and animals. In five years, Annie paid the farm mortgage by shooting game birds through the head and shipping them to the hotels in Cincinnati. Her quail were prime because diners knew that when they had one of Annie's birds, they wouldn't break a tooth on stray buckshot.

Her older, married sister, Lydia, invited Annie to visit Cincinnati when she was sixteen. The slender, modest girl asked to be taken to a hotel that was one of her best customers. The manager was enchanted to meet

Annie Oakley at the Chicago World Fair c. 1893 (courtesy of Buffalo Bill Historical Center, Cody, WY)

**Barbara Stanwyck as *Annie Oakley*
(1935 RKO)**

the young lady who had been supplying his tables with her superior shooting. He offered to introduce her to another grand marksman, Frank Butler, who was staying at the hotel until he could find someone who would dare to shoot against him in an exhibition. Annie was too shy to accept at first, but when she heard of the one hundred dollar prize, she overcame her timidity.

Frank E. Butler was born in Ireland in 1840, and he immigrated to New York in 1863. He did numerous jobs around the city until he was attracted to show business. His first act was a dog and pony show, but he watched the trick shooters and knew he could do better. Before long, he made a name for himself around New York as a trick shooter of extraordinary ability. He made several tours around the northern states before he came to Cincinnati, where he had a hard time finding anyone courageous enough to try their ability against his.

No one knows what Annie used for her side of the bet—perhaps the hotel manager covered the wager for her—but she matched Frank shot after shot until he finally missed a clay pigeon and she did not. Frank went on with his tour, but he didn't forget the small girl who had bested him in Cincinnati.

Annie didn't forget him either. He was tall, slim, and blue-eyed—the handsomest man she had ever seen—and he could shoot. They understood each other, and eventually they loved each other. In 1880 they married, and he became her manager on the circus tours he booked for them. He worked on their act, polishing it and teaching her the niceties of trick shooting with all kinds of pistols and rifles. Gradually he pushed her into the foreground as he stepped further and further back.

In 1885, Annie Oakley and her manager joined Buffalo Bill Cody's faltering Wild West. She was an instant hit and brought crowds into the show. She hadn't been in the show long when Chief Sitting Bull, the aging Sioux chieftain, watched her act. He called her, "Watanya cicilia," or

COWGIRLS AND SHARPSHOOTERS

Although women had punched cattle, broken horses and run ranches throughout the Old West of the Nineteenth century, the term "cowgirl" didn't come into general use until after 1900, when President Theodore Roosevelt applied it to champion roper and rider Lucille Mulhall. Lucille, then only fourteen years old, reportedly rode down and roped a wolf at Roosevelt's request.

Zack Mulhall, Lucille's father, started up his own Wild West show at the turn of the century on his Oklahoma ranch. Lucille not only starred in Mulhall's exhibitions, she also traveled with his other rodeo riders to compete in steer roping, bronc riding and other events. Her demonstration of her ability at a 101 Ranch rodeo in 1905 so impressed one observer, Geronimo, that the old Apache warrior gave her a beaded vest.

Like many of the media legends of the Wild West, that of the sharpshooting, hard-riding cowgirl got its start in the arena of Buffalo Bill Cody's Wild West. Annie Oakley was the first female star of the Wild West (as well as the First Lady of Cody's Wild West), but she wasn't the only woman to enter the Wild West ring. Oakley's specialty was shooting, not riding, and Cody hired other performers for horseback stunts—true cowgirls like Georgia Duffy, the "Rough Rider from Wyoming," and trick rider Emma Lake Hickok. By the time he took his show to Europe, Cody employed a coterie of trick-riding cowgirls who could rope, square dance and race better than any man.

Patrons fell in love with the ladies of the Wild West, with their daring deeds, their directness and their flamboyant costumes. Cody and his imitators fell in love with the profits they generated. The Miller Brothers' 101 Ranch claimed that the cowgirls in

Miss Lillian F. Smith, the "California Girl" Champion Rifle Shot Of The World c.1886 (courtesy of Buffalo Bill Historical Center, Cody, WY)

Adele von Ohl Parker, performing a flying mount c.1917 (courtesy of Buffalo Bill Historical Center, Cody, WY)

their roundup were all from the neighborhood of their Oklahoma ranch, but some of the "cowgirls" in the Miller troupe were probably there just to get into silent films. The Millers also featured their answer to Annie Oakley, a trick-riding and trick-shooting lady they titled "Princess Winnemucca."

In his Historical Wild West, Pawnee Bill (Gordon Lillie) featured his sharpshooting wife, May, along with "Indian Princess" Bright Star and the bronc-riding Bertha Blancett. Blancett, who grew up on a Colorado ranch, was a major influence in enabling women to cross over from Wild West show performing into rodeo sports.

Though women had ridden broncs in events at the Cheyenne (Wyoming) Frontier Days rodeo as early as 1897, it wasn't an accepted practice. In 1901, Prairie Rose Henderson, the

daughter of a Cheyenne rancher, challenged the judges when they told her women weren't allowed. In the end, Prairie Rose got her way and competed, and she rode broncs with no hobbles to the stirrups—just the way the men did it. She became so popular that many rodeos began to sponsor cowgirl bronc-riding events.

Many other Western women followed Prairie Rose and Lucille Mulhall in demanding that they be taken seriously—women like relay racer Vera McGinnis, bull-rider Tad Lucas, bulldogger Fox Hastings, and cutting horse rider Fern Sawyer. They cleared the way for today's women in rodeo and made "cowgirl" a coveted title.

"Little Missy Sure Shot," and Little Sure Shot became her second name. She so impressed the old chief that he adopted her into the Sioux nation; the young sharpshooter and the old veteran of the Indian Wars became fast friends.

Those first years were the wonder years. She was presented to Queen Victoria, and once she shot a cigarette from the lips of Crown Prince Wilhelm of Germany. In their European tours, it was Little Sure Shot who saved the day. The Europeans hadn't read the dime novels that had brought Buffalo Bill to fame in the U.S. On the continent, they looked at the rickety old stage coach, the whooping Indians and the galloping cowboys with disdain. One thing they understood was fine shooting.

Howard Keel as Frank Butler with Betty Hutton (right) as Annie Oakley in the 1950 MGM musical, *Annie Get Your Gun.*

Annie always began her act very quietly, walking calmly out to acknowledge the crowd and then standing while two assistants rode out to hold her targets. They held glass balls, which she broke with pistol and rifle. Then, with unbroken rhythm, she snuffed out the flames from a revolving wheel of lighted candles. With a shotgun, she broke clay pigeons that were tossed into the air in many directions. Her finale to the standing act was to toss two balls in the air, pick up the pistol and break both targets while they were still in the air. Her performances were characterized by grace and precision.

For the mounted portion of her act, she leaped aboard the back of a pinto pony as he galloped into the arena, then leaned down, Indian-style, to pluck a pistol from the ground. As she rode, she shattered glass ball after ball from the air. The European audiences were mesmerized by that small figure on the spotted horse, whirling, racing and shooting against the painted backdrop of the magnificent Montana mountains.

While Cody was the star and the master of ceremonies, Little Annie won the hearts of the audiences and kept the show afloat.

In October of 1901, during the early morning hours, a chartered train carrying Cody's Wild West through the North Carolina darkness crashed into a freight train. Annie was one of the severely injured; so severely that she could no longer travel with the show. Long months of hospitalization followed, but even her injuries couldn't stop Annie for long. In 1902 she returned to show business to play the lead in a stage melodrama called *The Western Girl.*

The years didn't dim Annie's shooting skills. In 1912, she and Frank

traveled with the farewell tour of Cody's Wild West. She worked as a trap-shooting instructor, and she gave demonstrations of shooting for the troops during World War I. For several years after she retired from public life, Annie and Frank lived in Leesburg, Florida, but she didn't like the hot, humid climate and longed to go back to Ohio. In 1926 they went back to Darke County, where they bought a home in nearby Dayton.

Annie Oakley died on November 2, 1926, in Dayton, and Frank died exactly twenty days later, but Little Sure Shot had made her mark on the legend of the West. As part of Cody's Wild West, she introduced that legend to the world, and since her death her story has been the subject of biographies and fiction, stage dramas and musicals, motion pictures and television. The better-known pictures were *Annie Oakley* (RKO, 1935) with Barbara Stanwyck and Preston Foster, and *Annie Get Your Gun* (MGM, 1950) with Betty Hutton and Howard Keel. The television series "Annie Oakley" ran from 1957 to 1960 and starred Gail Davis. Though the series, some movies and other fictional depictions have little to do with her actual life, Annie's true memorial is that all good shooters everywhere will always be compared to Annie Oakley—"Little Sure Shot." ■

RODEO, THE GREATEST SHOW IN THE WILD WEST

BY CENA GOLDER RICHESON

> "For good healthy exercise I would strongly recommend some of our gilded youth to go West and try a short course of riding bucking ponies, and assist at the branding of a lot of Texas steers."
>
> **THEODORE ROOSEVELT**

THE SPIRIT OF CODY'S WILD WEST LIVES ON IN THE WEST'S GREAT sport, rodeo. Each year, more than thirty-nine million spectators attend thirty-six hundred rodeos in the U.S. sponsored by high schools and colleges, Native Americans, the Women's Professional Rodeo Association, the Professional Rodeo Cowboys' Association, and other groups. Modern rodeo is a carefully honed sport with precise rules, but it maintains the daredevil, free-spirited image of the West. Even so, it's respectably tame compared to its original form.

About 1769, when Spanish Franciscan missionaries landed in California with their modest herds of cattle and fine horses, they found rich, green valleys in which their animals could flourish. Many of the Spanish *Californios* were the sons of nobility, and expert horsemen, but they needed help to manage their stock. The Indians they converted (usually by force) became the first cowboys, the *vaqueros,* adept livestock handlers. The Spanish-influenced *vaquero* developed the saddles, clothes and equipment that evolved into the gear used by the American cowboy. The later Anglo cowboy even Americanized *vaquero* as "buckaroo."

After each spring roundup—the laborious gathering of the widely scattered cattle from the range—the *vaqueros* engaged in competitive games of cowboy skill using horses and cattle. So was the rodeo born, a tradition carried on by the American cowboys who learned it from the *Californios* and Mexican *vaqueros.*

The cowboy's skills at riding and roping (mixed with trick shooting and showmanship) first came before the general public in the form of the Wild West shows. As early as 1872, Wild Bill Hickok starred with hard-riding Indians and Mexican *vaqueros* in "The Grand Buffalo Hunt," a showcase of their talents presented at Niagara Falls

Of course, the premiere showman and promoter of the Wild West was Buffalo Bill Cody. His Wild West and Congress of Rough Riders debuted in 1883 outside North Platte, Nebraska. Cody's Wild West featured daring

Cowboys at roundup roping a bronc (courtesy of Kansas State Historical Society, Topeka, KS)

cowboys, authentic Indians and sharpshooters, later on including Sitting Bull, and Cody's star attraction, Annie Oakley, re-enactments of gunfights and stagecoach robberies, and a herd of buffalo. The spectacle of Cody's shows popularized the fictional image of a glamourous, enviable cowboy lifestyle.

Others followed Cody's trail. Pawnee Bill, who was fluent in several Plains Indian languages, toured the same routes with his Historic Old West Show. His show bills advertised "daring Western girls" and "contests of equine skill." Eventually, his show merged with Cody's.

Rodeo events often featured Wild West show acts. The famous 2-Bar brand Wyoming cattle ranch, managed by Alec Swan, hosted a three-day rodeo that featured Butch Cassidy as a sharpshooter. Colonel Zach Mulhall of Oklahoma featured rodeo contests that starred his daughter Lucille as a trick roper. The Miller Brothers' 101 Ranch formed their 101 Ranch Real Wild West Show, and they took it on the road in a special train. The 101 featured Indian sharpshooters, the great bulldogger and

Wyoming bronc-rider Prairie Rose Henderson c. 1920 (courtesy of Rodeo Historical Society)

champion black cowboy, Bill Pickett, and celebrities such as Will Rogers, Tom Mix, Buck Jones, Tex Cooper and Hoot Gibson. The 101 Ranch was itself used as the location for several early Western movies.

The 1880s was a foundation decade, when the rodeo gained a life of its own and spread over the United States west of the Mississippi River, into Canada, and finally to the eastern United States. What was probably the first public rodeo that offered prizes for events from bronc riding to steer roping was held in Pecos, Texas, on July 4, 1883, in a field near the courthouse. The first rodeo that charged admission as well as awarding prizes to the winners was held at Prescott, Arizona Territory, on July 4, 1888. Independent little rodeos, often called stampedes, frontier days, or roundups, sprang up all across cattle country.

The first indoor rodeo was held in Ft. Worth, Texas, at the Stockyard Coliseum in 1917. After 1920, rodeo became a regular feature of annual county fairs. To cash in on rodeo's popularity, eastern sports magnates sponsored the first World Series Rodeo at Madison Square Garden in New York City.

The Rodeo Association of America formed in 1929 to set rules governing all rodeos, to schedule rodeos to prevent conflicting dates, and to promote public interest and professionalism. In the early 1940s, the newly organized Cowboy Turtles Association (CTA) sanctioned 150 rodeos; in 1945 it became the Rodeo Cowboys Association (RCA), and in 1974 changed its name to the Professional Rodeo Cowboys Association (PRCA). Today, the PRCA sanctions 600 pro rodeos and has over 5,000 cowboy members.

Certain performers' names stand out above all others in the history of rodeo, cowboys whose infallible courage laid the foundation for the sport. In the early days, at least one working American cowboy in six was black, Hispanic or Indian. Nat Love was born a slave in Tennessee in 1854, but as a free man he ventured to the Wild West. At age fifteen he found work as a trailhand in Dodge City, Kansas; then he drifted into Texas. He excelled as a wrangler, and he easily won bronc riding contests, earning fame for himself under the name of "Deadwood Dick."

Bill Pickett was one of a kind—a world champion cowboy and entertainer of mixed Anglo, black and Indian heritage. Western writer Homer Croy described him as "not only a good man everyone treated with respect, but he contributed more to rodeo entertainment than any one person." Pickett (also known as Will) invented what's known as steer wrestling, or "bulldogging." As a working cowboy in 1903, while he was trying to drive a testy steer into a corral, he leaped from his horse, grabbed the steer by its horns, clamped his teeth into its lower lip like a bulldog, and wrestled it to the ground. His style won him star billing with the 101 Ranch Real Wild West Show, and guaranteed him a place in rodeo history.

The roll call of modern rodeo greats who have followed the tradition begun by the old-time cowboys include champions like Casey Tibbs, Jim Shoulders, Harry Tompkins, Larry Mahan, Bill Linderman, Tom Ferguson, Dean Oliver, Joe Alexander, Homer Pettigrew, and Jim Rodriquez, Jr.

Modern rodeo is divided into several events.

Saddle Bronc Riding

Riding "green" horses, rodeo's oldest event, evolved from necessity. For a cowboy (or any horseback rider) to secure a gentle mount, the horse has to be tamed or "broke" to the saddle. Early competitions between bronc riders required the cowboy to remain in the saddle until "the horse was rode or the rider throwed."

Today's rider uses one hand to hold onto a six-foot "buck rein" that's attached to the bronc's halter while he uses the other hand to balance himself. The rider must spur over the break of the horse's shoulders as the animal's front hooves touch the ground at the first leap out of the chute. With toes turned out, the rider continues spurring forward and backward throughout the eight-second ride.

If the rider changes his grip on the rein from hand to hand, if he loses a stirrup, or if he touches himself or the horse with his free hand, or if he's thrown, he's disqualified. Judges tally the score for the quality of both horse and rider, with a possible fifty points for each.

Calf Roping

During every roundup, a lone cowboy had to chase down and brand or doctor the dogies. Unlike most modern cattlemen, who use cattle chutes, he used his lariat and his horse to catch up with the calf and restrain it.

The rodeo calf roper works as a team with his specially trained horse. The calf is released with a head start, then trips a string barrier to signal the cowboy and his mount to begin the chase. If the cowboy leaves the roping box prematurely, he suffers a ten-second penalty.

Using a twenty-five-foot lariat, the roper forms a loop, twirls it out, and throws it so that it snares the calf around the neck. Once the lariat hits its target, the cowboy loops his end of the lariat around his saddle horn and the horse slides to a stop to hold the calf. With a six-foot "piggin'" string gripped between his teeth, the cowboy dismounts and races toward his objective. His trained horse constantly watches and works the rope to keep out the slack until the cowboy reaches the calf. The cowboy throws the calf to the ground, gathers up three of its legs, ties them together with his piggin' string, then steps back and lifts his

Dan Mortensen, 1993 World Champion Saddle Bronc Rider (top); Joe Beaver, 1985, '87-88, '92-93 World Champion Calf Roper (bottom) (photos by Dan Hubbell courtesy of PRCA)

Steve Duhon, 1986-87, '93 World Champion Steer Wrestler (top); Ty Murray, 1993 World Champion Bull Rider (middle); Deb Greenough, 1993 World Champion Bareback Rider (bottom) (photos by Dan Hubbell courtesy of PRCA)

hands into the air. He then remounts his horse and nudges him forward to give the calf some slack. If he's still got the calf restrained six seconds later, the judges tally his time.

Steer Wrestling

Like calf roping, steer wrestling probably originated during roundup at the branding fire. The "'dogger" cowboy needs skillful coordination and timing, along with his "hazer," a fellow cowboy who rides parallel to the steer's off side to keep the animal running straight. The dogger and his horse cannot begin the chase until the steer crosses the score line. If the cowboy charges too early and his horse breaks the string barrier across the front of the chute, he gets a ten-second penalty.

The cowboy times his drop from horse to steer, keeping one foot in the stirrup until the last second. A 'dogging horse is trained to veer away as his rider drops. The cowboy grabs for the horns and stretches out his legs so that his boots serve as brakes. Once he stops the steer, he must throw it on its side with all four of its legs pointing in the same direction before the timers stop their watches. The cowboy who does it right in the shortest time wins.

Bull Riding

It's easy to see why bull riding is undisputedly the most dangerous rodeo event when one considers that the cowboy must ride unpredictable animals that weigh at least fifteen-hundred pounds—and the bulls are usually in a bad mood.

As the rider climbs into the chute and onto the bull, he wraps a flat rope, into which a handle is braided, around the animal. He tightens the rope, then wraps it around his gloved hand. The rope harness includes a cowbell that hangs under the bull's belly; the bell not only serves as a weight to pull the rope free when the eight-second ride is over, it also irritates the bull to make a better (rougher) ride. Once the ride starts, the rider can't touch the bull, himself, or his equipment with his free hand. When the final buzzer sounds, the rider bails out.

The rider's exit is liable to be abrupt and forceful, and he could be stunned and rattled by the experience. That comic bullfighter, the rodeo clown, distracts the angry bull to give the rider a chance to scramble for safety. Rodeo clowns have often risked their own lives to save injured or stunned bull riders.

Bareback Bronc Riding

The bareback rider has only a small ten-inch-wide surcingle as his "rigging" to keep him on his cayuse. He places his gloved hand into the rig-

2½-year-old Jimmy VanBelle, Enterprise, OR, in the mutton-riding event at a Joseph, OR, Junior Rodeo. (Photo courtesy of Janie Tippett)

ging's handle, and when he's ready, he says, "outside," or simply nods and hangs on for dear life. The chute opens, and he finds himself riding the "hurricane deck" of a mad bronc, all the while reminding himself to keep his toes turned out and to keep spurring. He can't touch the horse, himself, or his rigging with his free hand for the duration of the wild, eight-second ride.

The unsung heroes of the bronc ride are the pickup men who gallop their horses alongside the fighting bronc to help lift the rider to safety.

Barrel Racing

The women of the Women's Professional Rodeo Association (WPRA) dominate what may be rodeo's most popular event—the barrel race. From a running start, racer and horse weave a cloverleaf pattern around three individual barrels placed about 100 feet apart. They must make a complete circle around each barrel and then race to the finish line. An overturned barrel adds a five-second penalty. The rider with the fastest time wins.

At selected rodeos, the WPRA also sponsors competitions in bronc riding, roping, and bull riding.

In the century since its rough beginnings, rodeo has evolved into a modern sport for top professionals, who treat it as a business and a science, analyzing techniques and improving equipment to enhance performance. It's a "pay your money, take your chances" in which there are few winners. The risks are high, and there are no guarantees, but rodeo's magnetic attraction for dream-chasing contestants and its split-second action are addictive. Decades ago, it was a cowboy's goal to be the best roper or bronc buster on some remote ranch. Today's cowboy goes for broke, and his goal is to be the world champion who can wear the engraved silver buckle that has his name on it.

Rodeo draws loyal fans, from children to senior citizens, by virtue of its heart-stirring, attention-riveting drama. It's driven by apprehension and excitement; a contest stimulated, as in the days of the Wild West, by a cowboy's boasts of, "I can outride, outrope and outdo you!" Just as did Western artists like Remington and Russell; showmen like Cody; novelists like Zane Grey and Louis L'Amour; and actors, from Tom Mix to John Wayne, rodeo continues to preserve and romanticize the mythic image of the independent cowboy. It thrives because it is the embodiment of the wild American West. ■

(courtesy Kansas State Historical Society, Topeka, KS)

ACT II: DREAMERS, LIARS, AND POETS

THE FIRST WESTERN

BY BRIAN GARFIELD

YOU'VE PROBABLY NEVER HEARD OF CHARLES KING'S NOVEL, *THE Colonel's Daughter,* or of its author, but it has a strong claim to being the first Western ever written.

Any book's claim to be the first Western must be hedged with exceptions; there's no universally accepted definition of the Western. Some literary historians insist that the first Westerns were James Fenimore Cooper's novels of Natty Bumppo, but those—geographically at least—were "Easterns," and they predated the "Cowboys-and-Indians" era by half a century.

We can make a more sensible "first" claim for the frontier dime novels of Prentiss Ingraham, Ned Buntline and others. Their paperback entertainments, which featured lurid imaginary exploits of real-life heroes like Buffalo Bill Cody, Billy the Kid and Wild Bill Hickok, began to appear in the late 1860s. They were as widely popular with the literate common folk as they were widely condemned and vituperated by the clergy, the literary set and the educators of the day. The dime novels were exuberant, cheerful trash and made no pretense to be anything else—juvenile fictions, florid of prose, absurd of characterization, imbecilic of plot and contemptuous of plausibility—the nineteenth century's version of the comic book.

There's little doubt, however, that the first legitimate and respect-

PREVIOUS PAGE:
Detail from *Wind River Mountains,*
Alfred Jacob Miller (courtesy of
Joslyn Art Museum, Omaha, NE)

"The Wild West is tamed,
and its savage charms have
withered."

FRANCIS PARKMAN IN HIS 1892
INTRODUCTION TO *THE OREGON
TRAIL*

able novel of the Indian-fighting West was *The Colonel's Daughter; Or, Winning His Spurs,* written by Captain Charles King, U.S. Army, and published in 1882 by the J. B. Lippincott Company of Philadelphia. With its blue cloth binding and its plate illustrations by A. F. Harmer, the 440-page first edition sold out quickly at $1.25.

The *New York Tribune* greeted its publication as "a contribution so good that we hope he will give us another"—a spur that no doubt goaded King to write a sequel, *Marion's Faith* (1886), in the preface of which he wrote, "The kind reception accorded *The Colonel's Daughter* was a surprise and delight to the author." Indeed the reception was excellent, as were the sales. Best-seller lists didn't exist in the 1880s, but if they had, *The Colonel's Daughter* would certainly have been on them. It went quickly through numerous printings and remained in print for decades. My own copy of the book is the 1894 edition; it was still selling actively when Owen Wister's *The Virginian* was published in 1901. There's a certain wistful irony in that fact, and in that Wister himself wrote that Charles King was "the first that ever burst into the silent sea" (i.e., the Western)—wistful and ironic because Wister's novel today is so universally regarded as having been the first Western. Indeed, by the time Wister's book was published, King had written at least thirty novels, most of them Westerns and many of them the literary equals of Wister's tale.

King's frontier cavalry novels were the direct precursors of an entire school of Western literature that extends into the present. A close reading of the classic Indian-fighting Army novels of Ernest Haycox (*Bugles in the Afternoon, The Border Trumpet*) and James Warner Bellah (*She Wore a Yellow Ribbon, Fort Apache*) implies that both writers were intimate with, and strongly influenced by King's works.

That's only proper, since King was the only novelist of the Indian wars who wrote out of firsthand experience. He was a gallant cavalry officer who served under Crook in the campaigns against the Sioux and Apache, and under Merritt against the Nez Perce. His books, while bigoted racist romances, were realistic and authentic in every detail; they serve not only as entertainments and as typical examples of nineteenth century prose fiction, but also as rich sources of eyewitness information about frontier life. It's important to remember that *The Colonel's Daughter* is not a historical novel but a romantic contemporary account of thinly disguised current events; it accurately depicts the manners and attitudes of its time—some of which, to be sure, we find repugnant today.

It's odd how completely we have neglected King for the past several generations. Certainly it's past time he was rediscovered. *The Colonel's Daughter* is not only a fascinating book, but a time capsule and the fountainhead of the entire Western genre.

Charles King was born on October 12, 1844, in Albany, New York, but he grew up in Wisconsin, where his father edited the *Milwaukee Sentinel*. He came from a distinguished line of American statesmen (Rufus King, Sr., Charles King, Sr.) and military men.

King was sixteen at the outbreak of the Civil War. His father, a West Point graduate, assumed command of the famous Iron Brigade and rose to major general; young Charles served in the brigade as a mounted orderly until Abraham Lincoln gave him an appointment to West Point in 1862. At the academy the boy achieved the highest possible cadet office, cadet adjutant, but in 1865 a shocking theft scandal occurred and King was mistakenly implicated. He was suspended during the inquiry, damned by circumstantial evidence, and was only cleared and reinstated

Francis Parkman on The Oregon Trail

When he set out for the West, a young Bostonian named Francis Parkman didn't intend to write a travelogue but a history of the French and Indian War. He'd studied historical accounts and extensively explored the war's actual setting, but he wanted practical experience with Indians—wild, free Indians. He knew the eastern Indians wouldn't do; to understand the true Indian character, he'd have to meet the free plainsmen of the West—the Sioux, the Comanche and the Cheyenne.

So, in the spring of 1846, when Parkman was twenty-three, he left St. Louis for the Oregon Trail accompanied by his cousin, Quincy Adams Shaw, to explore the Wild West and to meet its inhabitants.

And he met them—not only the Indians but the mountain men, pioneers, soldiers, teamsters, trappers, explorers and the fortune hunters who for one reason or another were drawn to the West. He'd picked an opportune moment in history, just before the emigrant wagon trains turned into a flood, before the meeting of the native and immigrant cultures became a violent collision. The Plains Indians were at the zenith of their strength, not yet generally hostile to whites, and the French-Canadian trappers and the mountain men moved freely (with some exceptions) among them.

With skilled trapper and hunter Henry Chatillon as his guide, Parkman gained introduction to the lodges of the Oglallah Sioux. By joining the Sioux (the Dacotah, he called them) in their hunts and horse races and battles, in their triumphs and sorrows, by sitting down for talk over meals in their camps and lodges, he saw them neither as the noble or the savage. What he wrote of them later painted a picture of a robust people who accepted the challenges of their life with ruthless courage and a sense of humor, an image that defies modern stereotypes.

Parkman also saw the unspoiled Wild West, where millions of buffalo covered the prairies, dams hadn't yet tamed the rivers and axes hadn't touched the forest. He experienced the majestic power of the sacred Black Hills, shot the river rapids, and endured violent weather, incredible hardships and dangers as well as debilitating illness brought on by exposure and privation.

Though he later wrote the book he'd planned (*A Half-Century of Conflict*, 1892), his Western sojourn was foremost in his mind when he returned east. *The Oregon Trail*, the travel narrative he reconstructed from

Covered wagons on the Oregon Trail, 1992 (photo courtesy of Paul Rocheleau)

his journals and notes, is a highly personal story of a young man's adventure in a strange new land. Though some historians of the time criticized its lack of objectivity, it may be an enduring favorite for that very reason. Parkman preserved the reality of the Old West from an individual's perspective. Though it's non-fiction, *The Oregon Trail* reads like a boy's adventure tale, fired with the kind of youthful enthusiasm that created and promoted the mythology of the Wild West.

when another cadet confessed some months later.

For the rest of his life, King displayed an almost paranoid distrust of circumstantial evidence and the way it could be misread. His obsessive concern crops up in elements of the plot of *The Colonel's Daughter* and many of his other novels.

AFTER THE ARMY SHEEPISHLY CLEARED HIS RECORD AND COMmissioned him in 1886, King took command of a Gatling Gun platoon in New Orleans, where he was called upon to put down several Reconstruction riots. While stationed in Louisiana he met Adelaide Yorke, whom he married in 1872, on a return visit to New Orleans. In the meantime, he served briefly as an instructor at West Point, then in 1870 he shipped out to the West to join the 5th Cavalry in Nebraska—General Crook's regiment.

He served in the field in several Plains campaigns, then transferred to Arizona Territory in 1874 to take the field (again under Crook) against the Chiricahua and Mimbrenos Apache under Cochise and Geronimo. He fought at Diamond Butte and Black Mesa, and fought again at Sunset Pass, where a bullet shattered his right shoulder. It was a grievous injury that invalided him out of active service for a full year, and did nothing to reduce his almost hysterical (but typical of the period) hatred toward Indians. By 1876 he was back in battle, serving as Regimental Adjutant of the 5th Cavalry against the Sioux in Nebraska, Montana and Dakota; he was in the field with Crook when Custer was killed at Little Big Horn.

A year later King was transferred west to serve in the campaign against Chief Joseph's heroic Nez Perce, after which—troubled considerably by the crippling effects of the old wound to his shoulder—he retired temporarily in 1879 as a captain, and returned to his native Wisconsin.

But King couldn't stay out of uniform. Within months he joined the Wisconsin Militia (later to become the National Guard), where he soon rose to the rank of colonel, training weekend soldiers and administering the state organization. In the meantime he served as an aide to the governor and as Adjutant General of Wisconsin.

King was past fifty when the Spanish-American War broke out in 1898, but he took command of a brigade of volunteers—a short-lived job, for the Army soon relieved him of the command and sent him to Honolulu as the United States' first Commanding General of the new Military Department of Hawaii. King briskly organized the department, then took command of a front-line infantry brigade and steamed west across the Pacific to see considerable action against Moro rebels in the Philippine

> **"Last night as I lay on the prairie,**
> **And looked at the stars in the sky,**
> **I wondered if ever a cowboy**
> **Would drift to that sweet bye-and-bye."**
>
> **FROM "THE COWBOY'S DREAM"**

Insurrection. He experienced a number of hair-raising escapades during the Philippine adventure.

Finally he returned to Wisconsin as a brigadier general and remained there. In 1929 he was promoted to major general; he held his commission in the Wisconsin National Guard until 1932. In all, he served seventy years in the armed forces.

On March 17, 1933, at the age of eighty-eight, Charles King died. During his busy military and political career, King managed to write nearly sixty books as well as several hundred short stories and essays. His life was both industrious and productive; he sometimes carried three or four jobs at once. Despite his half-crippling injury, he was a robust and vigorously handsome man with a barrel chest and a remarkable facial resemblance to Theodore Roosevelt. His extraordinary strength and vitality help account for his sizable literary output, most of which dated from the period 1890-1909, with a few years out for service in Cuba, Hawaii and the Philippines—a period in which he produced more than thirty novels as well as a vast assortment of short prose pieces.

But nearly all his later work was inferior to the ten or eleven books he wrote before 1890, largely because in 1890 he bought an Ediphone dictating machine. Its use seems to have produced a marked deterioration of ingenuity and freshness, and his post-1890 books are quite repetitive and hoary now. It should be understood, however, that sloth didn't cause King to use the machine. His old arm injury was extremely troublesome—it was his writing arm—and he simply could not wield a pen for extended periods, although his handwriting (if his autographs are any indication) remained precise, bold and neatly legible clear to the end of his life.

The Colonel's Daughter was his first novel but not his first book. In 1880, King published a paperback-pamphlet limited edition of a nonfiction book titled *Campaigning with Crook,* containing a series of newspaper sketches that King had written for his father's newspaper, the *Milwaukee Sentinel.* The favorable reception garnered by this small but accurate account of his service in the Sioux Campaign of 1876 encouraged him to try his hand at the novel; in the meantime *Campaigning with Crook* was reprinted and became a fixture in libraries of the Indian Wars. It may be better known today than any of King's subsequent books.

Still, *The Colonel's Daughter* was his first novel, his first book written as a book, and was undeniably the first Western. After a four-year lapse, he followed it with the sequel, *Marion's Faith,* and then quickly wrote a succession of Westerns including *Captain Blake, Kitty's Conquest, Foes in Ambush, An Army Wife, A Daughter of the Sioux, An Apache Princess, Laramie* (subtitled *The Queen of Bedlam*) and the best-selling *The*

Deserter. His first dictated novel appeared in 1890. Significantly, it was titled *Sunset Pass,* which was the place where he had suffered the shoulder wound that made his dictation necessary.

After that he branched into other genres, although he continued to write Westerns. He wrote several juveniles about West Point cadet life and the like; later, after his turn-of-the-century active service, he wrote five novels about the Philippine Insurrection and seven concerning the Civil War and Reconstruction, as well as an aptly titled autobiography, *Memories of a Busy Life.* One of the freshest Westerns he wrote during that period, *Comrades in Arms* (1904), was a throwback to his earlier style.

Students should be cautioned that bibliographies of King's works aren't always trustworthy. He contributed introductions to a fair number of books written by other people; his name was more prominent than theirs, and often the books are credited to his canon. While on board the steamer *Kaiser Wilhelm II* of the North German Lloyd line, cruising the Atlantic and the Mediterranean in 1895, King rendered into good English prose an awkward translation from the German of a book by Ernst von Wildenbruch about German cadet life—*Noble Blood.* The actual translator was Anne Williston Ward, and the story was hardly King's, but his name appears on the dust jacket and title page. The book is credited to him in most bibliographies. According to the scholar-historian Don Russell, King actually wrote fifty-seven books; some bibliographies credit him with as many as seventy.

KING'S POPULARITY WANED AS THAT OF ZANE GREY WAXED. It has been alleged that audiences outgrew him in their sophistication, but a reading of King's novels puts the lie to that allegation; despite his avid bigotry, he was far more sophisticated, more witty and more mature a writer than Grey. What supplanted King was the same shift in public appetites that ruined William S. Hart—the first of the great movie cowboys.

Hart, whose films were melodramas set against shabbily realistic backgrounds, was supplanted in public favor by Tom Mix, who brought flamboyant costumes, circus acrobatics and childish adventures to the Western film, changing it from a genre of serious melodrama to one of wild juvenile fantasy. In the same way, King's novels—romantic but rooted in plausible actuality—were superseded in popularity by the wild flights of fancy of the fabulist Zane Grey and his pulp-magazine imitators. In a sense, Charles King gave birth to the Westerns of John Ford, while Zane Grey gave birth of those of Gene Autry.

Indeed, King wrote the screenplay for what may be the greatest *lost*

Western movie of the silent era—Buffalo Bill Cody's immense epic re-enactment of the Indian Wars, filmed in 1914, and never seen since.

These shifts in public favor occurred simultaneously in the genres of film and fiction. Tom Mix and Zane Grey rose to their greatest popularity in thedecade of the First World War, while William S. Hart and Charles King dwindled toward obscurity in that same decade. Hart and King lived on into the 1930s, but by then nobody remembered either of them.

King was a curiously economical stylist in an age when his colleagues wrote Byzantine baroque prose. His wit, while simple, was funny and straightforward; his narrative, while longwinded by present-day standards, is clear and unpretentious. It therefore stands up better, and is far easier to read, than that of Wister or Grey, both of whom came after him. Here, for example, is a passage chosen almost at random—the opening sentences of *Comrades in Arms* (1904):

"The first thing Pat Langham does when he gets a new uniform," said Captain Sparker reflectively, as he studied the approaching officer, "is to pay the photographer a visit."

"And the last thing Pat Langham does," drawled Lieutenant Crabbe significantly, "is to pay the tailor—anything."

One does not find the same polish or economy in *The Colonel's Daughter*—after all, it was a first effort, and King was yet to become an accomplished professional—but neither does one find hackneyed formula work in it. If there are cliches in the book, it's because the novel has been too often imitated. They weren't cliches when King wrote them, for he was the first. Indeed, the title itself has become a cliche by now.

The remarkable thing about *The Colonel's Daughter* is not that it seems a bit dated and familiar, but rather that it seems so curiously fresh, so vital, up-to-date and entertaining despite some of its redneck attitudes. The description of the hero, Jack Truscott, in the opening chapter might aptly fit the image of Clint Eastwood in his prime. It's a boy-meets-girl romance laced with speedy adventures and officer's mess intrigues, an excellent love story with exciting action sequences marked with the stamp of eyewitness authenticity. Its sense of humor is bright and brash, its characters are sophisticated, its language is simple but effective. It is, in short, a remarkably good novel for its day and a pretty good novel for *any* day.

The reader who comes to *The Colonel's Daughter* for the first time may find that he is astonished by how much King accomplished in his first book, and how little his successors were able to add to his contribution to literature—the publication of the first Western of all. ∎

THE WESTERN BOOK OF LISTS

Bugles in the Afternoon
by Ernest Haycox

Shane
Monte Walsh
by Jack Schaefer

Hondo
The Daybreakers
Sackett
Conagher
The Shadow Riders
by Louis L'Amour

Cheyenne Autumn
by Mari Sandoz

The Searchers
The Unforgiven
by Alan Le May

Hombre
Valdez is Coming
by Elmore Leonard

The Wonderful Country
by Tom Lea

Lone Star: A History of Texas and the Texans
by T. R. Fehrenbach

Little Big Man
by Thomas Berger

The Squaw Killers
From Where the Sun Now Stands
by Will Henry

True Grit
by Charles Portis

The Way to Rainy Mountain
by N. Scott Momaday

Bury My Heart at Wounded Knee
by Dee Brown

The Day the Cowboys Quit
The Wolf and the Buffalo
by Elmer Kelton

The Cowboys
by William Dale Jennings

Son of the Morning Star
by Evan S. Connell

Lonesome Dove
by Larry McMurtry

Dances With Wolves
by Michael Blake

Ten-Cent Homer: Ned Buntline and the Dime Novel

By Loren D. Estleman

"There's money in it, and you will prove a big card, as your character is a novelty on the stage."

NED BUNTLINE TO BUFFALO BILL CODY

A SIGN OUTSIDE THE ENTRANCE TO THE CATTLEMAN'S STEAKHOUSE in the Fort Worth stockyards reads: "Ned Buntline was hanged and shot inside." The simple elegance of that legend, so far removed from the florid bombast beloved of the man who inspired it, is symbolic of the many contradictions in the life of the inventor of the modern best-seller. It's also a lie, something of which he would approve most heartily.

He's popularly remembered for the design of a long-barreled revolver that never existed. A short, dumpy man with carroty hair and mustache and a rolling way of speech, he delivered temperance lectures for money throughout the West, and wrote his most famous work in four hours while under the influence of whiskey. He was fond of reliving his role in the siege of Montezuma during the Mexican War, a battle in which he didn't take part. Even the name "Ned Buntline" was a pseudonym borrowed from nautical terminology, as Mark Twain was for Samuel Clemens.

He was born Edward Zane Carroll Judson in Stamford, New York, in 1823, the son of a schoolmaster. He ran away to join the navy at age thirteen and was commissioned a midshipman at fifteen for his efforts to rescue the crew of a boat that capsized in the East River. A prankster and a savage satirist, he regularly hoisted shipmates under the Buntline *nom de plume* in the *Knickerbocker Magazine*.

In 1842 he left the sea to fight in the Seminole War—he later claimed to have served as U.S. Army Chief of Indian Scouts. A civilian stint as publisher of *Ned Buntline's Own,* a scandal sheet, ended abruptly in 1846 in Nashville, Tennessee, when a man named Robert Porterfield accused him of dallying with his wife. Buntline shot him to death, and Porterfield's brother then shot Buntline in the chest.

The wounded Buntline leaped from an upper-story window of the City Hotel to elude a mob, crippling one leg when he landed. Thereupon, so the story goes, the mob seized him and lynched him from an awning post.

Col. E.Z.C. Judson, a.k.a.
Ned Buntline

Someone cut him down and saved him from strangling.

Shortly thereafter he was arrested in New York City for inciting an anti-immigrant riot that killed thirty-four people and injured one hundred forty-one. A year and a day on Blackwell's Island failed to rehabilitate him; he jumped bail on another charge of inciting to riot in St. Louis, where he was a major figure in the xenophobic Know-Nothing Party.

His record in the Civil War is a subject of some controversy. He was either a hero or a deserter—it's difficult to imagine him as anything in between—and appears to have served most of his hitch as a member of the Invalid Reserves due to his game leg. This didn't prevent him from promoting himself to colonel after Appomattox, a title he carried to the end of his life.

Buntline was a prolific writer. Beginning in 1869, his publishers paid him a princely twenty thousand dollars a year for his flamboyant memoirs, and they sold them to a growing following of readers who had never ventured west of the Hudson River. The proceeds allowed Buntline to support four wives and a succession of mistresses, and they financed

JOACHIM MILLER'S SUNRISE

BY SCOTT CUPP

Joachim Miller was born Cincinnatus Hiner, near Liberty, Indiana, in September 1837, and he died in Oakland, California, in February 1913. Between these two dates, he established himself as the major romantic poet of the West, the self-proclaimed "Byron of the Rockies," a title he had printed on his business cards. He toured Europe in 1870, where his flamboyant clothes and exotic manners made him a big hit. He adopted the name Joachim out of reverence to the myth of Joaquin Murietta, whom he used as a character in several poems.

Miller's poetry suffered from the very excesses that made the poetry of the early Romantics so good. Where poets of the caliber of Byron and Shelley made it work, Miller's poems tended toward the maudlin and grotesque. Take as an example the opening section of "The Tale of the Tall Alcalde":

Where mountains repose in their
   blueness,
When the sun first lands in his
   newness,
And marshals in his beams and his
   lances
Ere down to the vale he advances
With visor erect, and rides swiftly

On the terrible night in his way
And slays him, and, dauntless and
   deftly,
Hews out the beautiful day
With his flashing sword of silver,
Lay nestled town of Renalda,
Far famed for its stately Alcalde
The iron judge of the mountain mine,
With heart like the heart of woman,
Humanity more than human;
Far famed for its gold and silver,
Fair maids and its mountain wine.

Miller takes sixteen confusing lines to tell the reader that the sun came up in Renalda, California, one morning. The poem goes on for another nine hundred similar, impossible lines. Miller published nine volumes of poetry in his career, including *Songs of the Sierras,* from which "The Tale of the Tall Alcalde" is acknowledged as the best.

PIONEERS TO THE GREAT EMERALD LAND

A POEM BY JOACHIM MILLER

Pioneers to the Great Emerald Land,
Emerald, emerald, emerald Land;
Land of the sun mists, land of the sea,
Stately and stainless and storied and grand
As closed mantled Hood in white majesty—
Mother of States, we are worn, we are gray—
Mother of men, we are going away.

Mother of States, tall mother of men,
Of cities, of churches, of home, of sweet rest,
We are going away, we must journey again,
As of old we journeyed to the vast, far West.
We tent by the river, our feet once more,
Please God, are set for the ultimate shore.

Mother, white mother, white Oregon
In emerald kilt, with star set crown
Of sapphire, say it is night? Is it dawn?
Say what of the night? Is it well up and down?
We are going away...From yon high watch tower,
Young men, strong men, say, what of the hour?

Young men, strong men, there is work to be done;
Faith is to be cherished, battles to fight,
Victories won were never well won
Save fearlessly won for God and the right.
These cities, these homes, sweet peace and her spell
Be ashes, but ashes, with the infidel.

Have Faith, such Faith as your fathers knew,
All else must follow if you have but Faith.
Be true to their faith, and you must be true.
"Lo! I will be with you," the Master saith.
Good by, dawn breaks; it is coming full day
And one by one we strike tent away.

Good bye. Slow folding our snow-white tents
Our dim eyes lift to the farther shore,
And never these riddled, gray regiments
Shall answer full roll call anymore.
Yet never a doubt, nay, never a fear
Of old, or now, knew the Pioneer.

his travels and a steam yacht on the East River, where he recuperated between Western excursions and eastern benders. His rotund frame and rumpled clothes were equally familiar sights in the opulence of Chicago's Palmer House and flyblown barracks in Kansas.

The dime novel, (Buntline himself preferred the term "popular fiction") captured the fancy of an industrial nation eager for stories from the frontier, and it found its way into parlors and saddlebags across the continent. Under bright serifed mastheads like *The New York Detective Monthly* and *Beadle's Dime Library,* their illustrated covers promised plenty of action and the lowdown on "Buffalo Bill's Double" and "The James Boys in California"—and their contents delivered. Invariably the stories dealt with saintly heroes and endangered virgins, villains of a depressingly reptilian sameness, bandits and rustlers and interchangeable savages. Inevitably he included a speech on temperance—Buntline's favorite subject—or appeals to patriotism or testaments of faith. All too frequently, they ended with gunfire. The bibulous Cody and the amoral Hickok seldom recognized themselves in Buntline's flowery prose.

Buntline wrote of Buffalo Bill, put him on stage in New York and Chicago, and planted in his imagination the seeds of the open-air exhibition that would marry forever the mystique of the historical frontier to the romance of Buntline's Arthurian vision. Together they invented the Wild West.

If Buntline had none of his heroes' social virtues, he shared their ingenuity. When the proprietor of Nixon's Amphitheater in Chicago, aghast to learn that there was still no script at the eleventh hour, pulled out of the production, the novelist-turned-playwright rented the auditorium himself and knocked out "Scouts of the Plains" in four alcoholic hours. He surrounded Cody with Bowery Indians, cast himself as a paunchy teetotaling scout, and ad-libbed the company through a hilariously disastrous opening night into theatrical legend. When a fresh crop of criminal charges threatened a lien against the play, Buntline changed its title and stayed away from the theater. In his place, Cody cast his friend Hickok.

Edward Zane Carroll Judson died at Stamford, his birthplace, in 1886. Today his fame is linked inexorably with the Buntline Special, a Colt revolver with an attenuated barrel and a detachable rifle stock, said to have been presented personally by Buntline to Wyatt Earp, Bat Masterson and Bill Tilghman. Ironically, the gun didn't exist until 1977, when the Colt Company began manufacturing a model by that name to satisfy popular demand. Biographer Stuart N. Lake created the myth of the weapon in *Wyatt Earp, Frontier Marshall,* published in 1931.

The dime novel traces its ancestry to the German horror pamphlet of the fifteenth century. With the economical printing processes of the Reconstruction and the prolixity of writers such as Buntline and Prentiss Ingraham, who once wrote thirty-five thousand words in twenty-four hours to meet a deadline, it became unstoppable. Schoolboys read the books behind barns in Maine, and desperadoes passed time with them while hiding out in the Dakota Badlands. Genuine Westerners imitated the characters' dress and speech, melding the lies into a kind of alloy that still confuses serious historians. The West the world remembers owes everything to the anonymous Samaritan who cut Buntline down from that awning post in Nashville. ■

MARK TWAIN IN THE WEST

When the Federals blockaded the Mississippi River at the outbreak of the Civil War, a young riverboat pilot named Sam Clemens found himself out of a job. After a disappointing stint in the Confederate militia, Sam, who was in spirit a Southerner but had ambivalent feelings abut the conflict, accompanied his brother, Orion Clemens, to the West. Orion had secured a position with Nevada Territorial Governor James W. Nye. The brothers arrived in the mining boom town of Carson City, Nevada on August 14, 1861.

When his attempt at mining proved a bust, Clemens indulged his literary leanings by writing letters to the newspapers. In September 1862, Clemens signed on as a reporter for the *Territorial Enterprise* in Virginia City, Nevada. Clemens first used his pen name of "Mark Twain" to sign his *Enterprise* columns in which he covered territorial legislature meetings. He expanded his range to cover local social events, from Indian raids to shoot-outs in the mining camps. His columns became popular throughout the West as California newspapers picked them up for reprint. His acid wit gained him fans and detractors, and upon occasion it got him into trouble.

While drinking one night in 1864, Twain wrote a sarcastic article—titled "How Is It?"—that questioned the ethics of the Sanitary Fund, a Civil War equivalent of the Red Cross that raised funds for military medical supplies. Though Twain claimed he'd written it as a joke never meant for publication, the article appeared in the *Enterprise*. It got Twain into a war of words and letters with James Laird, owner of the Virginia City *Daily Union*, a rival newspaper. Between lurid correspondences, vitriolic columns and heated words, the paper war threatened to turn into a deadly duel.

Early on the morning appointed for the duel, his *Enterprise* compatriots set up a target range for him against a barn door. Twain couldn't hit the barn door, much less the target. Frustrated by his student's lack of aptitude, Twain's close friend and second for the duel, Steve Gillis, grabbed the pistol and shot a flying sparrow out of the air. He'd no sooner handed the weapon back to Twain than Laird appeared with his party. Laird asked who had made the shot; Gillis replied that it was the man who held the gun. Laird and his seconds immediately withdrew from the field of honor.

Because Governor Nye's strict stance against dueling made it a crime to even solicit a duel, Twain and Gillis fled almost immediately for San Francisco. Though the paper war ended his career with the *Enterprise*,

Mark Twain, 1870 (courtesy of History Room, Wells Fargo Bank, San Francisco, CA)

Twain took with him a wealth of memories about the life of the wild mining towns, which he'd later recount in *Roughing It*, his memoir of the time. In California he found a publisher for his short story, "Jim Smiley and His Jumping Frog," eventually collected in *The Celebrated Jumping Frog of Calaveras County*. After an ocean voyage to the Sandwich Islands, he embarked on a speaking tour of the West which won him even greater fame as a humorist.

And so did the Wild West transform a transplanted, reluctant Southerner, who wanted only to be a riverboat pilot to the end of his days, into one of America's greatest storytellers.

Cooper's Rules of Storytelling

by Bill Crider

AS ANYONE WHO HAS READ MARK TWAIN'S ESSAY, "FENIMORE COOPer's Literary Offenses," is well aware, Twain was no admirer of Cooper's stories of the frontier. In fact, Twain accused Cooper of scoring 114 literary offenses out of a possible 115, not to mention violating eighteen of the nineteen rules that govern literary art in the realm of romantic fiction. In his pointed and hilarious essay, Twain destroyed his straw man with ease.

But the fair-minded reader will realize that Twain overlooked an important point. Despite his shortcomings, Cooper (his friends called him James rather than Fenimore) managed singlehandedly to create the fictional Western hero as we know him today.

Although *The Deerslayer* (1841) was the last novel Cooper wrote in his Leatherstocking series—the others were *The Pioneers* (1823), *The Last of the Mohicans* (1826), *The Prairie* (1827) and the *Pathfinder* (1840)—it features the earliest adventures of Cooper's hero, Natty Bumppo. Also known as Deerslayer, Hawkeye, Leatherstocking and Pathfinder, Bumppo explored not Tombstone or Dodge but central New York State—but it was the frontier nevertheless. And by writing the first book in the series last, Cooper made sure he got things right, thus putting in his debt all the writers of Western fiction who have come after him.

Twain discussed the rules that Cooper broke, but much more important were the rules that Cooper *made*—they established for all time the archetype of the Western hero.

RULE 1: The Western hero should have a faithful Indian companion. Where would the Lone Ranger be without Tonto? Red Ryder without Little Beaver? McMurphy without the Chief? It was Cooper who established the pattern with the friendship between Natty Bumppo and Chingachgook (pronounced, we may assume, as it is spelled, despite Twain's insistence that "Chicago" is correct). What affects Chingachgook affects the Deerslayer. When asked why he is interested in one of his friend's problems, the Deerslayer replies, "It all consarns me as all things

> **"By American literature in the proper sense we ought to mean literature written in an American way, with an American turn of language and an American cast of thought. The test is that it couldn't have been written anywhere else."**
>
> **STEPHEN BUTLER LEACOCK FROM "MARK TWAIN AS NATIONAL ASSET" (1932)**

"It was in the Klondike that I found myself. There, nobody talks. Everybody thinks. You get your perspective. I got mine."

JACK LONDON

that touches a fr'ind consarns a fr'ind." The two friends are still together when Chingachgook dies in a fire fifty years later. In the B Westerns of the 1940s, the Indian companion evolved (or devolved) into the Sidekick, but the principle remained the same.

RULE 2: The Western hero is morally straight. "I would dare to speak truth," Deerslayer tells Hurry Harry March, "consarning you, or any man that ever lived." Deerslayer also refuses to join Hurry Harry and Tom Hutter on a scalping expedition, although Hurry Harry explains that scalping Indians is perfectly legal and that, in fact, the colony pays a bounty for Indian scalps, just as it does for the ears of a wolf. "When the Colony's laws, or even the King's laws, run ag'in the laws of God," Deerslayer says, "they get to be onlawful and ought not to be obeyed." It's a statement with which even Henry David Thoreau could agree. The Western hero is always faithful to his own code, or to higher morality, even when he appears to be acting contrary to the "law."

RULE 3: The Western hero is a deadly shot. Of course, Natty Bumppo uses a muzzle-loading rifle instead of a pistol, but he's just as fast and just as accurate as any pistolero in the pages of the dime novels. When Deerslayer kills his first man, he needs only "a single moment and a single motion" in order "to cock and poise his rifle," and he fires almost without aiming. Of course the result is deadly for the redskin, who is so impressed by the Deerslayer's skill that he gives him the name, "Hawkeye." Even this feat of shooting pales beside some of Natty Bumppo's later exploits, all of which Twain more than adequately delineated in his essay.

It's also in the *The Deerslayer* that Natty Bumppo receives his legendary rifle, Killdeer, from the hands of a beautiful woman, with her admonition that he become "King of the Woods"—a hundred years or so before Roy Rogers became "King of the Cowboys."

RULE 4: The Western hero should avoid marriage. How many married heroes have there been in the annals of the fictional West? Could Matt Dillon ever have married Miss Kitty? Had he done so, we'd have had no more *Gunsmoke;* we'd have had *The Little House on the Prairie.* Cooper knew this very well. Natty Bumppo avoids the marriage trap twice in *The Deerslayer.* Once, when he's captured by the tribe of the man he killed, the Deerslayer is faced with a choice—suffer torture and death or marry the widow of the slain man. Naturally, he chooses torture and death. He tells the assembled tribe that he, "may never marry," and that Providence, having seen fit to put him in the woods, intended that he "should live single," without a home.

The second woman the Deerslayer avoids is Judith Hutter, who prac-

JACK LONDON IN THE KLONDIKE

He'd been an oyster pirate off the California coast, sailed the Pacific to Hawaii and Japan, and crossed America on foot as part of Coxey's march of the unemployed to Washington, but young Jack London's greatest adventure still awaited him in the frozen north. In the Klondike River country of the Canadian Yukon he found little real gold, but discovered the stuff that dreams are made of—literary gold.

His frail brother-in-law, Captain James Shepard, offered to finance a trip to the gold fields if London would carry most of the physical load. London, Shepard and three other partners traveled from San Francisco to Juneau, Alaska, by steamship. They arrived on August 2, 1897, then took Indian canoes up the Lynn Canal to the town of Dyea, which lay at the entrance to the deadly Chilcoot Pass, "the worst road this side of Hell." Shepard found the pass so daunting he decided to return to California.

London and his remaining partners managed to carry their required 5000 pounds of food and equipment through the pass at 150 pounds per trip. Beyond the pass lay miles of semi-frozen swamps and icy streams they had to cross to get to Lake Lindeman. They had to build their own boat to travel up a series of lakes that led to Dawson, and it was a race against time to complete it before the killing white winter set in. They fought their way through whirlpools, rapids and storms; even traffic jams as thousands of other Klondikers clogged the routes into gold country. Eventually they set up operations on Henderson Creek near the Stewart River.

Their cabin was a tiny, dirt-floored icebox thirteen feet square—they could break icicles off the ceiling to boil for water. They subsisted on the three "Bs," sourdough bread, beans and bacon; London came down with scurvy for a lack of fresh vegetables or fruit. Any illness or weakness could mean death, and in the long night of winter, many a Klondiker's cabin became a trap or tomb.

But London survived, and what he saw during the wild rush to the Yukon —the heartbreaking spectacle of thousands of pack animals left dead and dying beside the trail, the natural beauty of the glaciers and the rivers, the squalor and rowdiness of frontier Dawson, the awesome power of avalanches, the terror of the all-encompassing cold and the spirit that kept men slogging on despite absolute exhaustion and the despair of loneliness—fueled his writer's imagination.

In the spring of 1898, London and his companions gave up their quest for gold and began the long journey home. By that time young Jack had already begun to think that the true source of his hoped-for success lay in the writer's pen rather than the miner's pan. He was right. Even though he'd not struck it rich, he left for home loaded with the powerful images he later brought to life in his novels; *A Daughter of the Snows, The Call of the Wild, White Fang,* and his host of short stories. London not only discovered the greatest treasure of the last frontier, he shared it with us all.

Jack London (courtesy of History Room, Wells Fargo Bank, San Francisco, CA)

**"When you call me that,
smile!"**

OWEN WISTER FROM
THE VIRGINIAN (1902)

tically proposes to him. (Corollary 1: The Western hero is irresistible to women.) It takes Judith quite a while to make her proposal, for Deerslayer pretends not to understand what she means. Finally she asks point blank: "You will not accept me for your wife, Deerslayer?" Of course he won't. After all, his sweetheart is, "in the forest…hanging from the boughs of the trees, in a soft rain…in the dew on the open grass…the clouds that float about in the blue heavens…the birds that sing in the woods…in the sweet springs…and in all the other gifts of God's Providence!" What does he need with a mere woman?

RULE 5: The Western hero is a square shooter. He always plays fair and would never dream of taking unfair advantage of an opponent by, say, shooting him in the back, even though the opponent wouldn't think twice about killing the hero by any underhanded means available. After an Indian attempts to murder Deerslayer from ambush, Deerslayer slips into the forest and gets behind the Indian, who is reloading his rifle. Cooper points out, "nothing would be easier," than for Deerslayer to shoot the "unprepared foe, but [his] every feeling…revolted at such a step." Instead, Deerslayer steps from behind a tree and calls out to the Indian, "Thisaway, redskin; thisaway if you're looking for me."

Similar scenes repeated themselves for years in B Westerns—usually the hero disarms the villain and then refuses to gun him down. He always allows the villain to retrieve his weapon, then guns him down, but he always lets the villain draw first. The important thing—the only thing that really matters—is to give the opponent a fair chance. What happens after that is up to the individual's skill (See Rule 3).

RULE 6: The Western hero lives on the lone prairie, not in the stifling atmosphere of the settlements. In all the movies about Hopalong Cassidy, did Hoppy ever settle down? No, he just toured the countryside, riding Topper. Natty Bumppo doesn't ride, and he lives in the woods most of his life, but it's a similar case. At the end of his long career, fleeing the settlements, Bumppo finally comes to live on the plains. In a moving scene in *The Prairie,* he requests that he be buried far from the towns and that no verse be carved on his tombstone, though he would like to have the stone so that in some small way his name will be preserved.

Natty Bumppo need not have worried. Though not everyone knows his name, virtually anyone who has seen a Western movie or read a Western novel has seen an aspect of him, no matter how dimly represented. James Fenimore Cooper achieved a lasting place in American fiction by creating the first Western hero, the one in whose footsteps all the others follow. ■

THE MYTH AND THE MYTHMAKERS...

ON CANVAS, ON STAGE

The White Castles on the Missouri, Karl Bodmer
(courtesy of Joslyn Art Museum, Omaha, Nebraska)

The Chasm of the Colorado, 1873–74, Thomas Moran
(courtesy of National Museum of American Art,
Washington, DC/Art Resource, NY, lent by the U.S. Department
of the Interior, Office of the Secretary)

Last Chance or Bust, 1900, Charles M. Russell
(courtesy of C.M. Russell Museum, Great Falls,
Montana)

At the End of the Fight, Frederic Remington
(courtesy of Texas A&M University, Special
Collections and Archives)

Scenes of Summit Springs Rescue
c.1907, lithograph poster
Buffalo Bill Historical Center, Cody, WY

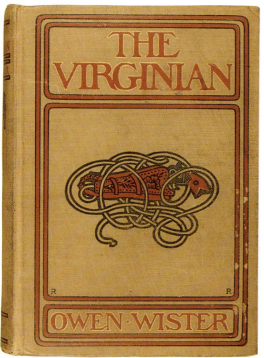

ABOVE: *The Virginian*, 1920,
Charles M. Russell (courtesy of C.M.
Russell Museum, Great Falls, Montana)

LEFT: First edition of *The Virginian*
by Owen Wister (courtesy of Texas
A&M University, Special Collections
and Archives)

OWEN WISTER: "SMILE!"

BY LEE SCHULTZ

Owen Wister at the age of forty

MOST PHOTOGRAPHS SHOW OWEN WISTER IN THE CLOTHING OF HIS success: a well tailored-suit, high-collar shirt, tie, even a vest. He wears hand crafted boots with a finish and a polish meant for civilized streets.

In the older photos he poses beside the fork of a huge twisted cedar; he has the looks of one who might have ridden with Billy Bonney or clinked glasses with Bat Masterson and Wyatt Earp. He might have ridden with Kit Carson or Custer.

In one photo he wears his weather-beaten, rolled-brim hat thrown back at a distinctly rakish angle, baring his forehead. He's rough shaven, with dark eyebrows and an untrimmed mustache. His beard swallows the lower part of his face, and he wears a large, light-colored bandanna about his neck. The twin tails of the neckerchief dangle down between the lapels of a soiled brush jacket, which is thrown wide. In one gloved hand he pinches what looks to be a hand-rolled cigarette. His other hand rests thumb-hooked over a large belt just in front of the plain leather holster for a large six-gun. He's tucked his old pants into rough work boots.

His picture wouldn't be out of place on a wanted poster.

The photograph was taken in 1887. Only five years prior, Wister had graduated *summa cum laude* and Phi Beta Kappa from Harvard, with a degree in music.

His ambition, backed up by considerable talent, was to be a composer. After graduating, he traveled to Europe to visit the greats of the profession. In Wagner's house in Bayreuth, Bavaria, he played his own composition of *Merlin and Vivien* for master composer Franz Liszt. Liszt was impressed—he wrote to Wister's grandmother that the American had a, "pronounced talent."

While at Harvard, Wister met Theodore Roosevelt, who would remain a lifelong friend and inspiration. He also kept company with the elite of society, politics and the arts—Frederic Remington, Oliver Wendell Holmes, Jr., Henry James, William Dean Howells, and later, even Rudyard Kipling and Ernest Hemingway rubbed elbows with the rough-shaven

> **"It may be there is no ordinary and wonder is true vision."**
> **ROBERT SERVICE**

cowboy in the photograph.

But Wister's father called him home from Europe and pressed him to begin a career in a Boston brokerage firm. That business floundered, and instead of being in a high position with Lee, Higginson & Company, Wister found himself sitting below stairs on a high stool in the Union Safe Deposit Vaults, computing interest rates on daily balances.

To keep his hand in, Wister completed a novel in his spare time. William Dean Howells, though impressed with the display of talent, advised him never to show it to a publisher. He followed Howells' advice.

At that point, Wister decided to return to Harvard to make a career of law. He explained to his father, "American respectability accepted lawyers, no matter how bad, which I was likely to be, and rejected composers, even if they were good, which I might possibly be."

BUT THEN HE HIT A TURNING POINT IN HIS LIFE. THE TENSION of beginning a new career and the disappointment of the end to his previous ambitions poised him on the brink of a nervous breakdown. In 1885, his doctor ordered him to visit some friends at their ranch in Wyoming. The change of atmosphere, scenery and new vistas provided an ecstatic adventure. He wrote in his journals, "I'm beginning to feel I'm something of an animal and not a stinking brain alone." He wondered why anyone would go back east after having been in the West for a few years.

He found a lyric serenity in Western solitude, and it healed him physically and psychologically. He returned home to enter Harvard again, and by 1888 he graduated with a law degree.

But his attachment to the West haunted him and finally claimed him. Before 1900, he made fourteen more trips to the West, and as early as 1889, he began to talk about a "great book" on the West. In 1902, he produced that book, *The Virginian,* in which he introduced the prototype of every Western hero and most of the Western plots that followed.

The Virginian became one of the great best-sellers of all time. In the five decades after its first publication, it sold 1.8 million copies; more living Americans had read it than any other novel. It would be difficult to find a written or performed Western with no similarities to *The Virginian's* hero or plot.

Wister's readers accepted his depiction of the cowboy and his West as "the way things were." Other writers copied his hero, his code of Western justice, his explanations of good and evil and love. Zane Grey, Max Brand, B. M. Bower, Louis L'Amour and a host of others wrote from what they found *true* in Wister's story.

Almost everyone recognizes one scene from the novel; it's become an American cliche. Dustin Farnum, William S. Hart, Kenneth Harlan, Gary Cooper and Joel McCrea are just some of the actors who have spoken the most famous line in a Western.

Focus in on a poker game in the saloon in Medicine Bow, Wyoming. The Virginian is joined by his friends; they josh each other and divine some pranks. One of his best friends, Steve, compliments him on his pranksmanship: "You're a son-of-a _____ when you get down to work." The Virginian takes the words as a friendly tribute.

But now enters Trampas, the evil plotter who has given the hero

ROBERT SERVICE, POET OF THE KLONDIKE

Lured by tales he'd read of Western adventure, a young Scotsman and novice poet named Robert Service left his job as a clerk at the Bank of Glasgow and took ship in 1896 for Canada. With his guitar on his shoulder and a copy of Robert Louis Stevenson's *An Amateur Emigrant* in his pocket, he followed his elusive muse, singing and tramping his way through the West. Often penniless, he paid his way working at odd jobs from British Columbia to San Francisco, from Colorado to Nevada, from Mexico to Arizona and back to the Northwest. All along the road, he set down in verse what he saw, and even published some of it when he found an occasional stopping place.

Although it wasn't the cowboy adventure he'd expected, Service found plenty to write about in the life of the open road. He worked side by side with the common laborers of America's orchards and fields, and he sometimes slept in hobo jungles. He shared in the hardships and despairs of the "great unemployed," and often saw the country's natural wonders

through eyes dulled by hunger or fever.

In 1903 Service got a job with British Columbia bank, but he wasn't drawn north so much by steady employment as by stories of the Yukon. Even though he'd missed the height of the 1889 Gold Rush, in 1904 he wangled a transfer to the bank's branch in Whitehorse in the Yukon territory. The bank manager, a former ship's captain, told the young poet stories of his adventurous life at sea and taught him the slang of the Yukon. Service joined readily in the social life of Whitehorse, which went on all night under the midnight sun. He took to the North country and found inspiration in the fragile beauty of its summers and the stark majesty of its winters.

When Service submitted some of his work to the *White Horse Star*, the editor asked him to write a piece for a church concert, something relevant to life in the North. In looking for something different from the standard dramatics, the former hobo balladeer turned to the music of the barroom piano as a dramatic device. A line flashed into his mind, an image of some of the boys "whooping it up" in the saloon. He decided to work on his composition late at night in his teller's cage in the bank, and it nearly cost him his life. The bookkeeper was sleeping in the guard room and, thinking Service a bank robber, took a shot at him.

Even as Service's ears still rang from the shot, he sat down to write the story it had suggested to him. If the bookkeeper hadn't fired, or if he hadn't missed, the life of the Yukon would never have been celebrated in "The Shooting of Dan McGrew," "The

Poet Robert Service

Cremation of Sam McGee" and the thirty-odd other poems in Service's *The Spell of the Yukon and Other Verses*. In those verses, Service chronicled both the hardship and the humor of North country life, and froze them forever in time. The vagabond poet had finally captured his muse. After Service left the Yukon, he turned his pen to other experiences, which he collected in *Rhymes of a Rolling Stone, Ballads of a Bohemian, Rhymes of a Red Cross Man* and many other books. Though literary success brought him fame and fortune and lured his restless boots away toward other roads, he never forgot the debt he owed to the land of the midnight sun.

trouble before. He half-heartedly sneers the same words: "You bet, you son-of-a _____." The Virginian draws his pistol, and in a voice "gentle as ever," says: "When you call me that, smile!"

You never learn his name; he's known only as "The Virginian." But you see his shadow behind every cowboy hero.

Wister, the musician-lawyer, may have created the Virginian as his alter ego. He took most of the characters and incidents in *The Virginian* from his own experiences during his travels in the West. The reality of those experiences were sometimes brutal.

In June of 1891, as Wister visited ranch owner David Tisdale, he watched helplessly as Tisdale committed an unspeakable act of cruelty to a horse. Tisdale first violently prodded the animal, then actually gouged out the horse's eye. In his journal, the meek Wister contemplated many actions he might have taken to protest the maiming. But Wister, a far cry from the desperado in his 1885 picture, did nothing.

In his short story, "Balaam and Pedro," which appeared in *Harper's* magazine, he faithfully recreated the incident. But instead of a helpless witness, Wister's hero is a strong, righteous individual who crushes Balaam's gunhand and leads the poor horse away with a lightened pack. Wister recycled the story as a scene in *The Virginian.*

So it was that the most famous cowboy of all may have been born as the alter ego of a gentleman, the musician-lawyer, Owen Wister. In the novel, the Virginian administers a severe beating to Balaam. In reply to the horse-abuser's screams, the Virginian replies, "If you are dead, I am glad of it."

President Theodore Roosevelt had strong objections to Wister's description of Balaam's act. In the short story, Wister describes Balaam's actions clearly, if not graphically. Roosevelt felt that "conscientious descriptions of the unspeakable" breached realism and disgusted readers, "not afflicted with the hysteria of bad taste."

Argue with the great Rough Rider though he did, Owen Wister accepted the criticism. In *The Virginian,* he left the details of the blinding to the imagination of his readers. After all, the Virginian's justified beating of the terrible miscreant was much more important than missing a detail or two.

Could it be that the transformation of a musician into a lawyer, of a lawyer into a cowboy, of a cowboy into *the cowboy,* the Virginian—all started on that first trip to Wyoming?

Just look at the picture of the young desperado Wister leaning against the tree. Watch his gunhand carefully and listen to his voice, "gentle as ever," tell you to *smile!* ■

HOPALONG CASSIDY, FROM PRINT TO PICTURES

BY ABRAHAM HOFFMAN

IN THE EARLY 1900s CLARENCE EDWARD MULFORD, A YOUNG CLERK in a Brooklyn, New York marriage license bureau, wrote a series of Western stories that were published in *Outing* magazine. The stories were then collected and published by Doubleday in 1907 under the title *Bar-20*.

Mulford's knowledge of the West was limited to library research, for he wouldn't make a trip to the West until 1924, well after he had established the popularity of his most famous protagonist, Hopalong Cassidy.

Born in Illinois and raised in New York, Mulford made up for his lack of first hand Western experience by writing action-packed stories full of gunfights and killings, with little attention to historical context. Hopalong was a hard-riding, hard-living cowboy who spoke Mulford's version of Western dialect, smoked, frequented saloons and shot to kill.

The formula worked for Mulford, and in the course of his career his Hopalong Cassidy stories sold well over a million copies. But it all begain with his first book, and a review of its contents reveals the tremendous contrast between Mulford's creation and Hopalong's transformation by motion pictures and television into someone else entirely.

Bar-20 begins with a violent confrontation between the cowhands of the Bar-20 and their neighbors and rivals, the cowboys at the C-80. Hard words are spoken, a young Bar-20 cowboy is too slow on the draw, and his friends take quick revenge. By the end of Chapter Three, at least a dozen more men have been killed, all from the C-80, and others wounded, including Cassidy and several of his friends. No mention whatsoever is made of lawful authority in Buckskin, the small town where the bloodbath takes place.

Cassidy and his friends, including Buck Peters, Red Connors, Johnny Nelson, and the other cowhands, relish the opportunity to eliminate a few rivals, and Mulford reports the affair in matter-of-fact fashion, as if such a battle were a common occurrence for the Bar-20 ranch hands.

Indeed it was—the narrative is continually punctuated by gunfights. In the course of the story, Hopalong is at one time or another shot in the arm, leg and collarbone, and the other Bar-20 men suffer similar wounds, but they all ultimately recover well enough to anticipate the next altercation with a sense of carefree anticipation.

Instead of a story line building to a dramatic climax in *Bar-20,* Mulford provided an episodic narrative. Three or four chapters traced an incident to its conclusion, then the story continued with another adventure. This, of course, reflects the original source of the book as a series of short stories. During these episodes, Cassidy and his Bar-20 cohorts perforate vagrant Indians, murderous outlaws, cowardly Mexicans, outrageous claim jumpers, nasty horse thieves, treacherous vigilantes and nefarious cattle rustlers, as well as anyone who transgressed their somewhat amorphous code of honor. The cowboys seldom work with cattle;

Hopalong Cassidy (William Boyd) holds his sidekick, Windy, (George Hayes) back in *Bar 20 Rides Again* (1935 Paramount)

in fact, there's only one brief scene in *Bar-20* in which they actually do so. They spend the rest of their time in Cowan's saloon in Buckskin or in saloons in other towns, or pursuing outlaws, rustlers or other evil-doers.

Mulford's Hopalong Cassidy in no way resembles the visual incarnation William Boyd gave him in motion pictures and television. In the first book, Cassidy was a youthful twenty-five, red-haired and possessed of a passionate personality, a tobacco-spitting practical joker with a quick trigger finger. He'd experienced the one love of his life at age eighteen, but when seven years later Cassidy heads south of the border to once again see his beloved Carmencita, he finds her married and very over-weight. Cassidy beats a quick retreat, but not before he shoots up the local saloon and wounds the sheriff. Mulford excused such exploits as youthful shenanigans.

Apart from the lost love Hopalong gives up without much regret, *Bar-20* is notable for its virtual absence of women. There's no love interest in the story, and except for Carmencita and the occasional mention of a "soiled dove," almost no female characters figure in the plot, not even the traditional schoolmarm. There is a brief appearance near the end by Miss Dean, a superficially respectable Easterner, but she turns out to be a con artist.

Mulford never mentions the owner of the Bar-20. Buck Peters, older than the other hands, is the ranch foreman, but the reader never learns if the Bar-20 is run by absentee owners or foreign investors. Mulford does give the reader a sense of place, although in point of time the story takes place in Western fiction's ambiguous 1870s. Buckskin and the Bar-20 are located in the Pecos Valley of Texas, and the Bar-20 men all have had experience in towns from Albuquerque to Cheyenne, and on ranches from Montana southward. The characters sweat freely, curse loudly and frequently play practical jokes on each other. The general impression Mulford gave was that the men of Bar-20 were not particularly intelligent, loved a good fight, were sorry when a friend was killed and carried their revenge to extremes.

Mulford insisted that his characters did have a code of honor: "They were real cowboys, which means, public opinion to the contrary notwith-standing, that they were not lawless, nor drunken, shooting bullies who held life cheaply, as their kind has been unjustly pictured, but while these men were naturally peaceable, they had to continually rub elbows with men who were not." Mulford blames the, "gamblers, criminals, bullies and the riffraff that fled from the protected East," as being the "class that caused the trouble." He excused the true cowboys who, "obeyed the greatest of all laws, that of self-preservation. Their fun was boisterous,

AN ELEGY FOR HICKOK

BY SCOTT CUPP

Captain Jack Crawford was far and away the *worst* of the serious poets of the West. Self-educated, he wrote maudlin drivel at the drop of a hat. When a man named Charlie Holt was killed in 1876 in the town of Custer, in the Dakota Territory, Crawford composed a poem for the funeral, even though he'd never met Holt:

Poor Charlie braved the wintry
    storms,
And footed it all the way;
And now he is a bleeding corpse—
He died at dawn today.

Imagine, if you will, the consolation that this deeply moving piece gave to the family—or how it would have been received at the gravesite.

Even more famous, or infamous, is the poem Crawford composed for Wild Bill Hickok's funeral:

Under the sod in the land of gold
We have laid the fearless Bill;
We called him Wild, yet a little child
Could bend his iron will.
With generous heart
he freely gave
To the poorly clad, unshod—
Think of it, pards
—of his noble traits—
When you cover him with the sod.

but they paid for all the damage they inflicted; their work was one of continual hardship, and the reaction of one extreme swings far toward the limit of its antithesis."

To the contrary, Mulford's heroes avoided work whenever possible, were seldom at the Bar-20 ranch, took any insult with the utmost seriousness, and held all non-Anglo peoples in contempt. Cassidy himself became so frenzied during a shoot-out that his behavior bordered on insanity. Mulford rescued his hero by having him calm down for a moment and exercise more caution as the bullets whizzed by.

It may well be that Mulford's first attempt at Western fiction was subtly satirical and that the public overlooked the undertone of cynicism modern readers can detect in the narrative. In any event, *Bar-20* was immediately popular, and Mulford spent the next few decades producing one sequel after another. Eventually he wrote twenty-eight books on the Bar-20 men, most of them featuring Hopalong Cassidy, out of a total career effort of over one hundred novels and short stories.

Inevitably, there were some contradictions in the stories. For example, Cassidy married—so much for Carmencita—and a later story portrayed him as a widower, with no explanation of how the change occurred.

Ironically, Mulford's literary success was eclipsed by his most popular character and how William Boyd portrayed him. A visually oriented generation of young people, weaned on B Westerns in the 1930s and 1940s, was followed by a television generation hungry for excitement on the small screen. The Hopalong Cassidy of movies and television evolved along lines rather different from the character created by Mulford.

In the motion picture versions, gone were the passionate revenge killings, the drunken sprees, the youthful exuberance. In their place came the ritualized cowboy styles of the 1930s B Western heroes. For Hopalong, the style included black clothing, a white horse named Topper, comical sidekicks and a patrician demeanor. In 1934, Paramount Studios hired William Boyd, age thirty-six, to play Hopalong; in Mulford's first book, Hopalong was a dozen years younger. Moreover, Boyd offered a much more sober portrayal than Mulford's original characterization. The love interest was left to Johnny Nelson, no longer Hopalong's peer, but now his apprentice. George "Gabby" Hayes and Andy Clyde provided the comic relief.

Aghast at what Hollywood was doing to his creation, Mulford saw only six of the Boyd/Cassidy films, sold off most of his rights to the character for a generous sum and retired to his Maine farm, there to build model steamboats, stagecoaches and covered wagons and to rake in even greater royalties when television rediscovered Hopalong. During

Mulford's career, he amassed a large collection of books and file cards on the West. He donated these materials to the Library of Congress in 1954, observing that in giving his collection away, he earned a tax writeoff of twenty thousand dollars—more than he would have netted had he sold it.

Television revived both William Boyd's career and the Hopalong Cassidy character, which by the late 1940s had run out of steam in the movies. An overnight craze for Hopalong Cassidy stories and paraphernalia resulted in some sixty-six television episodes, a Hopalong Cassidy radio program that ran for several years, personal appearances by Boyd dressed as Hoppy at openings of shopping centers and parades,

Hopalong Cassidy (William Boyd) and his faithful horse, Topper, in *The Unexpected Guest* (1947)

sales of bubble gum cards, cap pistols, hats and scarves and other artifacts. Ironically, the television success of Hopalong Cassidy resulted not in a reprinting of Mulford's Bar-20 books, but in their rewriting to fit better the character as personified by Boyd. Among the authors who wrote new Cassidy stories was a young Louis L'Amour.

Life even imitated art. Along with the Hopalong Cassidy comic book, Fawcett Publications, which churned out comics featuring an assortment of B Western stars in the early 1950s, even put out a series of Bill Boyd comics. This gave impressionable young readers the idea that when Boyd wasn't having adventures as Hopalong, he was having them as the actor who played him.

Mulford died in 1958. By that time it seemed that Hopalong Cassidy was dead too, for the Boyd/Hoppy craze, despite Boyd's personal appearances and the sale of bubble gum cards, had run its course. Unlike the Lone Ranger, Superman, Little Orphan Annie and Tarzan, no revival has boomed for Hopalong and the Bar-20, no major motion picture deal has been made. But there's always a chance. The television programs have aired on the Disney Channel, and some television or movie executive may just take it in his head to bring back beloved old Hoppy—while the original novels gather dust on library shelves. ■

PRICE, 10 CENTS.   **$1.00 A YEAR.**

Brann's Iconoclast.

VOL. 8.   WACO, TEXAS, U. S. A., MAY, 1898.   No. 4.

W. C. BRANN, Deceased.

Cover of May 1898 *Brann's Icono-clast* **(courtesy of William Cowper Brann Collection, The Texas Collection, Baylor University, Waco, TX)**

A BULLET FOR THE ICONOCLAST

BY THOMAS W. KNOWLES

THOUGH THE EXTRA EDITION OF THE *WACO DAILY TELEPHONE* WAS dated April 1, 1898, its shocking headline, "ANOTHER STREET DUEL" was no joke to the citizens of the self-proclaimed "Athens of Texas." The fierce gunbattle in the downtown commercial district had left principal duelists William Cowper Brann and Tom E. Davis fatally wounded, and three others injured. They were the final casualties of a long and bitter feud, not between rival gangs, but between the publisher and supporters of a crusading news magazine—*Brann's Iconoclast*—and the zealous defenders of Baylor University, the gem of the Baptist General Convention of Texas.

When William Cowper Brann resurrected the *Iconoclast* in Waco in 1895, he advertised it with a bold motto—"It Strikes to Kill!" "Iconoclast" translates literally as "idol-breaker"—one who destroys religious images or opposes their veneration. Brann redefined the word to fit his own obsessive pursuit of the absolute truth, his passion for exposing the moral and social hypocrisies of the late Victorian era. His acid wit and formidable literary skills were well-suited to such an occupation.

Brann was a self-educated writer and a gifted essayist. His precise style is readable even by modern standards. He could quote by memory from the classics, but like his beloved Shakespeare, he could wield vulgarisms, epithets and barnyard slang to devastating and sensational effect. He was also a product of his times, and not above its contradictions. His occasional racist diatribes were balanced by bitter condemnations of lynchings and disenfranchisement. He was at turns a defender of women's rights and a misogynist, a devoted husband and a paternal failure whose harsh words drove his thirteen-year-old daughter, Inez, to suicide in 1890.

He was born the son of a Presbyterian minister in Coles County, Illinois; after his mother's death, Brann was abandoned by his father to a succession of foster homes. He struck out on his own at age thirteen, and by the time he was twenty-one, he had worked as a traveling salesman, printer's devil, railway brakeman and fireman, a semi-pro baseball

Sat. Nov. 2nd

Hi Richard,

I'm in Bakersfield

So left you a note.

Have a great weekend

with Alex. Stay warm.
Maybe you could

take Alex for a walk

and show her the

morning glory vine

at the corner of 12th

and San Fernando.

Also, all the

Halloween decorations

we've seen!

See you Monday!

Your pal,
Diane

Saturday

pitcher and an opera company manager.

Neither his marriage to Carrie Belle Martin in 1877, nor the responsibilities of the family that soon followed, could root him to one place. He eventually left his reporter's post with the *St. Louis Globe-Democrat* to follow a long-held desire to emigrate to Texas. He worked as reporter, editor and columnist for many of the prominent Texas newspapers of the day, including the *Galveston Evening Tribune,* the *Galveston Post,* the *Houston Post,* and the *San Antonio Express.* His success as a writer was matched only by his inability to hold a job; the uncompromising nature that drove him to excellence always led him into disputes with his employers.

After the death of his daughter in 1890, Brann moved his family from

W.C. Brann at his desk (courtesy of William Cowper Brann Collection, The Texas Collection, Baylor University, Waco, TX)

GO WEST, YOUNG MAN!

BY DALE L. WALKER

Horace Greeley, onetime presidential candidate and publisher of the *New York Tribune,* is credited with this famous line, but didn't write it. It first appeared in print in the *Terre Haute* (Indiana) *Express* in 1851, in an article by John Babsone Lane Soule. Later, Greeley adopted the line when he wrote "Go west, young man, and grow up with the country," and tried his best to see that the admonition was properly attributed to Soule, even reprinting Soule's article in the *Tribune*.

Incidentally, Greeley took Soule's advice and went to the West in 1859, all the way to California. En route, he stopped off at Salt Lake City and spent some time interviewing Brigham Young. The story that resulted from his chat with the Mormon leader was printed in the *Tribune* and is a journalistic landmark: the first question and answer news story in American newspaper history.

Houston to the Texas state capital, Austin, where he started the *Austin Iconoclast* as a vehicle for a popular economic reform movement. When the venture failed, he sold his printing equipment for $250 to a friend, a young banker named William Sidney Porter. Porter would later be better known by his pseudonym, O. Henry.

In 1894, at age thirty-nine, Brann found himself faced with financial ruin and an uncertain future. He accepted a position with the *Waco Daily News.*

In 1894 Waco was a progressive city with a population of twenty-five thousand, an industrial and educational center that proudly claimed the title of "The Athens of Texas." In addition to Baylor University, it was the home of the Methodist Waco Female College, the Catholic Academy of the Sacred Heart, the African Methodist-Episcopal Church's Paul Quinn College, and several other private institutions.

Cotton was King, and yearly tribute was made to that monarch at the Cotton Palace Exposition. Waco's business district was served by modern electric streetcars, gas lighting and high-rise office buildings, while the rich industrial climate fostered a thriving textile industry. The dark side of this prosperity was reflected in the legalized "red-light" district and a slum known as Edgefield, an environment that later produced notorious bank robber Clyde Barrow.

Where not sixty years before the Waco Indians had encamped, the well-to-do-families lived in gracious homes and attended the opera, charity balls and art exhibits. These second- and third-generation Wacoans did their best to live down the town's less palatable sobriquet, "Six Shooter Junction," derived from their not-quite-forgotten habit of allowing Judge Colt to arbitrate personal disputes.

Baylor University was established in Independence, Texas, in 1845 by Judge R. E. B. Baylor, a former congressman from Kentucky. In 1861, Reverend Rufus C. Burleson moved the school to Waco and merged with the Waco Classical School to form Waco University. The founder's name was restored to the university in 1886. At the time of the Brann conflict, Baylor was a thriving co-educational classical/religious institution with an enrollment of five hundred and fifty. Modern Baylor University is the premiere learning center for the Southern Baptist Convention. The campus houses two of the Southwest's finest collections of historical and literary memorabilia—the Baylor Texas Collection and the Armstrong-Browning Library.

Waco's social life at the turn of the century quite naturally revolved around the university, but Brann found some of the less-progressive aspects of Baylor's influence on the religious, economic, and social development of the community disturbing. Those social foibles were perfect targets for his satirical pen. While other journalists either supported or declined to criticize the university, Brann enthusiastically attacked its prominence in Waco's affairs. He dismissed Baylor as a "great storm center of misinformation," and mercilessly ridiculed the darlings of Waco society.

As before, Brann found the conventions and restrictions of another's publication too confining. With pennies he scraped together from his salary, he resurrected the *Iconoclast*. The first Waco edition hit the streets in February 1895, and was an almost immediate financial and sensational success.

Battle lines were irrevocably drawn between Baylor and the *Iconoclast* in April of 1895. Brann attended a lecture meeting at Garland's Opera House in an attempt to interview the speaker, Reverend Slattery. An ex-priest turned traveling fire-and-brimstone Baptist against the "evils of the Catholic Church," Slattery represented an anti-Catholic, anti-Semitic organization known as the American Protective Association. The A.P.A. was devoted to the eradication of the "Roman Catholic influence in American education and government."

Brann's advocacy of religious tolerance had already earned him the title of "The Apostle," shorthand for "The Devil's Apostle." His sharp ques-

Waco Daily Telephone extra, 11/19/1897 (courtesy of William Cowper Brann Collection, The Texas Collection, Baylor University, Waco, TX)

tioning of the speaker earned him the applause of a major part of the audience, but he was forcibly ejected by Slattery's supporters, mostly Baylor students and faculty. His caustic editorials on the incident heightened the tensions and resulted in the first in a series of anonymous threats to his life.

Brann's work also began to win him fame among literary circles. The *Iconoclast* grew in circulation, with subscribers from as far away as

G.B. Gerald portrait (courtesy of William Cowper Brann Collection,The Texas Collection, Baylor University, Waco, TX)

Canada, Australia and Hawaii. As the *Iconoclast* prospered in the climate of controversy, so did Brann. For the first time in his life, he was able to provide Carrie Brann with a more permanent home than the series of boarding houses they'd inhabited for most of their married life. He purchased a roomy two-story house on Austin Avenue, and named it, "The Oaks."

In the summer of 1895, the *Waco Daily News* broke the scandal that would rock the university to its foundations, and lead to the violent deaths of four men—the sad affair of the rape of Antonia Teixeiria, a teenage Brazilian girl recruited by Baptist missionaries as a special student. While she attended five years of classes at Baylor in preparation for her career as a missionary, Antonia was to be a ward of the church and the university. Her welfare was President Burleson's direct responsibility.

Antonia accused Steen Morris, the brother of President Burleson's brother-in-law, of a series of assaults that culminated in rape in November 1894. Antonia claimed that no one in the Burleson family had paid heed to her complaints even though Morris had made his unwanted advances while he was visiting the Burleson household. She feared that she would not be believed, and only reported the rape when forced to do so by the evidence of her advancing pregnancy. Medical examinations bore out her testimony that she had been the victim of a brutal sexual assault. On this evidence, Steen Morris was charged with the crime.

Brann immediately put the *Iconoclast* at Antonia's defense—and to Baylor's prosecution. He baldly stated that his was the only earthly court in which the wronged Brazilian girl could expect justice. It may be that he saw in Antonia's plight a chance to redeem himself, to alleviate his guilt for his own daughter's fate.

It was Brann's greatest blow to Baylor's prestige and influence. He forced the university and the Burleson family to take the defensive, and they did it by attacking the victim. Though the words must have choked them, they swore that the physically and mentally abused fifteen-year-old girl was a thief, liar and harlot. It was that, or publicly admit they had failed miserably in their guardianship. For each of their accusations, the "Apostle" fired back a scathing rebuttal. With each defamation and slander of Antonia's character, the defenders of the faith readily convicted themselves.

In the *Iconoclast,* Brann recommended that parents not send their daughters to Baylor, citing Antonia's testimony that instead of being allowed to pursue her studies, she was made to serve in Burleson's kitchen while her guardians debated her fate. He staunchly defended her against barroom accusations that her pregnancy was the result of her

Old Corner Drugstore (courtesy of William Cowper Brann Collection, The Texas Collection, Baylor University, Waco, TX)

willing liaison with one of Burleson's black servants. That rumor was proven false by the birth of her child on June 17th, 1895. Her daughter, of obvious Anglo heritage, died within a few months.

Antonia eventually dropped the charges against Morris and returned to Brazil. In the September 1896 *Iconoclast,* Brann noted that Morris' defense attorney, R. L. Allen, had not only prepared Antonia's affidavit of Morris' exoneration, but he had also purchased the steamship ticket for her trip home.

The humiliation and damage to Baylor's credibility was incalculable; new enrollments, particularly of young women, began to fall. That the university and the *Iconoclast* could co-exist was no longer in question. It was only a matter of time and intolerance—and like Voltaire, Brann didn't know when to quit.

On Saturday, October 2, 1897, three Baylor students abducted Brann at gunpoint from the office of his printers, Knight and Womack. They bundled the publisher into a carriage and drove him to the campus mall. A reception committee awaited him. They roped him like a steer and pulled him toward the Main Hall, shouting, "Hang him! Hang the atheist!"

EXTRA.
Waco Daily Telephone.

WACO, TEXAS, FRIDAY NIGHT, NOV. 19, 1897.

GERALD - HARRIS STREET DUEL.

Three men Engaged in Deadly Comb.t on Austin Avenue.

W. A. HARRIS WAS KILLED

J. W. Harris was Mortally Wounded and G B. Gerald Has two Wounds---J. W. Harris Fired the First Shot.

At a time when the streets of Waco were crowded with men, women and children, this afternoon, a street duel participated in by three persons occurred on the most prominent business corner of this city, during which many shots were exchanged. One was killed and two wounded.

It is one of the most deplorable tragedies that has ever occurred. All by-standers and pedestrians escaped injury, with one exception, as the shooting seemed to be indiscriminate and occurred at a time when the streets were thronged.

When the firing began citizens rushed to cover and drove hurriedly away their vehicles. From other parts of the city curious people ran towards the scene but as they heard more firing they hesitated until it ceased. Within 60 seconds after the firing ceased several hundred persons rushed to the corner and it was with difficulty that Justice J. B. Earle could reach the inanimate form of W. A. Harris. Friends of all men engaged in the trouble were there

W. A. Harris, was across the street near the Citizens' National bank.

Judge Gerald crossed the intersection of the two streets and the firing began. The first shot came from the pistol of J. W. Harris and two were fired before Judge Gerald drew his pistol. He returned the fire and was then attacked by the brother, W. A. Harris. He turned to meet his new foe and in the exchange of shots, about 18 were fired. It was a street duel the like of which have never been seen in Texas since the days of border life, and at a time when the streets were crowded. Both men sought shelter from the leaden hail and stylish equipage with ladies at occupants moved swiftly from the scene. A panic occurred and within a short time the duelists had the street to themselves.

Judge Gerald was shot in the right side and in the left arm, his wounds are not fatal.

W. A. Harris was instantly killed and fell on the pavement of the Citizens' National bank, shot through the head and body.

was near me. He remarked: 'Get out of the way, I may have to do some shooting.' I stepped away and as I walked away Harris began shooting the first ball grazing the back of my head. As I walked away I saw Gerald crossing the street." Said Dr. Taylor crossing the street," said Dr. Taylor

"Who shot first," asked the reporter. "J. W. Harris fired first. He shot twice before Gerald pulled his pistol.

Judge Gerald said that he was attacked front and rear; and that J. W Harris fired first, and that he turned to defend himself; that when he fired at J. W. Harris W. A. Harris attacked him from the rear and he was forced to turn on him.

Judge Gerald walked away from the corpse to W. A. Harris and remarked "The cowards attacked me from behind. They were afraid to come out in the open."

The affair has created a great deal of excitement. The meeting between the men has not been unexpected, and when the reports of the pistols were heard every one said: "That is Harris and Gerald."

W. S. Jasper, a negro bystander, was shot in the fleshy part of the leg during the duel.

One person who saw the affray said "I was standing in front of the Citizens' National bank and started across the street towards the Old Corner Drug Store and the shooting began when I was about half way across. J. W. Harris was standing in the door of the Old Corner Drug Store apparently leaning up against the door jam and Gerald was standing on the curbstone, the two facing each other and both shooting. While they were shooting another man, now said to be W. A. Harris, who was standing in front of the Citizens' National bank, shot once at Gerald and once again but apparently the pistol snapped. He was seized by a policeman and Gerald ran across the street toward him. By the time he had reached the opposite side W. A. Harris had fallen and the policeman was on top of him, when Gerald, who had got over him shot him three times. Then a policeman seized Gerald and in the struggle both fell into the gutter."

From the statements of several people who met the principals prior to the shooting, the opinion is expressed that the meeting was not unexpected.

It is stated that Policeman Ballenfant had seized W. A. Harris after he shot at Judge Gerald and he was in custody when shot by the latter, who exclaimed as he fired the shots, "You ——— —— you shot me in the back."

At 5:30 this evening it was reported by the physicians in attendance upon J. W. Harris, and he was very low. They missed the bullet had evidently struck the cervical vertebrae and had caused paralysis from the hips down. It is stated that the condition of the wounded man admitted of little hope of his recovery. He was conscious and stated that he was bleeding internally

While they awaited the arrival of the tar and feathers, the mob began taking turns striking him, with fists at first, then with sticks and clubs. When it was discovered that someone had removed the tar and feathers from their hiding place, the cry went up once again for a hanging or a firing squad. Brann was saved only by the advent of three Baylor professors, Tanner, Brooks and Pool, who managed to cool the mob of students long enough for him to escape. He managed to drive away in the carriage, despite the pain of a severely injured right arm and the blood that flowed from his scalp into his eyes.

Brann's virulent words, typeset in lead, escalated to new promises of a different kind of exchange in that metal. He replied in print to the death threats, but he also took on a new partner—a revolver. The once-peaceful Central Texas community fractured into armed camps of Brann and Baylor supporters, with each side just waiting for someone to light the fuse.

The spark came from one of Brann's most loyal friends, Judge G. B. Gerrald, a battle-scarred ex-Confederate officer who had commanded the 18th Mississippi Regiment at Gettysburg. In his two terms as a McLennan County judge, he made his reputation—and many enemies—by personally smashing the equipment in a favorite gambling spot that was operating in defiance of his unpopular anti-gaming ordinance. His left arm was crippled by his war wounds, but he remained a quick-tempered man of action who invariably went armed and ready for trouble. His weapon of choice was a rare, .41-long caliber short-barreled version of the 1890's model Army Colt revolver known as "The Thunderer."

When J. W. Harris, editor of the *Waco Times Herald* and a staunch

Baylor supporter, refused to either print or return the original of Gerrald's letter to the editor condemning Brann's abduction, the 62-year-old judge confronted Harris in the *Times-Herald* office. Harris, a much larger and younger man, struck Gerrald with a cane and disarmed him. The ensuing struggle tumbled both men partway down the stairs, Gerrald getting the worst of it before they separated. As he left, Gerrald made it clear that he would seek retribution for the incident.

Gerrald later published a handbill in which he related his side of the encounter and branded Harris a coward, but promised not to "hunt him." Harris feared that the judge, despite his printed promise to the contrary, would take the initiative. Harris enlisted his brother William's aid in a plan to permanently resolve the conflict. They armed themselves with new .45 caliber Colt revolvers.

At about noon on November 19, 1897, the Harris brothers ambushed Judge Gerrald on Austin Avenue near Fourth Street and caught him between them in a vicious crossfire. J. W. Harris drew first and fired two shots from the doorway of the Old Corner Drug, one of which shattered the judge's left elbow. One of William Harris' shots struck an innocent bystander; another glanced off a metal button on the judge's coat and scored his side.

The brothers hadn't counted on the old Confederate's cool under fire. Disregarding his wounds and the hail of bullets centered on him, the judge drew his revolver and shot both the Harris brothers to death. He walked up to William and fired his final shot at such close range that it set William's coat collar on fire. Though his wounded arm was later amputated, Gerrald recovered and remained active until his death in 1914.

The incident horrified all but the most rabid from both camps. A brief cease-fire resulted, but almost everyone involved recognized it for what it was — the eye of the storm. Brann soon resumed his editorial scourging, and groups of Baylor students began gathering outside his house to rebuke him, once to the extent that fire hoses were used to disperse them.

Brann knew that his troubles were far from over, and he consulted Judge Gerrald. The old Confederate began tutoring him in secret in the finer points of pistol fighting. He evidently found Brann's weapon unsatisfactory, for he made him a loan of the .41 Colt Thunderer with which he had killed the Harris brothers.

The sensationalism of the abduction and the gunbattle popularized Brann's work on an international scale. He scheduled a lecture tour to begin on Saturday, April 2, 1898 in San Antonio. From there he planned to go on to Houston, Galveston, New Orleans and Chicago. He intended

Tom Davis np sketch (courtesy of William Cowper Brann Collection, The Texas Collection, Baylor University, Waco, TX)

to take advantage of the tour to treat his harried wife to a vacation from the constant harassment. He may also have sensed that it was time to give his enemies some breathing space.

The final act of the tragedy took place at about six o'clock in the evening of Friday, April 1, 1898. Brann spent most of that day with his family and his friends. At four in the afternoon, he had his driver drop him off downtown so he could complete his travel arrangements. He met his friend and business manager, W. H. Ward, at Fourth Street and Banker's Alley. They spoke for a while with John Guerin and Joe Earp, admirers of Brann's work, and then went into Laneri's Saloon. They left Laneri's a short time later and walked together down Fourth toward the depot, to meet Ward's brother and some friends who were arriving by train that evening.

As the two neared French's newsstand, fervent Baylor supporter Tom E. Davis stepped out from an office doorway behind them, an oath on his lips and a .45 Colt revolver in his hand. He fired into Brann's back, in Davis' own words, "where his suspenders crossed." Ward was confused by the surprise attack, but he managed to grab Davis' revolver by the barrel. He reeled back, shot through the hand.

Brann's wound was a mortal one—the bullet had entered between

WILDE GOES WEST

BY SCOTT CUPP

Oscar Wilde came to America in 1882 with the purpose of delivering a series of lectures on aesthetics. He was detained in customs at New York because of a rumor that he slept in frilly nightclothes. While a large crowd looked on, the customs inspectors searched but found no such items. When asked what he had to declare, Wilde replied, "Nothing. Nothing but my genius."

Wilde delivered his lectures in many cities, and some of them led to interesting incidents in the poets life. In Salt Lake City, Wilde wrote to a friend, "I have lectured to the Mormons. The Opera House at Salt Lake is an enormous affair about the size of Covent Garden, and holds with ease fourteen families. They sit like this:

and are very, very ugly."

In Leadville, Colorado, he read to an audience of miners from the autobiography of Benvenuto Cellini. The miners asked him to bring "Benny" with him on the next trip. He helped open a new mine, and the miners presented him with a silver drill bit that they called "the Oscar."

While traveling across the country, he received many more invitations to come and speak. One such invitation came from Griggsville, Kansas. Wilde was obliged to decline. He was then asked how the town could begin to improve their aesthetics. To which Wilde cabled back, "BEGIN BY CHANGING THE NAME OF YOUR TOWN."

Wilde arrived in St. Joseph, Missouri, just as Jesse James was killed.

Upon reading the papers, he was astonished to learn of the prices that mementoes of the outlaw were bringing, and compared the price for the one picture owned by Jesse James to that of a verified Titian.

The American West had never seen anything quite like Oscar Wilde, and the same could be said for him. Both were enriched by the visit.

his shoulder blades, punctured his lungs and exited through his right armpit. Still, he turned, drew the judge's revolver and returned fire with a deadly accuracy that put four shots through Tom Davis' body. Of the eight or nine shots fired by the two men, two struck passersby, including a musician and a streetcar motorman.

Davis was carried into the newsstand where a doctor worked in vain to save him. He was later moved into the Pacific Hotel. He made a statement to the D.A. in which he admitted to having shadowed Brann all that day with the vague intention of confronting the publisher about some slight or insult, real or imagined. He did have a daughter enrolled at Baylor at the time.

Not realizing that Brann had been back-shot, policemen on the scene arrested the stricken publisher. Officers Hall and Durie marched him to the courthouse over Ward's protests that blood was literally sloshing from their prisoner's shoes. It was only after the attending physician noted the placement of the entry wound that Brann was allowed to retire to his home.

Brann died at one fifty-five in the morning of April 2, while Davis held on in agony until his death at two-thirty in the afternoon. The funeral staged by the publisher's friends and supporters was the largest in Waco's history, and eulogies to the passing of the Iconoclast, the man and his publication, poured in from journalists and literary figures from across the nation and throughout the English-speaking world.

Brann stated in the February 1898 issue, "There are not Baptists enough in Texas to drive it [the *Iconoclast*] out of town. If they kill the editor, another and a better man will step into his shoes and continue the old fight against the hypocrites and humbugs..." This was proven only partly true. There *were* other good men who stepped forward. Judge Gerrald, Bill Ward and Mrs. Brann attempted to keep the *Iconoclast* alive, but it could not survive the loss of Brann's vitriolic genius. The May issue, composed by Ward as a tribute to his friend and partner, was the last.

The subject of the *Iconoclast* remains controversial even beyond the living memory of those involved. By unofficial tradition, freshmen Baylor journalism students assemble at Brann's grave in Oakwood Cemetery to hear the *Iconoclast's* story as they look upon the final evidence of the bitter conflict. Brann's profile, carved into his tombstone under a marble lamp that symbolizes Truth, still bears the scar of some unforgiving critic's pistol bullet on its temple. ◼

Note: A shorter version of this article originally appeared in the Summer 1989 issue of Persimmon Hill Magazine, *published by the National Cowboy Hall of Fame and Western Heritage Center in Oklahoma City, Oklahoma.*

W.C. Brann's tombstone (courtesy of William Cowper Brann Collection, The Texas Collection, Baylor University, Waco, TX)

Frederick Faust (Max Brand) (courtesy of Robert Easton)

FREDERICK WHO?
OH, YOU MEAN MAX BRAND

BY WILLIAM F. NOLAN

UNTIL 1938, WHEN EDWARD H. DODD, JR. REVEALED THE TRUTH IN *Publisher's Weekly,* the identity of "Max Brand" was a mystery. The reading public had never heard of Frederick S. Faust, but they had celebrated Max Brand as the "King of the Western Pulps" since 1919, when his first major pulp novel, *The Untamed,* had found an immediate audience.

The irony of Faust's rise to lasting fame in the Western genre is that he spent the entirety of his creative life in the unsuccessful pursuit of classical verse. Prose fiction (and he wrote extensively in a dozen genres) was simply his way of supporting his family.[1] In doing so, he became one of the most prolific storytellers of the twentieth century, averaging a million words annually over a twenty-seven-year writing career.

The mythic Western characters he created, from Harry Destry to the Montana Kid, have taken their place in the canon of genuine folk heroes. As Max Brand, Faust stands today with the giants of Western fiction.

His Western output was staggering. As of 1991, 220 Faust books were published, of which 180 were Westerns. The other 40 ranged from secret service novels to sword sagas to crime adventures to slim-backed volumes of his poetry. Faust's main passion as a writer was rooted, as always, in the creation of his classical verse. His lifelong obsession with Arthurian knights and Greek gods formed the "backbone" of his highly romantic fiction. Faust's Westerns were never "real," despite his carefully collected encyclopedic background knowledge of the Old West; this research served only as stage dressing. He preferred myth-making to truth-telling, and had no interest whatever in portraying the Old West as it actually was.[2] His horses were noble, winged creatures; his heroes were gods-with-a-sixgun; his women were pure and ever-patient; his landscape was a timeless, unchanging painted stage. He wrote at full gallop, with a narrative thrust that swept his readers along from first page to last, giving them scant time to think along the way. Action was the thing, and Faust was its master.

Born in 1892 in Seattle, Washington, and having grown to manhood working on farms in California, Faust began his professional writing career for the Frank A. Munsey pulp empire early in 1917 in New York. He turned out a half-dozen conventional pulp tales before he sold his first Western story, "The Adopted Son," to *All-Story Weekly.* It appeared under his new pen name of "Max Brand" in October of that year.

Unable to sell his verse, he had turned to pulp fiction to keep from starving. Metro Pictures Corporation was looking for star vehicle material for silent-film idol Francis X. Bushman, and purchased motion picture rights to "The Adopted Son" while the story was still in manuscript. This proved to the young Faust that the Western genre was profitable. By 1918 he had completed his first full-length Western serial for Munsey, *The Untamed,* and this mythic drama proved so successful with readers (in both magazine and book format) that Faust wrote three sequels—a series that launched Max Brand's career as a Western fictioneer.

And yet it was not until 1921, when Faust began turning out massive amounts of prose for Street and Smith's *Western Story Magazine,* that his talent really asserted itself. Munsey had overstocked, so Faust had placed a serial with *Western Story's* editor, Frank Blackwell, late in 1920. The magazine had just gone weekly, and Blackwell was wide open for material. Faust realized that he'd found a steady market to tap, and by 1921 he was solidly committed. He began an assault on the pulp Western not equaled before or since, making no less than 834 appearances in 622 weekly issues of *Western Story* in the following fourteen years, and producing a mind-boggling *thirteen million words* for Blackwell at premium rates. Faust got as much as five cents a word in a penny-a-word era—which meant four thousand dollars for a single serial.

Faust's back was always against the financial wall due to his lavish lifestyle—fine foods, vintage wines, fast cars, a classic library, a villa in Italy—and he needed every dollar he could earn from his colorful six-gun sagas. Luckily, his powers of production continued to be awesome; he was quite capable of writing a full-length Western novel in five days, and he once wrote three in under two weeks. For years he *averaged* a book every two weeks for *Western Story.* Blackwell bought everything Faust could write, spreading this incredible output through his magazine under eleven Faust pen names. It was a mother lode of wordage, and publishers are still mining it today, six decades later, for their "new" Max Brand titles.

Several Faust pen names were retained when the stories made their translation to book format, and some half a hundred Faust Western novels were published under pseudonyms other than Max Brand: nine-

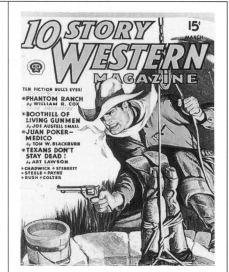

Max Brand reigned over pulps like these.

> "Bret Harte was one of the pleasantest men I have ever known. He was also one of the unpleasantest men I have ever known…"
>
> MARK TWAIN

teen by "David Manning," fourteen by "George Owen Baxter," eleven by "Evan Evans," three by "Frank Austin," two each by "Peter Henry Morland" and "John Frederick."

His peak year for Blackwell was 1932, when his work appeared (under five names) in every weekly issue of *Western Story.* By the year's end, however, Faust complained to his agent, "I have exhausted my potential for Western fiction," and he did not see how he could continue. But a bad heart, marital problems and a growing family (three children) put fresh pressures on him. Continue he did, producing his most extensive Western series, more than a dozen "Silvertip" novels, by mid-1934. By

THE LUCK OF BRET HARTE

Bret Harte's luck as a writer was a series of paradoxes, as was his life. One of the foremost creators of the myth of the Wild West, Harte was never at home in the West. Considered a dandy and a dude by Westerners, and an amusing curiosity by Easterners, Harte—a transplanted New Yorker—found the mining camps and boom towns of California too rude and unruly for his tastes. Once he established himself as a writer, he left the West, never to return. He wrote most eloquently of the West's natural beauty while he lived out the later years of his life as an expatriate in Great Britain.

By the end of his career, the English revered Harte as a great American of letters, but most of his countrymen considered him a simple storyteller of little note. If two of his stories, "The Luck of Roaring Camp" and "The Outcasts of Poker Flat," hadn't made the required reading lists for American school children in the early twentieth century, Harte would probably have been relegated to literary obscurity.

And yet, in those two stories and many others, Harte first brought to life the classic fictional Western characters, from sentimental miners to gentlemen gamblers, from tart schoolmarms to shady ladies with hearts of gold. Harte's characters were the originals, drawn with a finer eye to detail, closer to the raw myth of the West in not to the reality. The later dime-novel stereotypes of fainting, delicate females were poor copies of Harte's pragmatic and outspoken frontier women, and even his comic characters stretched beyond the two-dimensional range of the pulps.

For a time Harte became the literary darling of the Victorian Gilded Age, but his early success and the arrogance it engendered in him made him a target for envy. His disdain for the social conventions of the Victorian era also brought him censure. Harte was never satisfied in his personal or his professional life, and he expressed his dissatisfaction in excesses of behavior. He was at turns known as a model husband and family man, and condemned as a wife-beater and a drunken womanizer. As his public image suffered, so did his career.

As the first editor for the *Overland Monthly* magazine from 1868 to 1871, Harte was a driving force in the new literature of the West and a mentor to young writers. He was also a harsh and unforgiving critic, a master of literary sarcasm that he wasn't slow to exercise on friend or foe. Moody and prone to personal slights, he'd often ignore people he knew if he met them on the street. He could deal out criticism with ease, but he didn't take it well. He eventually retreated into exile in England, where he found a willing audience.

Harte's great early friendship with

Bret Harte as editor of the Overland Monthly *(courtesy of History Room, Wells Fargo Bank, San Francisco, CA)*

Mark Twain soured into a particularly bitter enmity, and Twain's condemnations dogged Harte throughout his literary career. Even so, Twain grudgingly admitted that he owed much of his success as a writer to what he'd learned from Harte—great praise indeed from the stubborn Missourian. Twain's ambivalence is the best illustration of the contradictory nature of Harte's life. Like his misfits in "The Outcasts of Poker Flat," Bret Harte could never quite get life to deal him a pat hand.

the close of that year, however, the Depression forced Blackwell to reduce Faust's rate to two cents a word; this put an end to their long association. Only two Faust tales appeared in *Western Story* in 1935.

He subsequently sold a few shorter Westerns, one of which was the notable and often-reprinted classic, "Wine on the Desert" from the June 1936 issue of *This Week*, but Faust's Western fiction career had run its course. One of his last published Westerns, the novelette *Señor Coyote*, appeared in a mid-1938 issue of *Argosy.* By then, Faust was in Hollywood developing the "Dr. Kildare" series for MGM.

Despite his film success with non-Western material, Hollywood refused to allow him to completely abandon the six-gun genre. He wrote three Westerns directly for major studios as "screen originals." The first was never produced, but the others served as the basis for the 1943 Randolph Scott/Glenn Ford vehicle, *The Desperadoes,* and the 1950 Errol Flynn epic, *Montana.*

Some three dozen Western films based on Faust's works were released by Hollywood from 1917 into the 1950s. Twenty were based on his novels, several others on his published novelettes. The most famous was *Destry Rides Again,* based on Faust's classic novel, originally published in *Western Story.* Universal secured the film rights in 1930 for the shockingly low price of fifteen hundred dollars.

Tom Mix based six of his silent films on Faust properties, including 1920s versions of *The Untamed* and *The Night Horseman.* His first "talkie" role was as Destry in the 1932 Universal version of *Destry Rides Again,* which was much closer to Faust's novel than the 1939 comic version starring James Stewart.

Faust left Hollywood in 1944 to serve as a war correspondent; he was killed at the Italian front just prior to his 52nd birthday in May of that year. In all, he had sold some 400 Westerns—serials, novelettes, short stories—a wordage equal to 230 books. Some 150 of these tales still remain in magazine format, meaning that there are another fifty books waiting to be published up to the year 2044, a *full century* beyond his death. What other Western writer can touch his incredible record?

Frederick Faust, the failed poet, remains unknown, but Max Brand rides again. And again.

And again.   ∎

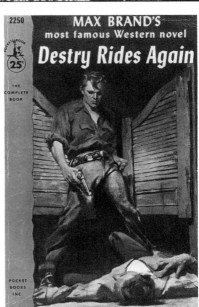

TOP: Claudia Dell and Tom Mix in *Destry Rides Again* (1932 Universal), Mix's first sound picture

BOTTOM: Made into a movie three times, *Destry Rides Again* has been continuously in print since first published in hardcover in 1930

[1]In the 1920s, just from pulp writing, Faust earned one hundred thousand dollars per year. In contrast, during this same period the yearly earnings of F. Scott Fitzgerald, who was in his prime as one of the most successful of the Jazz Age authors, averaged twenty-five thousand dollars per year.

[2]The only exceptions to this are his more than fifteen "Indian" novels, which reflect his careful research, particularly in regard to the history of the Cheyenne.

ZANE GREY, WRITER OF THE PURPLE SAGE

BY CENA GOLDER RICHESON

ONE OF THE MOST PROLIFIC AND SUCCESSFUL WRITERS OF THE TWEN-tieth century was Pearl Zane Grey. After a fractious childhood fraught with defending his first name, and a brief half-hearted attempt at maintaining a dental practice, Pearl switched to full-time authorship. He adopted the British spelling of Gray (Grey) and dropped his first name to embark on his new career; thus he began a life that was every bit as exciting and romantic as any character he ever created on paper.

Born in Zanesville, Ohio, on December 31, 1872, Grey developed a lifetime love of adventure in the great outdoors. He spent his halcyon youth occasionally playing hooky in the nearby woods next to the banks of the Muskingum River. A daydreamy kid in school, he was poor at ciphering and a disappointment to his music teacher, but he perked up during history and geography lessons. As biographer Norris F. Schneider stated, these subjects, "opened windows to his dreams." Undoubtedly they fanned the flames of his illuminative imagination.

The future author was an avid reader of Wild West novels, Harry Castleman's *Robinson Crusoe* and *Swiss Family Robinson,* and James Fenimore Cooper's works. His first creative attempt on record ended up in school chum Anna Oldham's autograph album. Young Grey penned a lovelorn advice poem. He suggested that Anna find a "good beau" and if he by chance slipped away, to "catch another and let him rip."

Grey and a gang of friends held clandestine meetings in a cave. With animal hides and weapons for inspirational atmosphere, the boys read the likes of Beadle's dime novels by oil lamplight. It was here Grey's brimming, creative mind impelled him to write "Jim of the Cave." Unfortunately, Dr. Lewis Gray (Zane's father) had no patience for such time-frittering. Once he learned of the boy's preoccupation, he went to the hideout. When he found items that had been pilfered from his wife's kitchen, he was furious. Finding his son's story only heightened his anger. Picking up a strip of carpet (also pirated from the Gray home), Dr. Gray tanned the aspiring writer's hide, hoping to beat some sense into him.

Soon after this incident, Zane's father decided the boy needed more discipline, less frivolity. He put him to work at the dental office. Washing windows and cleaning dental equipment was sheer drudgery to young Zane. Even so, he learned the basics of his father's work by being around it. He lived for the slack times when his dad would give him days off.

Besides reading and telling stories, young Zane developed two other passions: baseball and fishing. Athletic and strong, he eventually reached semi-professional status. In the summers, baseball earned him good money. As for his diversion with fishing, he worked as diligently at that sport, and with as much gusto, as he did his writing. He eventually held ten world records for big-game fishing.

Zane followed his father's advice and took the University of Pennsylvania's dental course. In 1896, a new dental shingle, among the already existing thousands in New York City, proclaimed him "Dr. P. Zane Gray, D.D.S." He chose New York because the major publishing companies were there. Even as he mundanely extracted or drilled patients' teeth, he never gave up his longing to be an author. Often the pressures of the city and the distasteful (to him) profession he chose drove him to close up shop and run off to the country for fishing trips. One of his favorite spots was on the Delaware River, the boundary between New York and Pennsylvania.

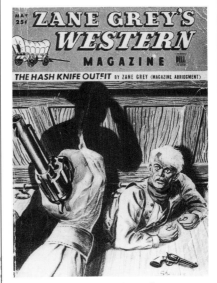

Zane Grey Western Magazine

In August 1900, Zane and his younger brother, Romer, went on a canoeing trip on the Lackawaxen River. This is where they became acquainted with Lina Roth, later known as Dolly Grey. She and her recently widowed mother had come to this idyllic setting conducive to the solitude a grieving heart craves.

Mature beyond her seventeen years, Lina shared Zane Grey's love of literature. She not only sympathized with his desire to become an established author, she reinforced the faith within him that said his dream could become reality.

In 1902, *Recreation Magazine* paid Grey ten dollars for one of his fishing stories. Publication affirmed his desire to become a serious writer. Romer gave him the idea for *Betty Zane,* a fictionalized account of their great-great aunt, Elizabeth Zane, the heroine who had saved Fort Henry from Indians and the British by transporting gunpowder in her apron. Though Zane was afire with enthusiasm for his story, his inexperience was an exasperating barrier. Recalling later, he said, "I wrote *Betty Zane* in a dingy flat on a kitchen table under a flickering light. All...winter I labored...suffered and hoped, was lifted up, and again plunged into despair." He carried his finished manuscript by hand to three publishers. All rejected it, but one "damned it with faint praise."

After more rejections, Grey finally self-published the work in 1903. Lina loaned him the money. She also corrected his spelling and grammar chapter by chapter. For the rest of his life, she served as his editor/confidante and morale supporter. After their marriage in 1905, the couple lived in Lackawaxen, Pennsylvania, on Dolly's inheritance from her physician father, as Zane continued writing. Again employing a real-life hero as protagonist (Lewis Wetzel), Grey at last wrote a book a New York publisher accepted.

The Spirit of the Border was published in 1906. By the time he published *The Last Trail* and a baseball novel called *The Short Stop,* Zane Grey was on his way.

THE WINTER OF 1906-07 SET THE STAGE TO TRANSFORM ZANE Grey into a Westerner. He met a fascinating man named Colonel Charles Jesse "Buffalo" Jones who was lecturing (and showing movies) on Yellowstone Park's wild game. Jones was also trying to cross breed animals with Black Galloway cattle. When the speaker told of roping mountain lions in the Grand Canyon, the laughter and jeers of the skeptical audience drowned out his words. But Zane Grey believed the Bunyanesque tales of the buckskin-clad holdover from the previous century.

Grey became obsessed with the idea of going to the West with Jones and re-living the frontier escapades he'd just heard about. He convinced Jones that his publicity-aimed chronicles would certainly provide needed funds. After he sold Jones on the idea, he had to discuss his brainstorm with Dolly. After all, it would mean gambling their entire future and savings. Wavering, Zane's conscience screamed out against using the last of his wife's money. He told Dolly it was time he gave up his foolish notions of earning a living by writing, that he'd return to dentistry and forget the whole business about Arizona.

But Dolly was a rare woman indeed. She had the blind faith, or perhaps foresight, to realize the venture would be a turning point in her husband's life. She insisted, "I'll get along somehow," and implored him not to let Buffalo Jones down.

Dolly's sacrifice and intuition were amply rewarded. That trip to the West began a long, highly successful career most writers only wistfully dream about. Grey's travels took him to remote regions of the West, where he met up with local historical heroes. He relished and absorbed the stories he heard, he learned all he could about the history of the region, and he examined the topography firsthand. He hired guides and packed into the mountains on horseback, lived the Western life, took copious notes and recorded much in photographs. He stored up his ever-

A Western Dime-Novelist (as described by a western dime-novelist).

increasing knowledge, returned home and put it all down on paper.

To write, Grey sat in a Morris chair with a lapboard across its arms; he spent marathon sessions handwriting manuscripts. In later years he had Morris chairs set up in several places, so that wherever he resided or traveled, he kept his method of creativity. After putting the ending on a manuscript, he would turn the bulky work over to Dolly. After she completed her expert polishing, she had a hired secretary type the manuscript before submitting it to a publisher.

Dr. G. M. Farley, a leading authority on Zane Grey, wrote, "Zane Grey was an individualist. He wrote what he wanted the way he wanted to write it. He did not compromise for the sake of praise. Fortunately, the public loved it; critics condemned it."

Zane's own definition of genius certainly applied to himself. He said, "Genius is sustained attention." Though Grey was away from home and hearth a great deal, he and Dolly kept in close contact by mail several times a week. There's no question that he would never have enjoyed the success and wealth he attained through his literary efforts without Dolly's dedication and business acumen. His impressive body of work includes over sixty Western novels, six juvenile novels, two baseball novels, and many nonfiction books on fishing and hunting, as well as short stories, anthologies and a long list of magazine articles. Over one hundred Hollywood movies based on his books and one hundred forty-five television shows written by others in his tradition gives us a substantial visual legacy as well. Even now, in bookstores, Zane Grey novels wearing new covers are lined up next to Louis L'Amour's books.

It all began winding down in 1937 when he and his eldest son, Romer, were on a fishing trip on the Umpqua River in Oregon. In the wilderness he suffered a stroke that sent him to hospital. Though he recovered and resumed writing, he died in 1939 at age sixty-seven.

In her diary Dolly numbly recorded, "Z. G. died this morning at seven-thirty." Two years later she told her diary, "Things are not right around here without Z. G."

Dolly took care of her husband's business until her death. In 1952, she said to a *New Yorker Magazine* interviewer, "…He just wouldn't edit. After he'd finished a first draft, he'd hand the manuscript over to me. I'm still doing his editing." Grey had left behind a good supply of unpublished manuscripts.

On July 26, 1957, Dolly followed her husband in death in a like manner, by heart attack. Today they rest side by side in a shady cemetery on the banks of the Delaware River, not far from where they met, married, struggled, mapped out their lives and lived them to the fullest. ◼

Note: An earlier version of this article appeared in the April 1990 issue of The Tombstone Epitaph.

THE MOST ENDURING CHARACTERS IN PRINT

Shane; the Virginian; Rooster Cogburn in *True Grit*; Tom Destry in *Destry Rides Again*; Lassiter in *Riders of the Purple Sage*; Hondo Lane in *Hondo*; Monte Walsh; Zorro in *The Mark of Zorro*; Hopalong Cassidy; the Cisco Kid from the O. Henry stories; Bob Valdez in *Valdez is Coming*; Charlie Flagg in *The Time It Never Rained*.

1940's pulp magazines

THE WESTERN PULPS

BY BILL PRONZINI

FOR MUCH OF THE FIRST HALF OF THIS CENTURY, PULP MAGAZINES were the leading supplier of popular fiction to the masses—not only in the United States, but in Canada and England as well. They were seven by ten inches in size, printed on untrimmed woodpulp paper, and had gaudy enameled covers that depicted scenes of high melodrama. The stories they contained were (for the most part) just as gaudy and melodramatic as their artwork. Successors to the dime novels and story weeklies of the nineteenth century, they were mass-produced to provide inexpensive escapist reading for imaginative young adults and the so-called "common man," selling for a nickel or a dime in their early years and a quarter in their final ones. At the height of their popularity, in the mid-thirties, there were more than 200 different titles on the market—magazines specializing in stories of mystery, detection, adventure, war on land and sea and in the air, life and death in the Old West, sports, romance, science fiction, fantasy, and sometimes sadistic horror.

Far and away the most popular pulps were Westerns. Such titles as *Western Story, Wild West Weekly, Ranch Romances, Texas Rangers,* and *Dime Western* perennially outsold those in all other categories throughout most of the pulp era. This is hardly surprising when one considers that the Western story is a uniquely American art form, and that as a result, Americans have not only embraced fictional chronicles of the great Westward expansion, but elevated them to the lofty status of myth. During this century the Western has been a symbol of all that America stands for: freedom, justice, self-reliance, the pioneer spirit. And in the Depression thirties and the war-torn forties, Americans needed that myth to sustain them. The Western pulps, then, were more than just cheap entertainment, more than just an escape into the past; they were a hope for the future.

The first Western pulp was established by Street & Smith, the dime-novel kings. In 1919 Street & Smith revamped one of their dime-novel periodicals, *New Buffalo Bill Weekly,* into the pulp format, and retitled the new bi-weekly *Western Story Magazine.* At that time pulp magazines had been around for nearly twenty years. Frank A. Munsey had restructured *Argosy* into a pulp in the mid-1890s, and soon afterward brought out numerous other pulp titles, among them *All-Story Weekly, Popular Magazine,* and *The Railroad Man's Magazine.* The circulation of *Western Story,* which sold for ten cents, burgeoned in the 1920s, when Street & Smith made it into a weekly, and it remained one of the two or three top-selling titles throughout its three decades of life.

One of the primary reasons for *Western Story's* success was the authentic Western flavor of the stories it published—stories by such born-and-bred Westerners as Walt Coburn, W. C. Tuttle, Stephen Payne, Jay

Ned Buntline set the tone in the 1880's for the nineteenth century dime novel (British version) of *Buffalo Bill and the Wandering Jew* (from the collection of Michael Moorcock)

Lucas, Ney N. Geer, and Raymond S. Spears.

The success of *Western Story* inspired imitations and variations, of course. Doubleday brought out *West* and *Frontier Stories,* which would also prove to be long-running titles; William Clayton started *Cowboy Stories, Ace-High Western, Ranch Romances,* and *Western Adventures;* Fiction House produced *Lariat;* and Street & Smith added *Far West, Wild West Weekly,* and *Pete Rice Magazine* to its stable. (Pistol Pete Rice, a rough-and-tumble Arizona sheriff with a coterie of deputies, was the first Western pulp hero to have his own magazine.) In the 1930s Ned Pines and his editorial director, Leo Margulies, started the Thrilling Group, which included such titles as *Thrilling Western, Popular Western, Texas Rangers,* and three Pete Rice rivals: *Masked Rider, Range Riders,* and *Rio Kid.* Harry Steeger's Popular Publications, eventually the largest and most active of the pulp chain publishers, also jumped on the bandwagon with *Dime Western, .44 Western, New Western, Star Western,* and *Big-Book Western,* among others. And there were numerous other titles produced by independent and small-chain outfits, some of which flourished for a while, but most of which were short-lived; among these were *Ace Western*

> "There was much to be seen, though it was a small place, for the ends of the earth's iniquity had gathered in Ogalalla."
>
> ANDY ADAMS FROM *THE LOG OF A COWBOY*

ANDY ADAMS AND THE LOG OF A COWBOY

Much like Francis Parkman, Andy Adams went West as a young man and wrote about what he saw and how he lived. Unlike Parkman, Adams wasn't an eastern scholar doing research for a book. His family moved from Georgia to the San Antonio River valley of south Texas to escape the aftermath of the Civil War, so Adams grew up in cattle country. He could ride, he spoke Spanish and was, by his own admission, a pretty good fiddle player.

At age twenty Adams signed on with Don Lovell's Circle Dot ranch for a cattle drive from the Rio Grande River in Texas to the Blackfoot Indian reservation in Montana. The drive lasted from March to September of 1882; the herd traversed hundreds of miles through plains and mountains and rugged badlands while the cowboys endured through drought and flood and storms.

In *The Log of a Cowboy,* Adams relates the story of the latter days of the great trail drives from his working cowboy's perspective. Even though he writes about his outfit's visits to some of the still-wild frontier towns like Ogallala and Frenchman's Ford, he concentrates more on the day-to-day life of the trail than on six-gun dramatics.

Adams describes the working life of a cowboy, from river crossings and other hardships of the trail to the camaraderie of the campfire. Along with his own observations about the horses of the *remuda,* the countryside and camp cooking, he records the personal stories related to him by other experienced cowboys. Because he uses a cowboy's language, his story reads like a Western novel. His words conjure vivid images of the Indians, emigrants and soldiers he meets, as well as of the mining camps, forts and cowtowns he visits, and he punctuates his narratives with snatches of cowboy songs and poetry. *The Log of a Cowboy* presents an accurate picture of the West of the 1880s.

More realistic for the lack of reckless gunplay, Adams' story still contains scenes played out in countless Western novels and movies. Though there are no bloody Indian fights, there's a scene on the North Fork of the Red River in which Adams and the foreman must use Spanish to negotiate with a Comanche chief for passage through his country. When the cowboys run into a bear and her cubs, they try roping her for fun. When a cowboy drowns in the flooded Platte thirty-five miles from Fort Laramie, the hands search downstream until they find his body, then ride to the fort for a coffin. They recruit a minister from a nearby emigrant train to perform the burial service, and the minister's granddaughters sing a simple hymn over the cowboy's lonely grave.

These are scenes that can be found in Westerns from *Red River* to *Lonesome Dove;* the movies obviously owe a lot to a young cowboy who turned writer.

and *Mammoth Western.*

A successful adjunct to the Western pulps of this period were those magazines devoted wholly or in large part to "Northerns"—stories set in the wide-open frontier days of Alaska, the Yukon, and the Canadian Barrens. The first and most popular of these was Fiction House's *North West Stories* (later *Northwest Romances*), which in its early years proclaimed itself "the world's only all Western and Northern story magazine," and modestly announced that what it published were "vigorous, tingling epics of the great SNOW FRONTIER and the IMMORTAL WEST!" The magazine lasted more than twenty-five years and featured the work of such writers as Jack London, Robert W. Service, James B. Hendryx, William Byron Mowery, W. Ryerson Johnson, and Dan Cushman. Northerns also appeared frequently in other Western pulps, and of course both Westerns and Northerns were regularly found in *Argosy, Adventure, Short Stories,* and other adventure pulps.

"Ranch Romances" magazine (courtesy of Texas A&M University Special Collections and Archives, Dykes Collection)

The paper shortage of World War II killed off a large number of pulp titles, including many marginal Western books. Of the survivors, a handful were purchased by the healthier chain publishers, such as Popular and Thrilling and thus underwent changes in editorial policy. A few new titles were introduced during and after the war, and into the early fifties, among them two named after Western pulp giants: *Max Brand's Western Magazine* and *Walt Coburn's Western Magazine.* But the handwriting was on the wall: the pulps were doomed. The advent of war might have ended the Depression in this country, but it also began the decline and fall of the pulp kingdom; and in the war's aftermath, things began to change rapidly and radically everywhere. The publishing industry was especially vulnerable. Television and paperback books were the coming forms of inexpensive entertainment for the masses; there was little room for the pulps in the new and changing society.

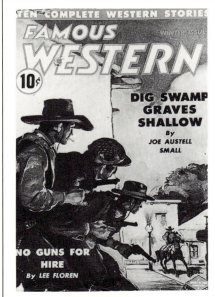

1940's pulp magazines

Most titles were extinct by 1950. A hardy few hung on a little longer: *Dime Western, Thrilling Western, Big-Book Western, Fifteen Western Tales,* and *.44 Western* until 1954; *Western Short Stories, Complete Western Book, Texas Rangers,* and *2-Gun Western* until 1957-58. *Ranch Romances,* amazingly enough, lasted until 1970 (though it was a mere shadow of itself at the end, publishing reprints almost exclusively), thus earning the distinction of being the longest-surviving pulp title.

The "Digest" Pulps

Although technically not pulp magazines, the digest-sized Western periodicals of the past fifty years were in fact pulps in every major respect: aim, content, even the paper on which they were printed. The only appreciable difference was size.

The first digest Western was the short-lived *Pocket Western,* which appeared in the late thirties. The title was revived in 1950 by Trojan Magazines, and again proved to be short-lived. So did a companion magazine, *Six-Gun Western.* Street & Smith had the first success with the digest format during World War II when the paper shortage led to a decision to shrink such pulp titles as *Western Story* and *Romantic Range,* as well as *Detective Story, Doc Savage,* and *The Shadow.* The format proved so popular with the readers that even after the war Street & Smith continued to publish *Western Story* as a digest until the magazine's demise in 1949.

Other publishers followed Street & Smith's lead in reducing full-sized pulps to the smaller size, though without nearly as much success. Early in 1950 Dell relaunched one of its old pulp titles, *All-Western,* as a digest, but it lasted only a few issues. Stadium Publishing briefly reduced *Best Western* in 1951, then returned it to the standard pulp format for the remaining few years of its life. And in 1958, Robert A.W. Lowndes' Columbia Publications shrank all of its pulp titles, among them *Famous Western, Double-Action Western, Western Action,* and *Real Western.* These remained digest-sized until their group demise in 1960.

The best of the Western magazines that began and ended in the digest format—and one of the best of all the Western fiction periodicals—commenced publication in November 1946. It was *Zane Grey's Western Magazine.* Under the editorship of Don Ward, ZGWM published original fiction by most of the major names in the Western field, as well as classic reprints of Zane Grey, and a number of nonfiction features. Ward was especially good at developing new writers; among his "finds" were Elmore Leonard and Lewis B. Patten. He even persuaded science fiction and fantasy writer Theodore Sturgeon to concoct a few Western stories, and later collaborated with Sturgeon on a couple of others. Throughout its relatively short life—its final issue appeared early in 1954—ZGWM remained a showcase for some of the most interesting and entertaining short fiction of its era.

Another quality publication appearing in 1953 from Flying Eagle Publications was *Gunsmoke.* It was an "adult" Western magazine in the sense that it offered stories of a much grimmer and more elemental nature than most pulp Western fare. Flying Eagle also published *Manhunt,* a successful crime fiction magazine devoted to modern stories of the "seamier side of life." Although *Gunsmoke* featured some outstanding stories by such writers as Jack Schaefer, A. B. Guthrie, Jr., Frank O'Rourke, Elmore Leonard, Nelson Nye, H. A. DeRosso, Bill Gulick, and Evan Hunter, it lasted only two issues. Readers of the time were evidently not ready to embrace the seamier side of frontier life.

A few other digest Westerns appeared in the 1950s, among them *Luke Short's Western Magazine* (also edited by Don Ward), *TOPS in Western Stories, Blazing Guns Western Story Magazine, Western Magazine,* and *3-Book Western.* None of these survived more than three years; the last and longest-lived of them, Harry Widmer's *Western Magazine,* ceased publication late in 1957. In 1960 a pulp-size magazine called *Wagon Train,* after the then-popular TV show, made a one-issue appearance; it was the

THE WORLD'S FIRST ADULT WESTERN

BY ED GORMAN

I don't know who Glen Low is or was, but it seems he holds a rather dubious record in Western literature—he wrote the world's first "adult" Western. As you can see in the accompanying photo, the cover of his *Virgin Bounty* contains a small inset that reads, "an ADULT Western."

It's copyrighted 1959; back then, Jake Logan was probably still a virgin. So, what about the book itself?

Novel Books of Chicago published some tomes of distinction in the crime field; their Ennis Willie novels were first-rate. Obviously, their luck with the Western was less inspiring, at least where Glen Low was concerned.

Glen specialized in awkward verbs, as in, "The vultures flopped up and away," and, "He straddled down and went to work." How does a vulture "flop up," and how does one "straddle down?"

Low's story is literally incomprehensible. The cover blurb is a masterpiece of overstated and awkward narrative: "The odds—three hired killers, a sadistic sex maniac, and a pair of greed-ridden prostitutes—were heavy against Rand McKeever. But the stakes were even bigger. Reward. Revenge. And 118 pounds of pulsating, naked VIRGIN BOUNTY!" Did Rand McKeever carry a scale in his saddlebags?

The sex in *Virgin Bounty* is, of course, tame by the standard of today's "adult" Western novels, and the writing is turgid and lurid, but Glen Low's little epic was apparently the first of its kind—a very special type of book that more than a few authors have written but few have written well.

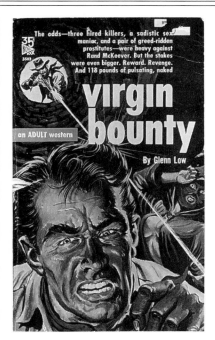

Virgin Bounty, *an adult western in paperback (courtesy of Ed Gorman)*

only Western fiction periodical to be published between mid-1960 and 1969, when Leo Margulies revived *Zane Grey's Western Magazine* in a monthly digest-sized format. The new ZGWM featured a novella in each issue based on such Zane Grey characters as Arizona Ames and Laramie Nelson, and was purportedly written by Grey's son, Romer. Each issue also contained classic reprints, as well as new fiction. This version on ZGWM lived just four years, only the first two as a digest; in its final years it was transformed into the large, flat format used by nonfiction magazines such as *True West,* and devoted as much space to fact articles as to fiction.

In 1978 the California-based *Far West Magazine* commenced publication; but after a promising beginning (its first issue contained a new story by Louis L'Amour), poor distribution and a misguided change to the large, flat format doomed it to extinction. By 1981 the last Western fiction magazine was dead.

The pulps may be gone, but they're not forgotten. Not only did they provide entertainment for millions of readers; they provided a training ground for scores of writers who eventually went on to bigger and better literary endeavors. Stephen Crane, Jack London, Theodore Dreiser, Sinclair Lewis, Tennessee Williams, Horace McCoy, Paul Gallico, Dashiell Hammett, Raymond Chandler, Isaac Asimov, Ray Bradbury, Edgar Rice Burroughs, John D. MacDonald, Cornell Woolrich, John Jakes, Evan Hunter, Erle Stanley Garner, and Rex Stout, among many others, wrote for the pulp-paper magazines. And in the Western field, in addition to those already mentioned, so did such luminaries as Louis L'Amour, Luke Short, William MacLeod Raine, Clarence E. Mulford, Ernest Haycox, Charles Alden Seltzer, Fred Gipson, Wayne D. Overholser, Frank Bonham, Norman A. Fox, Les Savage, Jr., Steve Frazee, Tom W. Blackburn, William R. Cox, Elmer Kelton, John Reese, Todhunter Ballard, T. V. Olsen, and Clifton Adams.

Much pulp fiction was of poor quality, to be sure; the stories were hastily written—many by hacks and many more by amateurs, in order to satisfy the annual demand for millions upon millions of words during the boom years. But there is also much that is of quality, surprisingly high quality in some instances; much that has been reprinted in anthologies and single-author collections for the entertainment of modern readers and the enlightenment of popular-culture scholars.

It is no exaggeration to say that if the Western pulps had never existed, popular Western literature would not be nearly as rich or as vital as it is today. ◼

Note: Originally published in The Best Western Stories of Bill Pronzini.

HEAVEN IN FOUR COLORS: THE WESTERN IN COMICS FORM

BY SCOTT CUPP

DURING THE LAST SIXTY YEARS, TWO MEDIUMS HAVE SET THE STAGE for the way in which most of the world perceives the West—the cinema and the comic book/comic strip. Both are intensely visual and bring to the reader scenes that were as foreign to some parts of the United States as was the landscape of Oz.

The early Western films depicted a time that wasn't too far removed from the present and yet different—and from the Great Depression through the fifties, they provided a world-view that distracted their audiences from the problems that plagued them. They were a time machine to a world where heroes righted the various wrongs wrought by the railroaders, the cattle barons and the bankers. Every boy in America wanted to be Tom Mix or Roy Rogers or Gene Autry.

But those initial films were in black and white, and that great, imaginary country of the West was color and light. It took the Western comic book and daily strip to make the logical step, to be the first to color the excitement and the glamor of the West as it was meant to be. The daily strips splashed their color across the Sunday pages and used them to paint recurring characters and story lines that could be built meticulously from month to month. Syndicated strips like Stan Lynde's "Latigo" and Tom Ryan's "Tumbleweeds" still appear each week.

From the strips sprang literally hundreds of Western comic book titles, series that endured for years. Nineteen eighty-six marked the first year since 1937 when there wasn't a regular Western comic book series being published. The last of the regular titles, *Jonah Hex,* converted to a science fiction theme in late 1985, died, and then was resurrected for a Western mini-series in 1993. Also in 1985, *The Rawhide Kid* reappeared for a four issue mini-series dealing with his late life adventures.

The early comics pages flourished with a variety of daily strips that on a regular basis featured Western settings. There were strips like "Bronco Bill and Little Joe" that gave readers a brief look at life in the

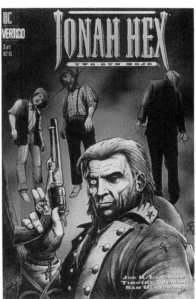

Two Gun Kid **#77, September 1965 (courtesy of Marvel Comics, Inc./artist Dick Ayers), and** *Jonah Hex: Two Gun Mojo* **#3 of 5, October 1993 (courtesy of D.C. Comics/artist Timothy Truman/writer Joe R. Lansdale)**

West. But it was the Western hero strips that really developed the images that we've carried forward from childhood—strips like "Red Ryder," "King of the Royal Mounted" and "Hopalong Cassidy" served as the early introduction of the Western hero to the daily page.

These strips owed a much of their form to the movie serials and to the various merits (and faults) of the handling of a daily adventure strip. Some came to the strips from the movie screen—though Hopalong had existed in the Clarence Mulford novels prior to his screen immortalization by William Boyd—and one went on to become a screen favorite in more than twenty Red Ryder movies.

Some characters fared well in the dailies, and some didn't. Roy Rogers and Gene Autry were unable to repeat their screen successes on the daily page, while "The Lone Ranger" fared well and continued to be published long after most of his contemporaries ceased to appear.

The appearance of the super-hero comic during the late 1930s helped to shape the future of the medium and the Western comic book character. Western heroes appeared in every shape and form. Some lasted a long time; some appeared only once or twice. They offered a continuity of sorts, and a story that could be sustained past the three- or four-panel limitations of the daily strip. They also offered color on more than just Sunday—in the comic book, it was color on every panel of every page.

And the titles proliferated. Every Western star of merit (and some of no merit) had his own book. There was Lash LaRue, Roy Rogers, Dale Evans, Buster Crabbe, John Wayne and even Tim Tyler and Rex Allen. Some of the books contained excellent art by artists such as Frank Frazetta and Fred Guardineer; most did not.

The Western comic hit its stride in the late 1940s and early 1950s with the introduction of the various "Kid" books. Books such as *Kid Colt, Outlaw, Two Gun Kid, The Rawhide Kid* and *The Apache Kid* featured work by a variety of comic book greats like Stan Lee, Reed Crendall, Doug Wildey, Jack Kirby and Al Williamson. The stories concentrated on a strong sense of justice and action, emphasizing moral victories as the most important aspect of Western life. They brought the life of the Western outlaw into some perspective, though it still held far too much glamor for its detractors. *Cowboy Love* and *Cowboy Romances* were published in an effort to reach and combine two popular audiences, but neither succeeded.

The mid-1950s were a trying time for the comics industry. Through the efforts of Dr. Frederick Wertham and his book, *Seduction of the Innocent,* the medium of comics found itself thrust into the forefront of a modern cultural controversy and under scrutiny by a Senate Committee chaired by Estes Kefauver. The concentration of the committee on

THE CISCO KID

By JOSE SALINAS and ROD REED

the violence and the sexual aspects of stories in comics sent shock waves through the industry. Publishers found titles being burned in city squares, and with the creation of the Comics Code, many titles were discontinued.

Oddly, during this period, the Western thrived. The super-heroes of the 1940s were gone, most with the passing of World War II. The horror comics that had been in vogue were in serious jeopardy. The new wave of super-heroes was still several years down the road. And television was rapidly becoming America's favorite medium of entertainment.

The drama and the spectacle that had developed over the years in the movie houses was now available in the privacy of one's own home

TOP: "The Cisco Kid" (courtesy of King Features Syndicate, Inc., ©1952)

BOTTOM: "Tumbleweeds" (courtesy of The Register and Tribune Syndicate, ©1971)

Rawhide Kid #81, November 1970 (courtesy of Marvel Comics, Inc./artist Larry Lieber)

and (if you had television) it was free! The Western became the most popular form of television entertainment and remained so through the 1960s, and television's success spun off into the comics.

Baby-boomers found that they could both watch and read about the adventures of Hopalong Cassidy and The Lone Ranger. They could mentally add the voices of Bill Boyd and Clayton Moore to the character on the printed page and make the comic live even more. During this period, many television characters found themselves transferred to the comic page, much as had their big-screen predecessors.

But a bust follows every boom. The influx of the super-hero comics following the appearance of a re-designed Flash in *Showcase Comics* and the debut of the *Fantastic Four* ushered in the so-called "Silver Age of Comics." During the period from late 1961 through early 1984 it seemed that a new hero appeared every month or, at least, a hero from the 1940s was re-tailored for the 1960s. The Westerns continued to appear, but their popularity waned with each passing month. Comics began to change to reflect "relevance" to the lifestyle of the 1960s, and the simple morality plays of the Western comics didn't fit in. Some writers tried to develop Western comics that featured blacks and Indians as major characters, but they never caught on.

As for the Western daily strips, the action continued to progress through six daily strips and a Sunday page. The Lone Ranger and Red Ryder still caught the bad guys and justice triumphed. During this period, the only new strip of any importance and staying power was Stan Lynde's "Rick O'Shay," which alternated between humorous stories and action tales. In 1965, "Tumbleweeds" took the humorous strip out West for a permanent location. Other humorous strips had used Western locales, but "Tumbleweeds" was the first important Western humor daily strip. The reason? None of the other strips was inhabited by such an engaging cast of oddballs. Gordon Bess soon followed with his "Redeye."

Comics corporations are very conscious of the trends in modern culture and never hesitate to incorporate some of the most ridiculous ideas into comics. Occasionally, one goes right. Clint Eastwood's extreme popularity in the Western movies of the late 1960s led DC Comics, never a company to miss a chance, to create *Jonah Hex*. Hex was a sort of Jekyll and Hyde of the West, a Western antihero designed by creators Tony de Zuniga and Michael Fleischer to resemble the Man With No Name and Josey Wales and to bring the intensity of the Sergio Leone Westerns to the comic book. Dressed in his ragged, dusty Confederate uniform, a grotesque facial scar marring his appearance, Hex made quite a visual impression. The writing was lean and the look was fresh.

DC Comics tried another unusual Western title in *Showcase Comics* when they presented *Bat Lash*. The initial trial was good and the title soon earned its own book. Written by Sergio Aragones and penciled by Nick Cardy, *Bat Lash* relied heavily on mood and characterization rather than the action that distinguished other Western titles. Despite fine

WESTERN COMICS SUGGESTED READING LIST

BY SCOTT CUPP

Good Western strips and magazines are still out there for those who are up to the challenge of finding them. You may have to sift a prairie wagon full of chaff to find the good ones, but it's worth it! Here's a list of titles that are almost always worth reading (limited to English-language titles because foreign titles vary so widely in terms of content and quality). Check 'em out—variety is the spice of life, especially Western life.

Bat Lash
appears in the *Showcase Comics* debut and seven issues of *Bat Lash*. The writing is twistedly humorous and the art from journeyman artist Nick Cardy has to be seen to be believed. One perfect scene involves Bat attempting to flee a shotgun wedding, aided by town kids who drop rats from the church ceiling on all of the wedding guests, allowing the hero to flee to safety.

The Durango Kid
This title is interesting only if you're able to find the issues that contain the Frank Frazetta "White Indian" stories. Frazetta's fine anatomic art is among the best to ever grace comic pages. You can see other strong Frazetta work in some issues of *Ghost Rider*.

Tumbleweeds
What can we say about this strip that hasn't been said before? It's a side-splitter, from the regular selections for "Indian of the Month," to Hildegard Hamhockers repeated attempts to get the faithful 'Weeds to the altar, to the Undertaker's—advertising "You Plug 'Em, We Plant 'Em."

Red Ryder
Fred Harmen's early *Red Ryder* work is graphically stunning with a great feel for the regions depicted. The daily strips were long on character and action, and the early comic books reprint the Harmen strips. The later comics were often illustrated by others even though they retained the Harmen signature.

Early Marvel titles
The Rawhide Kid; Two-Gun Kid; and *Kid Colt, Outlaw;* they all had their various merits and faults. Read back to back, they become repetitive, but, for sheer six-guns-blazing, posse-on-your-trail action, they can't be beat. Later Marvel titles such as *The Gunhawks* did not offer much new.

Drago
This strip from Burne Hogarth features the same detailed styling and color that made the *Tarzan* strips the delight they were. Given the option between this strip and most others, "Drago" will not lead you wrong.

Rick O'Shay and **Latigo**
Both of Stan Lynde's daily strips are well worth any attention you can give to them. The "Rick O'Shay" strips tended to have a little more humor in them than "Latigo," which concentrated on a faster moving story. "Rick O'Shay" Christmas Sunday pages were always beautiful and profound.

scripts and sometimes brilliant art, the book failed after seven issues.

Disney characters also had a fondness for the West. Stories such as Donald Duck in "The Sheriff of Bullet Valley" and "Mickey Mouse and the Bat Bandit" certainly colored many a young mind's vision of the West. The latter title was later satirized in the underground comic *Air Pirate Funnies,* which was itself a very *weird* Western.

Visions of the West in comics haven't just been limited to the American papers, or even the American West. Western daily strips have been extremely popular in Italy, France, Spain, England and Germany. Among the more interesting strips was Morris' "Lucky Luke," which, for a time, was handled by Maurice de Bevere (Morris) and Rene Goscinny, who later went on to create the popular *Asterix.* The strip featured unusual depictions of standard Western heroes and villains, such as Roy Bean, Billy the Kid and Jesse James, while carrying a strong humorous element. Also of extreme importance is "Lieutenant Blueberry," created by Gir (Jean Giraud, also known as Moebius for his science fiction work) and Jean-Michel Charlier. The fast-moving scripts and breathtaking art were combined with an innovative layout to help advance the story.

The West depicted in comics (particularly those set in modern times) didn't always reflect the reality that faced many people day in and day out, but neither did the West we saw in most films. West Texas was not Monument Valley. Cowboys didn't regularly ride the range in chaps, singing songs about lonesome cattle, or shoot a rattlesnake or gila monster every few minutes.

But to generations of readers, the West the comics created was every bit as valid as the "real" West. That comic book West came to life in the minds of children everywhere. We saw it month after month in living color. We heard owlhoots talking wild in the saloon; we broke the bronc that no one could ride; we sat around the campfire in the company of heroes; and we rode out with the posse to head the outlaws off at the pass.

Heaven is wherever you can find it. For many of us, it was inked in two to four colors on cheap pulp paper along with purple prose and art that was passable at best. But for us, it was the West brought home and up close, and that made us happy. ■

ACT III: THE ARTISTS' EYE

THE TWO GREAT POWERS OF THE WEST: RUSSELL AND REMINGTON

BY JOE FENTON

THEIR COMBINED WORKS FROZE THE WEST IN TIME—THE TIME OF the cowboy, the Indian, and the soldier, along with the other bit players and co-stars who lived in one of the most romantic eras in American history. They were the two great powers in the art of the West, Charles M. Russell and Frederic Remington.

They were born just at the right time to be the visual chroniclers of the Wild West, during the period known in the South as the War Between the States—Remington at the War's beginning, October 4, 1861, and Russell at its end, March 19, 1864. As children they rebelled against the restrictions of school and society, though unlike Russell, Remington managed to complete some formal training in art. They found an outlet for their talents and their free spirits on a frontier that was already vanishing. Because of their shared obsession for the American West, they preserved and publicised it by the most accurate and aesthetic means possible. They built on the works of earlier Europeans and Easterners who had come to paint the West, combined it with their vision of the real West, and set the stage for the multitude of Western artists who followed.

Although they were total opposites in most areas, the parallels in their lives and their work produced a panorama of the grand days of the Wild West with accurate details of dress, guns and gear. Both were avid letter writers, and they illustrated their letters with sketches that are masterpieces of detail. Remington personalized his earlier sketches with self portraits, and Russell enlivened his stories with his alter-ego, Rawhide Rawlins.

PREVIOUS PAGE:
**Detail from *Burning the Range,*
Frederic Remington (*Harper's
New Monthly*) (courtesy of Texas
A&M University Special Collec-
tions and Archives)**

In addition to their sweeping views of the sky and the land, they also scrutinized the everyday life of the frontier. They provided future generations with art so realistic and powerful that the smells and sounds seemed to explode from the canvas and the bronze.

The unique attraction of their work lies in the accurate pictorial stories that they spun with brush and clay. Russell was sometimes criticized for being an anecdotal painter, but to his admirers, that was his greatest gift. Remington was more of a classic painter, and although he wasn't the storyteller Russell was, his work always had a theme. Remington started out as a pure realist and an illustrator, but in later years the lines of his work blurred and took on an impressionist style. Russell began as a primitive artist, but his techniques evolved until he became an almost graphic realist. Unlike many artists, they both achieved financial and critical success during their lifetimes, and the popularity of their work disseminated their vision of the West throughout the world. Artistic sophisticates appreciated their art, but the common man found it even more accessible.

Remington and Russell owed much of their success and popularity to their wives, who provided the business sense and stability in their relationships. The artists considered themselves outdoorsmen, flamboyant characters, and they enjoyed living and dressing for the part. They wore distinctive gear as their trademarks—Remington's pith helmet, and Russell's sash with its specially tied knot. They lived hard and failed to take care of their health. Russell's early drinking and the hardships he faced on the plains eventually caught up with him, as did Remington's prodigious overeating. But that's the way they wanted to take life—in big bites, full of color and flavor—and that's the way they painted it. They captured the taste and tempo of America's growing years, and they added to it their own ingredients of humor, charm and flair.

Russell and Remington came along at just the right time to preserve the West, to interpret the spirit and the sense of it from their own unique viewpoints, and to leave us the rich legacy of their memories in shape, form, and living color.

Charlie Russell, the Cowboy Artist
The third of six children of an affluent family in St. Louis, Missouri, Charles M. Russell could have been anything he chose to be, but he was driven to be a cowboy. He was an avid reader and devoured every action-packed thriller the pulp writers poured out. He loved the stories he overheard from the mule skinners, trappers and mountain men who moved silent and strong through the mobs along the docks. These giants had come from up-river and from out West. The wild smell of ad-

Charles M. Russell in his studio
(courtesy of C.M. Russell Museum,
Great Falls, MT)

venture, tobacco, woodsmoke and danger left an odor of wildness in their wake.

Charlie fought school like a green-broke colt fights a halter and saddle. His father tried everything, and finally hired a tutor for regular studies and enrolled him in art school.

Charlie didn't stay there until the water got hot, though. He came home, bringing his clay and supplies with him, and informed his exasperated father, "I'm through with art school. That instructor wanted me to draw a plaster foot over and over and he wouldn't tell me what was wrong with my drawing, just do it over!"

It was the only formal art school Charlie ever attended. From that time on he created with pure raw talent and experience. After several attempts to run away from home to follow his dream, he got the surprise of his life. In the early part of March 1880, just before Charlie's sixteenth birthday, his father asked, "Charlie, how would you like to go West?" No doubt he thought a few weeks of roughing it on a sheep ranch in Montana would bring the boy to appreciate properly the comforts of home. But like Br'er Rabbit in the briar patch, the young adventurer thrived on the wildness of the country. The further he rode from civilization, the better he liked it.

While Frederic Remington was back east making money with his stylish renditions of the Wild West as he imagined it, Charles Russell was at Pike Miller and Jack Waite's ranch in the Judith Basin of Montana, working with clay from riverbanks and creating quick, loose watercolors. About the only thing Charlie hated about the job was the sheep he tended—he said, "I'd lose the damn things as soon as they'd put 'em on the ranch." He drew, painted and modeled all the natural things he saw around him—except for the sheep.

He found that he could effectively burn the clay from the bottom lands of upper Waite Creek, and he learned to fire it to the proper hardness without ruining the object. He turned that knowledge loose and began to create animals and other figures. He listened for hours to the stories told by ranchers, then drew and modeled the characters in the stories, bringing them all to life.

By the time he was sixteen, he was penniless, lonesome and discouraged. That's when he met Jake Hoover—trapper, hunter and one of the

George Catlin, the Soul Catcher

Assisted and welcomed by the great explorer, William Clark, self-taught artist George Catlin made his way to the West beyond the Mississippi in 1830. Though he'd painted the Indians in the east, Catlin was determined to meet the wild Indians of the plains and preserve their images on canvas before they were "corrupted by civilization." Under the Indian Relocation Act of 1830, the eastern tribes were being pushed out into the West, displacing the Plains tribes and disrupting their cultures. Catlin arrived on the scene just in time.

He traveled with several expeditions, exploring the West from the Mississippi to the Red to the Upper Missouri, painting landscapes and portraits as he went. In the summer of 1832, Catlin traced the route of the 1804 Lewis and Clark expedition for two thousand miles along the Missouri River, and in 1834 he accompanied a military expedition to Fort Gibson on the Arkansas River in Indian territo-

ry. In 1836, he visited the quarry in Minnesota from which the Indians obtained their sacred pipestone; mineralogist Dr. Charles Thomas Jackson of Boston named the newly-classified compound "catlinite" in his honor.

Catlin subscribed to the image of the Indian as the noble savage, "man in the simplicity and loftiness of his nature, unrestrained by the disguises of art." Despite his naive attitude, or perhaps because of it, he made friends easily among the Indians. He painted portraits of many famous men and women among the Sioux, Blackfoot, Assiniboine, Cree, Arikara and Mandan, and even among the Kiowa and Comanche of the Southwest. He was particularly fascinated by the Mandan—by their customs, their huge communal lodges and their self-torture rituals.

As early as 1833, Catlin began exhibiting his paintings in his native Pennsylvania, and by 1837 he had a one-man show in New York. He became adept at promoting his work, to the point that the American public couldn't get enough of his images of the exotic life of the Plains Indians. He self-published a book on his experiences, *Letters and Notes on the Manners, Customs and Condition of the North American Indians*, and he illustrated it with engravings from his paintings.

His show in England in 1839 was a great success, followed by an exhibi-

tion in Paris in 1845. King Louis Philippe of France even requested a special showing of Catlin's work in the Louvre.

Though Catlin was sometimes careless in detail of costume and accoutrements, and though his style grew awkward when it came to complete human figures, his work demonstrated simplistic genius and a powerful insight into his subjects. He often sketched action scenes at the moment they occurred, imparting a unique immediacy. Though he often exaggerated the lines of his landscapes, that in itself emphasized the natural power and expanse of the West.

But he was primarily a portrait artist, and at that he excelled. Using only a few bold strokes, he could accurately reflect the character of his Indian subject. A Catlin portrait is like a photograph of his subject's personality rather than just of his face—perhaps giving rise to the old legend that an artist could capture his subject's soul on canvas.

Though some of his successors were more technically proficient, Catlin's work certainly influenced the way in which they depicted the West. It could be said that Catlin most faithfully documented the spirit that rested just beneath the surface of the Wild West.

last of the mountain men. It was during the two years he lived, hunted and trapped with Hoover that he began to gain his profound knowledge of the animals of the mountain and plains. It was in Jake's mountain cabin that the young artist did his earliest serious work with watercolors, of which work there is known to be but a solitary surviving example.

His first-hand study of nature, which included skinning animals for the trapper, afforded him a better study of anatomy than any art school could have offered. He felt that the only way to be proficient in any craft was to constantly work to produce accurate material. His love for animals led him to sit for hours at lakes, water holes and salt licks, studying every move and characteristic to the point where he could reproduce what he saw with lifelike accuracy. It was his love for animals that kept him from often actually hunting with his friends. He would go only to draw and paint what he observed.

In March of 1881 he went back to St. Louis to see his folks, but he found the city too crowded and stayed only a few weeks. As soon as he got back out West, a wrangling job came open, and he jumped at it. He loved the job and decided to follow the cowboy lifestyle. It's well to note that as Charlie grew and became proficient in the cowboy life he loved, he also matured as an artist. He drew, painted and modeled in a rather nonchalant way, having fun with his craft. Riding night herd left him with plenty of daylight hours for his art.

Russell wrangled for the Bar-R outfit at a time of bitter history for the Montana cowman. Cattlemen were faced with many disasters, but none as devastating as the killer winter of 1886-87. A small watercolor sketch Charlie made hurriedly by lamplight on a bunkhouse kitchen table was his ticket to world-wide recognition, even though he didn't realize it at the time. He titled the picture "Waiting for a Chinook," but it was equally known as "The Last of the Five Thousand." The postcard-size painting conveyed the full measure of the disaster, a message that was beyond the power of words to convey.

Charlie's happy days were those spent as a carefree cowboy working cattle, playing pranks on his friends and exchanging wild stories. He was a wonderful storyteller and loved to tell funny stories about himself. He made his tales more believable with his colorful artwork and models. He used the same ball of wax he carried in his pocket over and over to illustrate a certain story, modeling as he talked. As the story progressed, he'd destroy one piece of sculpture to make another one. For that reason, there's no way of knowing just how many works of art Charlie created.

The American Indian was a most important subject for Charles Russell. He visited with Indians and learned their ways. He became

"I vow that nothing short of the loss of my life shall prevent me from visiting their country, and becoming their historian."

GEORGE CATLIN ON HIS INTENTION TO PRESERVE THE IMAGE OF THE WESTERN INDIANS ON CANVAS extremely proficient in sign language. It was said that "as a sign talker, he was all Indian." He saw the Indians as his friends and hated the way the white man treated them. In his paintings, he glorified the Indians and portrayed them as warriors in format bigger than life. He lived with the Blood Indians of Canada and for a time he went native, turning his back on civilization. The Blood gave him an Indian name, *Ah-wah-cous,* Antelope.

Charlie spent time with the freighters and picked up more stories and visual material about that part of the West. But soon, with his two favorite horses, Monte and Grey Eagle, he left the freighters and headed for his old stomping grounds. When he got there, he was startled by the change in the cow business. That "damned bobwire" was everywhere; nesters and farmers were plowing up the plains. Towns were springing up overnight, and hordes of lawyers, doctors, merchants, thieves and all other accessories of civilization were pouring into his beautiful land. Freedom was on its way out, and he knew he must somehow preserve it, save some part of it.

CHARLIE WORKED ON AND OFF DURING THE YEARS 1889 THROUGH 1892 for various outfits north of the Missouri River, in the vicinity of Chinook and Big Sandy. It was about this time that his art took on a new importance, mainly because of experience and notoriety. Still, top money for his work was twenty-five dollars and drinks for his friends. Sometimes he painted for food and lodging.

Even as he wintered with his old friend Jake Hoover, his work was getting noticed. In 1887, the Helena *Independent* first nicknamed him "the cowboy artist," and a Chicago company issued a lithograph of one of his paintings. But Charlie was pleased to paint just for amusement. If someone admired his work, he gave it to them. Because he painted for drinks to treat his friends or gave them as gifts to saloon girls, many of his paintings landed in saloons. If someone was willing to pay for his creations, he called them suckers. Once a drummer admired a clay model of a bear Charlie had sculpted, and when asked the price Charlie said twenty dollars. The drummer said he only had ten dollars, so Charlie crushed the model, cut the clay in half and quickly modeled a half-size bear for half price.

Wintering was hard on cowboys, who were always broke and restless. If they spent the winter in town they ended up having to take some cheap little job. Charlie put in with a bunch of cowpunchers, a roundup cook and an out-of-work prize fighter, then decided to be a free agent and try painting for his living.

Many of the pictures Charlie painted from 1893 to 1896 he gave to

KARL BODMER AND THE SCHOLAR PRINCE

When German soldier-scholar Prince Maximilian of Wied-Neuwied decided to explore the American West in 1832, he picked a young Swiss artist named Karl Bodmer to accompany him to visually document the journey. They studied George Catlin's work and contacted General William Clark for information and passports to Indian country. At St. Louis in 1833, they even took passage on the same American Fur Company steamboat, the *Yellowstone,* on which Catlin had traveled the Missouri River route the year before.

But unlike Catlin, Bodmer and the prince didn't turn back with the steamboat at Fort Union at the mouth of the Yellowstone River. They continued on by keelboat, following Louis and Clark's return route until they came to Fort McKenzie at the mouth of the Marias River. This made Bodmer the first trained white artist to travel among the Blackfoot and paint portraits of them. On their return route, they stopped to winter at Fort Clark, where they stayed in a large, glass-windowed, one-room guest house so poorly insulated that Bodmer's paints and pencils froze. He simply warmed his materials with hot water and continued to work.

In all, from Europe to America and back, their journey lasted more than two years.

For all his relative youth, Bodmer was a far more able and well-rounded artist than Catlin; he could reproduce the complete human form with ease and accuracy. Like a modern graphic artist, he paid meticulous attention to detail, and he made intricate sketches before he began painting. So accurate are the details in Bodmer's depictions of the Indians he met and befriend-ed—Mandan, Blackfoot, Cree, Assiniboine and others—that ethnologists and anthropologists can recognize the tribe and period by the facial features, clothing and artifacts of his subjects. And he not only faithfully preserved images of Indians both individually and in groups, but also of their burial customs, their battles, their homes, their hunts and their ceremonial dances. His painting of the *Dance Leader of the Hidatsa Dog's Society* is a masterpiece of portraiture, detail and action.

When the prince published his excellent account of the journey, Karl Bodmer's incredible illustrations accompanied and illuminated it. Bodmer settled in France, where exhibitions of his work won him awards and fame in all the major artistic venues of Europe. Though he sometimes produced new illustrations based on American scenes, he never returned to America.

Citadel Rock on the Upper Missouri, *Karl Bodmer (courtesy of Joslyn Art Museum, Omaha, NE; Gift of the Enron Art Foundation)*

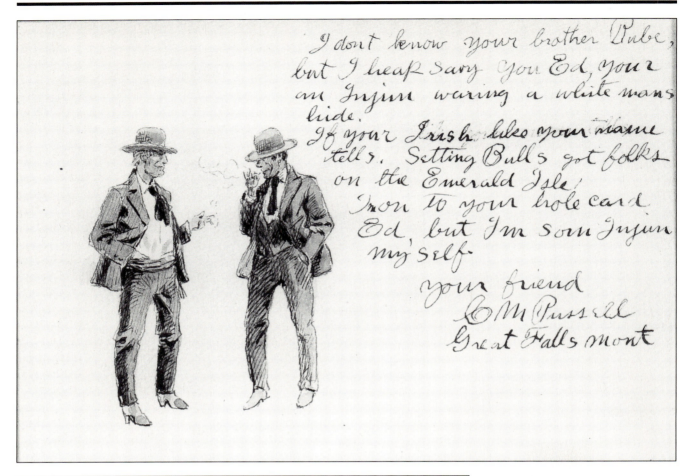

I dont know your brother Rube, but I heap savy you Ed, your an Injun waring a white mans hide.

If your Irish likes your name tells. Setting Bulls got folks on the Emerald Isle,

Nion to your hole card Ed, but Im som Injun my self.

your friend
C M Russell
Great Falls Mont

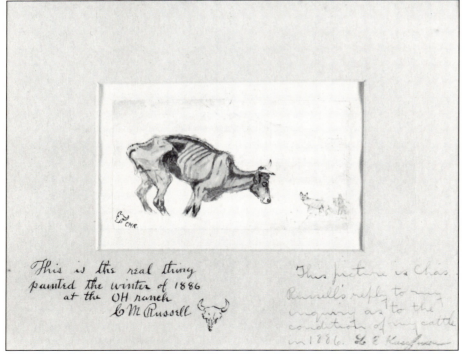

This is the real thing painted the winter of 1886 at the OH ranch
C M Russell

This picture is Chas. Russell's reply to my inquiry as to the condition of my cattle in 1886. L E Kaufman

ABOVE:
Ed Borein, Charles M. Russell (courtesy of Buffalo Bill Historical Center, Cody, WY, Gift of William E. Weiss)

LEFT:
Waiting for a Chinook, Charles M. Russell (The Last of the 5,000) (Montana Stockgrower's Association, courtesy of Montana Historical Society)

To Friend Tex, Charles M. Russell
(courtesy of Buffalo Bill Historical
Center, Cody, WY)

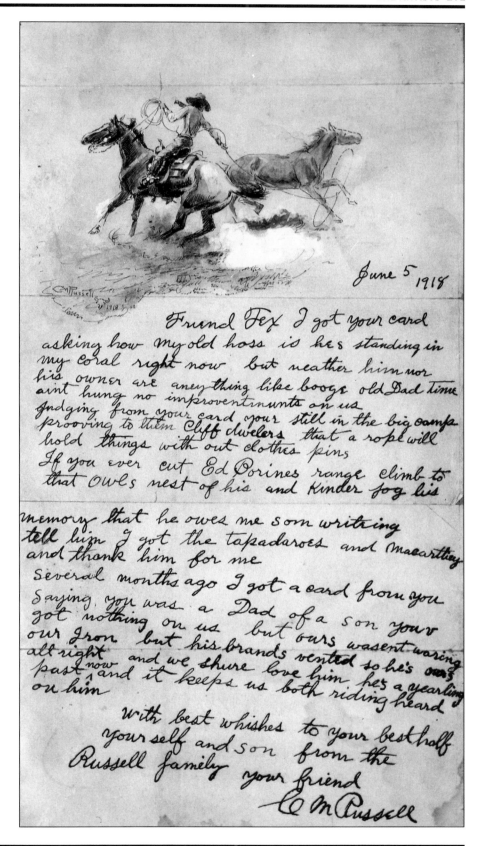

June 5 1918

Friend Tex I got your card
asking how my old hoss is hes standing in
my coral right now but neather him nor
his owner are aneything like boogs old Dad time
aint hung no improventinunts on us
gudging from your card your still in the big camp
prooving to them Cliff dwelers that a rope will
hold things with out clothes pins
   If you ever cut Ed Porines range climb to
that Owls nest of his and kinder jog his

memory that he owes me som writing
tell him I got the tapadaroes and macarthey
and thank him for me
   Several months ago I got a card from you
saying you was a Dad of a son your
got nothing on us but ours wasent waring
our Iron but his brands vented so he's ours
all right and we shure love him hes a yearling
past now and it keeps us both riding heard
on him

   with best whishes to your best half
your self and son from the
Russell family your friend
   C M Russell

ABOVE:
Bronco Busters Saddling, **Frederic Remington (*Harper's New Monthly*) (courtesy of Texas A&M University Special Collections and Archives)**

RIGHT:
Detail from *A Fantasy from the Pony War Dance,* Frederic Remington (*Harper's New Monthly*) (courtesy of Texas A&M University Special Collections and Archives)

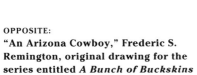

OPPOSITE:
"An Arizona Cowboy," Frederic S. Remington, original drawing for the series entitled *A Bunch of Buckskins* (courtesy of Rockwell Museum, Corning, NY)

friends; he sold only a small number of them to local buyers and a few outsiders. In 1893, he rode a cattle train to Chicago and stopped off to visit his family in St. Louis. He also visited William Niedringhaus, who owned one of the Montana ranches where he'd worked, and Niedringhaus commissioned several works. Charlie returned to the West and eventually set up a studio in a courtroom in Cascade, Montana. In two years, he produced twenty oil paintings and over forty watercolors.

It was in 1895 that Charlie fell in love with young Miss Nancy Cooper, something that drastically changed his life. There had been only one other special girl in his life, a puppy love affair with Lollie Edgar. To keep their daughter from getting involved with "that ornery kid Russell," the Edgar family had sent her back to St. Louis to enter college. Charlie and Lollie corresponded for quite a while, and he even went to St. Louis to see her, but her folks managed to turn her mind away from the cowboy. Charlie's broken heart had kept him away from serious love affairs, so his friends were flabbergasted when he gave Nancy his horse, Monte. They knew that he'd have to marry her "to get his hoss back." "That little Cooper gal" fooled a lot of folks when she came up with Charlie's ring.

Charlie was fourteen years older than Nancy, and living in rough and tumble cow camps for most of his life had left him lacking in the proposal department. One night while strolling on the bridge across the Missouri River, Charlie said, "Nancy, don't y'u want to throw in with me? I think I kin scrape up 'enough grub to eat on for a while."

She interpreted his unromantic proposal as an offer to just move in and live with him. She let him know that she was not that kind of girl, and he had to do some fast talking to let her know he meant marriage. Charlie was thirty-two and Nancy was eighteen when they were married on September 9, 1896. There were only nine guests at the ceremony.

It can honestly be said that the Russell marriage was also the major turning point in his artistic career. Nancy made him cut back on his drinking and roistering with his old cronies. He turned out fewer paintings, but his finished works were of finer workmanship. He spent more time in planning, and his technique improved. Nancy also took over the business and promotional end of the partnership. Charlie despised and hated business transactions. Growing up in the free world of the cowboy, where trust and a hand shake meant something, he didn't trust the fast-talking, slick hustlers in the marketplace. He turned everything over to Mame, as he called his wife, and asked her for money when he needed it—he never carried any on him. Charlie once said, "Mame's the business end, and I just paint. We're partners. She lives for tomorrow an' I live for yesterday."

Nancy's management propelled him into the big time, a major change.

Charles Russell begins painting a landscape and ends with a charging band of Indians.

ALFRED JACOB MILLER AND THE LAIRD OF THE ROCKIES

"The Lost Green Horn," Alfred Jacob Miller (courtesy of Joslyn Art Museum, Omaha, NE)

It was a lucky day for Alfred Jacob Miller when a retired Scots soldier walked into the drygoods store in New Orleans where the struggling young artist had set up his studio. Though William Drummond Stewart was a wealthy nobleman in his homeland, he'd also spent most of the years after his service to Wellington at Waterloo as a sojourner among the wild noblemen of the frontier—the mountain men. Stewart planned to return once more to his beloved Rockies, and he asked Miller to accompany him in order to preserve the images of the trappers' life in the mountains: the *rendezvous* and the hunt.

Stewart and Miller set out with a supply caravan from Westport (near present-day Kansas City) and forded the Kansas River in the spring of 1837. With them went a party of Delaware Indians and veteran mountain man Thomas Fitzpatrick as a guide. They headed northwest across the Kansas plains, then turned to the West at the north fork of the Platte, onto the future route of the Oregon Trail. They traveled past Sublette's fort on the Laramie River, up into the South Pass through the Continental Divide, on to the great summer *rendezvous* of the mountain men on the Green River. There Miller met living legends like Jim Bridger and witnessed Indian ceremonies and councils no white artist had seen before. After the *rendezvous* the party hunted through the rugged Wind River country, then began the trek back to St. Louis.

Miller kept a faithful record of their progress in over 200 sepia ink sketches and vivid watercolors: drawings of their caravan stretched out in a line across a sea of grass; portraits of the members of the party and of the Indians and mountain men they met; and sketches and watercolors of the trading posts, Indian villages and rugged mountain passes.

In anticipation of Charlie Russell's anecdotal style, Miller's sketches often depicted the stories behind his subjects; in *The Lost Green Horn,* he related how Stewart's English cook, who foolishly took off to hunt buffalo on his own, became bewildered by the vastness of the prairie. He sketched the buckskinned trappers riding unconcerned, sitting unposed at their camp tasks or setting their beaver traps in mountain streams.

As it had that of other artists, the immensity of the Western landscape affected Miller's sense of space. The best example is his allegorical watercolor of the *Wind River Mountains.* Ice-clad peaks tower into an endless yellow sky above mirror waters. Most of the color remains in the foreground in the reds and ochers of the foliage and in the robes of the tiny figures of horsemen along the riverbank. Miller allowed the land to overshadow the people, to become the main character in his story—like a John Ford Western.

After the expedition, Stewart returned to Scotland to assume his title and Murthly Castle. Miller went with him. While in residence at Stewart's estate the young artist produced almost four hundred finished works based on his field sketches.

Miller had a city kid's fascination and naivete when it came to Indians and the frontier. Like Catlin, he tended to idealize his subjects, both white and red. One of his most famous oil paintings, *The Trapper's Bride,* is a sentimental and romantic depiction of a trapper purchasing his Indian bride from her father. Even so, Miller accurately reproduced the details of the trapper's craft and recorded images of the life of the mountain Indians Catlin and Bodmer never met.

"The jaunty tilt of his sombrero, long yellowish beard, and portfolio under his arm marked the artistic type, with something of local color imparted by a rifle hung from his saddle horn."

PHOTOGRAPHER WILLIAM H. JACKSON'S DESCRIPTION OF ARTIST THOMAS MORAN, 1871

His style went from primitive to impressionistic, from realistic to illustrative. He became more careful of detail and accuracy.

When the Russells moved from Cascade to Great Falls in 1897, Charlie found that he needed a better place to work besides the kitchen table. He designed a little log cabin made out of telephone poles, with a huge stone fireplace at the end of the spacious twenty-four by thirty-foot room. Buffalo, bear and wolf skins covered the floor—part studio, part a man's paradise. He kept all of his supplies where he could put his hands on them as he painted. When he invited his friends over, they cooked over an open fire and dutch oven. There was always plenty of coffee and friendship.

Charlie couldn't stay cooped up too long at a time—he headed for the mountains every summer. From late June until the snow fell in early fall, he painted and worked in his second studio in the mountains. His trademark and signature, a horned buffalo skull, gave him the name for his second studio, Bull Head Lodge. He designed a dream studio, "Trail's End," built in Pasadena, California, but he died before he could move in.

About 1903 some of his expert friends insisted that he needed to go to New York—"the big camp," as Charlie called it—to further his career. In some ways it was probably the most miserable time in his life. He felt lost in the big city. For a while Charlie kept a small studio, but the expense was just too much. He enjoyed talking art and stories with those he met—including Will Rogers—but he needed his country living. He said there were, "just too many tall tepees," in New York, and he didn't much care for New York bartenders.

Charlie hit pay dirt when illustrator John Marchand introduced him to the New York magazine art editors. In his happy cowboy days he had painted for amusement, but as an illustrator for books and magazines, he carefully portrayed the West he loved as an artist. His work gained popularity, became sought after, and the money flowed into Nancy's hands in large sums. He told Nancy that it was, "dead men's wages," because most artists had to die before their work drew big prices.

Since he didn't try to be a portrait or landscape artist, he didn't need to pose models. He reached down inside and pulled up pure, raw Western history from his soul. He depicted the West as living, breathing reality. His art invited the viewers in, made them a part of the process. That alone made him popular with the common man.

When he became tired of civilization or perplexed with a painting problem, he would saddle one of his horses and ride to Jake Hoover's place or go see Con Price, his oldest and best friend from the Judith Basin. He would return to work filled with ideas; he would lay out as many as three or four paintings in a week, paintings about the rough and tumble world of the wrangler. Because he'd been thrown, stomped and kicked many a time, he knew what it felt like. He'd even physically act out the fall. His wife would find him rolling on the floor, making sketches of his arms and legs and how their position related to the composition of the painting.

During the sketching and study phase he'd remain silent, but when he started painting he'd smoke and visit with his friends. As he talked, the paint flowed and the canvas came to life. He knew the West firsthand from the time when it was real all the way to the time of the Wild West shows and rodeos—his work was accurate as well as entertaining and informative. As he painted, he shared his experiences with those around him. His trips to the Indian reservations, ranches and national parks fed details into his brain and soul. Coupled with his natural ability as a storyteller, his camera eye brought the reality to life. The critics Charlie painted for were his fellow cowboys, and they verified every stroke of his brush. The accuracy of his finished pieces was perfect even to those

THOMAS MORAN'S VISIONARY WEST

Thomas Moran hadn't yet been to the West when he first illustrated the features of the Yellowstone region for a *Scribner's* article by a member of the Montana Surveyor General's 1870 expedition. The prospect of seeing the region for himself so fired the frail, thirty-four-year-old artist's imagination that he signed on for Dr. Ferdinand Hayden's geological survey in 1871.

Though Moran had never ridden a horse or roughed it, he took to it well. He also made a lifelong friend of the expedition's pioneer photographer, William H. Jackson. The party set out from Virginia City, Montana, in July of 1871, accompanied by a military escort from Fort Ellis. They made their way into the Yellowstone River Valley, packing in after the country grew too rough for their wagons.

Moran was awed and amazed by the strange, beautiful country first discovered by mountain man John Colter and still believed by many to be just one of Jim Bridger's tall tales. For thirty-eight days he sketched and painted at a furious pace to record the marvels of the Yellowstone: the terraces of Mammoth Hot Springs; the incredible colors of the Grand Canyon of the Yellowstone; the great plumes of the geysers; and the great expanse of Lake Yellowstone with its many wooded islands, framed by the peaks of the snowy Absarokas. Easterners later criticized Moran for the brilliant range of colors he used, but it was the equivalent of dismissing Bridger as a liar. Moran was accurate to his subject—eastern critics just hadn't seen the Yellowstone.

He brought back a full portfolio of sketches from which he produced some of his most impressive works. It's evident that the haunting natural beauty of the Yellowstone left an indelible impression in Moran's mind, and his artist's eye translated what he saw into images of simultaneous destruction and creation—as when the plume of his painting of *Castle Geyser* throws itself into a heaven vaulted by white mountains and sulfurous steam. From a later expedition to the Grand Canyon of the Colorado, he produced his dramatic oil *The Chasm of the Colorado*. In it, the air boils above an eerie landscape of jagged rock cloven and shattered by the river's power.

Moran painted landscapes on huge canvasses which attracted the notice of the government and commanded huge prices—the U.S. Congress purchased *The Chasm of the Colorado*, which eventually ended up in the U.S. Department of the Interior Museum. Not only did Moran's works make his fortune, they established him as a voice for conservation. His illustrations of Ferdinand Hayden's article in the February 1872 issue of *Scribner's* and his 1876 portfolio of lithographs had a profound influence on public opinion and in the government's decision to preserve the Yellowstone and other areas as national parks.

Moran traveled with subsequent expeditions to the Yosemite, Utah, Colorado and Arizona. Years after the Hayden Survey named a peak in the Grand Teton Range in his honor, he traveled there to make sketches he turned into *The Teton Range* and *Mount Moran*.

By the time Moran died (1924), much of the country he'd preserved on canvas—the Yellowstone, Yosemite, the Grand Canyon and Devil's Tower—was also preserved in a system of National Parks.

"An Indian or a cowboy could take the average park rider off from his horse, scalp him, hang him on a bush, and never break a gallop."

FREDERIC REMINGTON

who couldn't tell the difference.

His 1911 exhibition at the Folsom Galleries in New York gained him worldwide recognition, and he followed it with shows in Canada at the Calgary Stampede, in London in 1914, and in other American cities from Washington D.C. to San Francisco. The backdrops for his one-man shows included such spectacular settings as Yellowstone and Glacier National Park. Nancy sold one of his paintings in 1921 for ten thousand dollars, the largest price ever commanded by a living American artist. She broke that record a year later by securing thirty thousand dollars for a commission.

Some collectors and admirers of Russell art believe he found his greatest artistic expression in his sculpture rather than his painting. There is no way of knowing how many countless small works he modeled in wax and clay and then destroyed. Turning models into bronze was an expensive process. Only a few of the originals remain; probably fewer than fifty of the priceless little creations exist in their original form, only twenty or so of the larger pieces. When Charlie captured a slice of history in bronze, it was a time capsule that preserved that particular point in time for the world to come look at and enjoy.

If there was anything larger than his talent, it was Charlie's heart. To his friends, he was the greatest man who ever lived. Because his generosity and caring was reflected in his work, the world learned of the reality of the West, knew the Indian's sense of loss, and came to appreciate the cowboy rather than to ridicule him.

During his later years Charlie made friends with nearly every celebrity in the West and the art world, from Will Rogers to William S. Hart and Douglas Fairbanks. His likable and friendly manner made him an instant hit with movie stars just as it did with the common folks. As a writer and a poet, Charlie could turn a phrase with the best of them. He wrote wonderful letters—"paper talk"—and always added a personal touch by doing a quick sketch relating to the subject.

Will Rogers once said, "Charlie is the greatest storyteller I ever heard, and most of them are on himself." That was quite a compliment to come from one of the great American storytellers of all time. Charlie's own style was warm and uncomplicated, filled with humor and down to earth philosophy. He told his stories through Rawhide Rawlins, his fictitious character. Charlie started his yarns, "Rawhide Rawlins sez." His book, *Trails Plowed Under,* is a perfect example of his ability to paint with words. His descriptions were as accurate as his painting, and just as full of his unique sense of humor.

Charlie's health began to deteriorate in 1923, but he continued to work up until he suffered a fatal heart attack at his home in Great Falls in October of 1926. He was just sixty-two years old, his artistic ability at its peak, but as he saw his death approaching, Charlie said, "I'm glad I lived when I did—not twenty years later. I saw things when they were new." Nancy arranged the funeral procession, which included a horse-drawn hearse and Charlie's saddle on a riderless horse.

Charlie Russell was born with a great talent and with a love for the animals and peoples of the West. His art was an extension of his personality. He was a free spirit who lived his life to the fullest, sharing laughter with his many friends from all walks of life. With every brush stroke and strike of the pen, Charlie exhibited his ability as an historian. His accurate modeling in wax and clay verified the time and era in which he lived. His words, his art and his soul captured the West as it was and preserved it for all mankind.

He painted to the very end and died with dignity and honor.

Frederic Remington's Classic West

In comparison to Russell, Remington had a rather normal childhood. Born in Grandma Remington's house on Court Street in Canton, New York, Frederic S. Remington was the only child of newspaper publisher Pierre Remington and his wife, Clara.

Frederic was a hyperactive, physically oriented boy. He fished, hunted and camped with his friends. While playing cowboys and Indians with friends, he once acted out a scalping by forcibly cutting the hair from a playmate's head. No one was surprised when he painted one girl's cat green. He hated formal schooling and did poorly even at the elementary level. Not only did his parents find it difficult to get him into school, they found it virtually impossible to keep him there.

In 1876, Remington transferred to Highland Military Academy in Worchester, Massachusetts, and found it to his liking. He got to wear a uniform, gained the nickname "Bud," and played football. His inner happiness, his generosity and his ability to draw caricatures of the officers and teachers made him popular with the other students. Drawing came easy to Remington, and he always gave his sketches to friends.

He did manage to stay in school long enough to complete his formal education, but he refused his family's wish that he study business. He went on to study at the Yale Art School and the Art Students League in New York City. When Remington entered Yale at age sixteen, he was the only first-year student to enroll in art. There he gained the invaluable technical knowledge and background information on the old masters that would make him a master of his craft. Even so, at the time his family considered his art as something by the wayside, merely a personal entertainment.

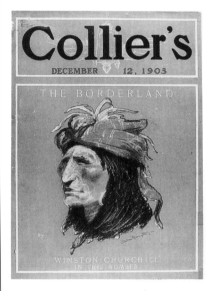

Collier's, December 12, 1903 issue with Remington cover (courtesy of Texas A&M University Special Collections and Archives)

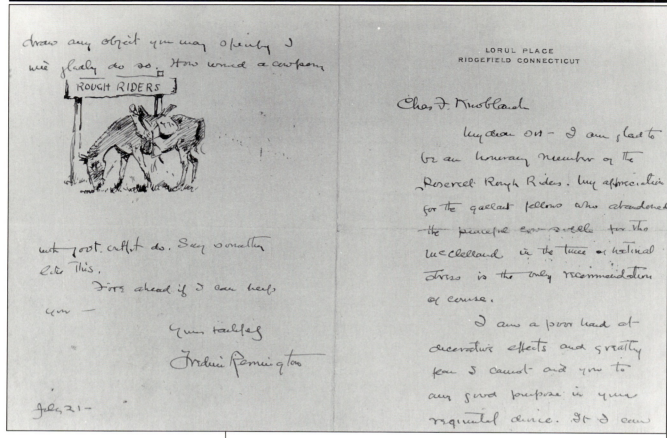

"Rough Riders," Frederic S. Remington (courtesy of Rockwell Museum, Corning, NY)

After his father died, Remington tired of classical training. In 1880, after he failed at standard work and at persuading the father of his true love, Eva Adelle Clayton, to allow her to marry him, he headed out to the still wild and woolly West. Though he went West ostensibly for his health and to try his hand at sheepherding, he took along his pen and brush. He found he hated sheep as much as did Russell, and though he was only nineteen, he soon began producing the illustrations that would eventually appear in *Harper's Weekly* and *Outing* magazine.

He fell in love with the West. He rode through Montana and over the site of the Battle of the Little Bighorn, and made friends among the cowboys. He spent his inheritance to buy a sheep ranch near Kansas City, but spent most of his time adventuring, riding and hunting. As he toured the Southwest, he sketched the people of the frontier, the American cowboys and the Mexican *vaqueros,* reservation Indians and Apaches fresh in from the wild.

On his travels out West, Remington made sketches of subjects and collected materials for his painting and sculpture. He took these ideas and images back to his studio, where they became his great masterpieces. In this transition from actuality to fantasy, his vision of the West sometimes lost a little of its flair and flavor. That's why so many of his horses lacked character. Technically, the Remington horse was correct in every way but lacked individuality.

He sometimes used horses from the race track or New York police mounts as models. They had the look of the thoroughbred rather than that of the rangy Indian pony or the hard-used cavalry horse of the Western plains. Some critics compared Remington's horses to those of a merry-go-round, for one of his most-used action sequences depicted the horse with all four hooves off the ground. In one of his bronze sculptures, "Coming Through the Rye," only five of the sixteen hooves touch the base.

Even so, he had an eye for detail, and he painted the frontier as he saw it. One could identify the individual tribes represented by the Indians in Remington's work by the details of their war paint, weapons and clothing. But from Remington's viewpoint, unlike Russell's, the Indian was a savage who couldn't adjust to the white man's "taking over the West"—so that's how he painted him. It wasn't that he had so much against the Indian, it was simply that Remington was more interested in the cowboy and soldier.

Remington's father had served the Union as a cavalry officer, and it was his military accomplishments that inspired Remington to glorify the United States Cavalry in his work. Remington immortalized the American horse soldier. His soldiers wore their headgear at a cavalier cant; they were swashbuckling, hard-charging heroes who galloped into battle with their carbines, pistols and sabers ready for action. He handled his cowboys in very much the same way. He emphasized composition and professional technique in every detail, sometimes at the expense of absolute authenticity. Many years later, the great Western movie director John Ford had his camera crews study Remington's paintings of cavalry to translate the look and feel of the artist's dramatic vision from canvas to film.

Eva Clayton's father eventually gave in, and Remington married her on October 1, 1884. It was a love match from the beginning. He claimed to be twenty-five although he was not yet twenty-three, and besides that, the clerk got the wedding date wrong. In New York, the newly-responsible Remington tried to market his illustrations to make a living, but the magazine publishers turned him down. He left his new wife with her parents and returned to the Southwest to add to his portfolio.

He returned and took Eva to live with him in Brooklyn while he again made the rounds of the publishers. By 1885, life began to improve for the Remingtons. He published a full-page illustration in *Harper's Weekly* in the January 6, 1886 issue, and followed it up with publications in *Outing* magazine, *Youth's Companion* and many others. He became a regular

One of the Old-time 'Long-Haired Men' of the West, **Frederic Remington (*Harper's New Monthly*) (courtesy of Texas A&M University Special Collections and Archives)**

Authentic Western Art

contributor, eventually publishing illustrations in more than 40 magazines and 140 books.

He published over two hundred of his illustrations in 1888, the year he "came to do the wild tribes," to paint the hostile Indian and bring back to the civilized world his view of the dangerous West. Critical and financial success followed his first major individual show in New York in 1893, and he started construction on a house and studio in New Rochelle. It was in that studio, which was fitted with barn doors to allow entry for his equine models, that Remington would produce most of his 2,700 paintings, drawings and sculptures.

Remington based the first of his 24 sculptured bronzes on one of his paintings, "The Bronco Buster." The result was fifty pounds of detailed metal; it forever immortalized the grim determination of cowboy to cling to the back of a sunfishing horse. He said of it, "I wanted to do something which a burglar wouldn't have, moths eat, or time blacken."

As an illustrative journalist Remington traveled the frontiers, painting the scenes of battle with a flourish and fervor seen by few. As a correspondent for *Harper's Weekly,* he saw the last gasp of Plains Indians resistance during the Ghost Dance. While covering revolution and war in Cuba in 1898 as a correspondent for Hearst's *New York Journal,* he contracted malaria.

In later years, he devoted himself mainly to sculpture and writing. He began with essays on horses and Indians and articles to go along with his war correspondence illustrations, then moved on to short stories and books. He collected his stories in *Pony Tracks* in 1895, then followed it with *Crooked Trails, Sundown LeFlare* and *John Ermine of Yellowstone.*

Remington turned away from illustration to sculpture perhaps because his painting style had evolved. He'd started as a graphic realist but eventually began to find it more difficult to focus his thoughts on canvas. His work drifted into the realms of the impressionistic, and in a fit of depression and anger, he burned many of his paintings in a giant bonfire.

After a particularly successful show in New York, Remington developed appendicitis. He allowed his illness to go untreated until it was too late. He was just forty-eight when he died on December 26, 1909.

As author Owen Wister had said, "Remington is a national treasure." And though his time was all too short, Remington preserved the wealth of his vision in a prodigious number of masterpieces. The Wild West breathes yet through the heroic lines and colors of his sketches and paintings, and is frozen for all time in the dramatic curves and angles of his sculptures. ■

ACT IV: LARGER THAN LIFE

WILLIAM S. HART ON LOCATION

BY ABRAHAM HOFFMAN

ONCE UPON A TIME, WHEN THE OLD WEST WAS STILL A LIVING MEMORY, and memories were a business for the young and ambitious, a stage actor named William S. Hart successfully bridged both worlds, bringing enjoyment to millions of people around the world. Speak to anyone over sixty-five years of age about William S. Hart and you will more than likely revive a sense of nostalgia. "Yes, I saw his films when I was a kid," would be a typical reply.

Bill Hart stood at the head of a logical progression of actors known for their roles as taciturn, courageous men, bound by a code of honor to which they adhered regardless of which side of the law they were on. Randolph Scott, Gary Cooper, John Wayne and Clint Eastwood all fit this mold, with Henry Fonda and James Stewart to a lesser extent, only because Fonda and Stewart played more diversified roles.

Despite their fame, Tom Mix, Gene Autry, Roy Rogers and any "cowboy" actor who catered primarily to a juvenile audience weren't in the same league as Hart. Young people, especially boys, idolized Hart, but he was the first major film star to appear in what the 1950s era referred to as "adult Westerns." Hart believed in recreating an authentic West in his films, or as near to authenticity as he could conceptualize. Hart considered unrealistic those cowboy stars with fancy costumes who ascribed to Gene Autry's "cowboy code of conduct," with its restrictions on smoking, drinking and stretching the truth,.

Perhaps Gene Autry has had the last word on Western film history— the new museum at Griffith Park in Los Angeles is named for him, since he put up most of the millions of dollars necessary to get it built, and the joke is that he took the money out of petty cash. Hart didn't make

PREVIOUS PAGE:
John Wayne in "Hondo"

a fortieth of what Gene Autry earned. The best he could do, at the height of his fame, was to buy a ranch in Newhall and retire to it after his star faded. At Hart's Horseshoe Ranch, children who have never seen a Hart movie tour his fourteen-room home and look at the paintings and decorations with no real understanding of who Hart was or why his home is now a county park.

Hart has faded from public memory because he appeared in silent films. His motion pictures are unavailable to the public except at occasional film festivals. But an increasing number of Hart films are appearing on videocassette, making it possible to see Hart on the small screen.

Nevertheless, Hart's brand is on our hides, whether we know it or not, in the formula he established for his heroic roles, in the authentic look he brought to his films and in the locations where he made his pictures. Many of Hart's early films were shot in Inceville, the studio town built by Thomas Ince near the beach at Santa Monica. Hart also used the Hollywood Hills, the hills around Chatsworth in the San Fernando Valley, and, to a very limited degree, the Newhall area.

Not all of Hart's films were Westerns, and locations at the San Francisco docks, in the forests around Santa Cruz, the town of Sonora, and

BRONCO BILLY ANDERSON

BY BILL O'NEAL

Bronco Billy and the Baby, a short film made in 1908, starred Hollywood's first real cowboy hero, Bronco Billy Anderson. It was a one-reeler shot around Golden, Colorado, on an eight hundred dollar budget and based on a Peter B. Kyne story originally published in the *Saturday Evening Post*. The story was eventually filmed a total of six times; John Ford directed the most popular version, *The Three Godfathers*, with John Wayne, in 1948.

Bronco Billy's version was a huge hit; it earned fifty thousand dollars in its first release and generated hundreds of other Bronco Billy Westerns, including *Bronco Billy's Last Spree*,

Why Bronco Billy Left Bear Country, The Treachery of Bronco Billy's Pal, Bronco Billy's Love Affair and many others.

So just who was Bronco Billy? He was Max Aronson, born in Little Rock, Arkansas in 1882. In 1903, under the alias of G. M. Anderson, he claimed he could ride a horse like a Texas Ranger and talked his way into an appearance in the landmark silent Western, *The Great Train Robbery*. He mounted on the wrong side of his horse and promptly fell off, so decided to take riding lessons at a Texas dude ranch. Convinced that Western pictures had tremendous potential, he directed a few movies in New Jersey, tried his luck at filmmaking in Chicago, then headed for California.

Weather conditions and scenic locations in California proved ideal for Western films, and with screen equipment distributor George K. Speer as a partner, Anderson formed the Essanay motion picture company. Drawing on the dime novel tradition, Anderson realized that a continuing character would sustain popular interest in a series of films. As producer-director, he couldn't find an actor to suit the role,

so he paved the way for William S. Hart, Tom Mix, Hoot Gibson, Ken Maynard, William Boyd, Gene Autry, Roy Rogers and a host of other Western stars who basically played themselves.

With his chunky build, Anderson wasn't handsome, and he never became a graceful rider, but his rugged physique made him quite believable in fight scenes. In time he even grew expert with a lariat. He used scruffy, realistic sets and costumes, partly because the real Old West hadn't quite passed into myth. Starting with *Bronco Billy and the Baby*, he established the more realistic good-badman character that became the staple of non-juvenile Westerns.

By 1920, Hart and Mix and the other, more stylized cowboys replaced Bronco Billy and the other realistic cowboy stars. Anderson produced Laurel and Hardy comedies for a time, then he left the movie business. He died in 1971, the first and the last of the true pioneers of the Western movies.

such faraway places as New Orleans and Chicago served as sites for Hart pictures. Location shooting for his outdoor epics varied from Griffith Park to the Grand Canyon. One of the first films in which Hart acted for Thomas Ince, for example, had some location shots at the Grand Canyon. In contrast to the canyon's scenic grandeur, Hart found Griffith Park a very convenient location when outdoor scenes didn't require spectacular vistas. Griffith Park was barely a mile away from Hart's studio when he ran his own company in the 1918-1921 period.

During these years, Hart leased the Mack Sennett studio at Fountain Avenue and Bates Street. When the need arose, Hart's crew headed for Griffith Park and its available canyons and chaparral. At the end of the day, everyone rode horses back to the studio, where the animals were stabled on the bottom floor of the studio building.

A film might contain bits and pieces of location shots from widely separated areas, put together by the magic and sweat of the film editor. It would be very difficult to identify the exact locations used by Hart in his motion pictures, just as would be the case for any movies, except such obvious places as Vasquez Rocks, the Alabama Hills or Monument Valley. We needn't spend time looking for the Mojave Desert in *Shark Monroe,* a sea story, or in *John Petticoats,* in which Hart played a lumberjack who inherits a New Orleans dress shop. If the latter scenario doesn't sound at all like the "two-gun Bill" image by which Hart is largely remembered, we should note that Hart did appear in a variety of motion picture plots.

The early heyday of Victorville as a center for Hart films coincided pretty much with Hart's peak as an international movie star. Hart was also breaking free of the influence of Thomas Ince, the pioneering producer to whom he felt he owed a debt for getting him off the stage and in front of the camera. Hart gradually realized Ince was paying him far less than he was entitled by his celebrity status. Hart finally extricated himself from his contractual obligations to Ince, but only with great difficulty.

With a very favorable contract with Famous Players-Lasky, now better known as Paramount Studios, Hart found himself in a position to produce his own films as well as star in them. In December 1918, the William S. Hart Company began operation in the studio owned by Mack Sennett. The company worked at a rapid pace in 1919, making films bigger in budget than Hart's previous efforts. For *Breed of Men,* Hart went to the Chicago stockyards. *The Poppy Girls's Husband,* a non-Western, used exteriors in San Francisco. To stage a rodeo scene for *The Money Corral,* Hart built rodeo facilities right in Hollywood and invited the public to attend, thereby getting his action scenes and his spectators all at once.

THE WESTERN'S WORLD RECORD

BY JEFF BANKS

No less an authority than the Trivial Pursuit game informs us that the character most often portrayed in films is Sherlock Holmes. The game is a pretty reliable source, but can anyone be right all the time?

The most extravagant published claim for Holmes movies is "close to 300," and perhaps "more than" might be accurate today. Yet according to Fenin and Everson's authoritative survey, *The Western, From the Silents to the Seventies* (2nd ed., 1973) Bronco Billy, the screen's first Western series hero, appeared in 400 to 500 one- and two-reel silents and even a few silent feature-length films. G. M. Anderson, the only actor to portray the hero, was also probably Hollywood's first and best example of type-casting. After he appeared in *The Great Train Robbery* and several lesser-known silent Westerns, he bought rights to the character of Bronco Billy and for most of the rest of his life went by the name of Bronco Billy Anderson.

Note: Clint Eastwood's Bronco Billy was connected to this first and certainly most-often-portrayed Western hero only by a similarity of name.

The film that followed *The Money Corral,* a Western titled *Square Deal Sanderson,* is the first film Hart made that shows the Mojave Desert in location shooting. Whatever earlier films Hart appeared in, it was now his company making the pictures, and he was responsible for the behavior of his cast and crew as well as their performances.

Hart hired a young agent named Paul Conlon as his studio's publicity director. Conlon had served as a reporter for the *Los Angeles Times* before hiring on as publicity agent for Fatty Arbuckle, the comedian whose career was later ruined by scandal. Hart lured Conlon away from Arbuckle, and the star quickly realized he had a live-wire publicity director. Conlon planted numerous stories about Hart in newspapers and magazines—not gossip stories, but substantive descriptions of Hart's Western background, his expertise on the West, his patriotism and his literary accomplishments. Conlon's influence shaped the Hart image as it's remembered today.

Conlon enjoyed going on location, although he often found it strenuous. Hart's company spent weeks at a time in isolated locales. Conlon later claimed that Hart

William S. Hart gets down to business in "The Gunfighter"

preferred location shooting in Victorville before other companies realized its many advantages, including the rail line, proximity to Los Angeles and a desert vista that embraced the Mojave River, huge rock formations and yucca and Joshua trees. The honeymoon must have been a brief one, for by the end of 1919, other companies were scouting the Mojave Desert locations in the Victorville area.

Square Dean Sanderson deals with mistaken identity, false imprisonment and a ruthless cattle baron who gets his comeuppance from Hart as a two-gun hero. Allegedly set in Arizona, the firm utilized the Mojave Desert. "Fade in on long shot of typical Arizona country," read the start of the shooting script. "Show a lone rider coming off a distant hill at a fairly good pace. If possible show just a speck and the dust cloud he is raising." Hart's love interest in the film was actress Ann Little, who at the end of the silent film era went on to manage for many years the famous Chateau Marmont hotel on the Sunset Strip. The company camped out in the desert near Victorville for two weeks. One publicity release observed that Miss Little was the only woman in the cast.

Hart found the Mojave area ideal for his story requirements. Working with cameraman Joe August, Hart located spots where water sparkled in a streambed and light and shade contrasted in a grove of cottonwoods. Diane Koszarski, author of *The Complete Films of William S. Hart,* wrote that, "Hart consistently placed scenes of romance in such attractive natural settings. Even the most forbidding countryside provides a natural bower for pledges of love, and such graceful interludes provide a refreshing visual texture to the gritty realism of the boomtowns, with their rough timber shacks and dusty side trails."

Hart followed *Square Deal Sanderson* with *Wagon Tracks,* a film for which he made a far greater commitment to location shooting than ever before. Set in the 1850s, *Wagon Tracks* featured a wagon train of emigrants led across the desert by Hart's character. The hero's younger brother was allegedly killed by actress Jane Novak's character. The real murderer is Novak's no-good brother, and after the usual misunderstandings and conflicts, all comes out right in the end, except that Hart rejects Novak in favor of returning to the desert and his work as a guide.

To film *Wagon Tracks,* Hart brought a company of 135 people and a train of covered wagons to Victorville. He filmed some river scenes on the Sacramento River, an indication of the moviemaker's lack of concern about editing together two points naturally separated by hundreds of miles. On May 10, 1919, the company entrained for Victorville. The three weeks on site proved taxing even for the energetic Conlon, who returned to Los Angeles on the May 14th for a brief respite from the rigors of camping in the desert. Hart named his encampment Cactus Center, proclaimed himself mayor, and declared co-star Jane Novak as sheriff.

After spending long hours in the desert heat, without any urban amenities, Hart and his employees were ready for whatever amusements individual ingenuity could provide. One of the most popular pastimes was holding kangaroo courts, with the somewhat sadistic punishment of "chapping" alleged offenders. "We had kangaroo courts on every location," recalled Conlon. "If you were the defendant, you were always guilty in the kangaroo court." "Chapping" consisted of a punishment where the victim bent over and was whacked five or ten times on the rear end by a pair of leather cowboy chaps, naturally wielded by an enthusiastic member of the "court."

No one was exempt from the punishment, not even Hart himself, who apparently got as good as he gave. Conlon remembered that during the location recreation for *Riddle Gawne,* Hart was chapped so hard he was "hardly able to sit down for days." On another occasion Hart was chapped, "for loaning his leading lady five dollars with which she got in the crap game and took money away from honest cowboys." For severe offenses, they first soaked the chaps in water. "And you may take my word for it," asserted a woman reporter visiting a location encampment, "that a man wants to reform when he has once had a taste of damp leather."

Other fun and games were slightly more civilized. The stuntmen and wranglers were usually cowboys who had discovered that working in the movies paid better than working cattle, though the work was often similar to the sweat and hazards of cowpunching.

Hart and Lambert Hillyer, the director of many Hart films, frequently competed in marksmanship matches. They spent evenings playing poker, shooting craps, swapping outrageous tales and playing a form of tag Hart learned in childhood from Sioux playmates, a game he called "Indian Blind Man Bugg." The rules are unfortunately unavailable.

Much of the camaraderie around the encampment was due to the ultra-democratic atmosphere Hart endorsed on location. High-salaried stars shared equal footing with cowboys and lesser workmen in doing the chores. Interestingly enough, Hart claimed that Indian extras seemed to have little resistance to the bitterly cold desert nights. He told one reporter that he worked as rapidly as possible with his Indian scenes in order to return the extras to Los Angeles before they caught cold.

Location life required everyone to live in tents, from stars to stuntmen. A chuckwagon provided well-cooked meals of beef, beans, potatoes, peas, and corn, with pie for dessert. Everyone lined up at dinnertime with tin mugs and plates, sharing fellowship and friendship.

Considerations of water and shade were important in a desert location; Hart kept an eye out for water in the proximity of the scenes to be filmed. Cowpunchers built rough corrals to house the livestock, horses and mules, while other crew members lugged the bulky filmmaking equipment—cameras, reflectors, and props, as well as artificial lighting for shooting campfire scenes and special lighting effects.

Making *Wagon Tracks* in the Mojave Desert resulted in an unexpected and unusual problem. The usual procedure in filmmaking is to shoot the story out of sequence, clustering scenes in the same area to save time and money. The Hart company purchased brand-new covered wagons for the desert trek scenes, but the wear and tear on the prairie schooners gave them an inconsistent look, forcing the crew to either clean them up or to make them look dirty, depending on when the particular scene fit. As the shooting progressed, the condition of the wagons deteriorated.

No sooner did he complete *Wagon Tracks* than Hart moved on to his next project, *John Petticoats,* the story of the lumberjack who inherited the dress shop. For the lumber scenes, the Hart company went to Santa Cruz and its famous redwoods, and in June 1919, they were off to New Orleans. Without any let-up, Hart kept up the production pace, starting his first picture to be done under his lucrative new contract with Famous Players-Lasky—*Sand.* It took Hart back to Victorville and more Mojave Desert location work.

TOM MIX

BY BILL O'NEAL

From circus performer to stunt man to star, Tom Mix came to personify the romantic (though unrealistic) image of the golden age cowboy movie star. Like others who followed him, he made the most of the Hollywood publicity mill and practically rewrote his life story to fit the image.

He was born on January 6, 1880, in Mix Run, Pennsylvania, and in his boyhood he learned to love horses and the outdoors. When he was only ten he attended a performance of Buffalo Bill Cody's Wild West; it fired his imagination and put him on the trail to cowboy stardom.

Though Mix did enlist in the Army for the Spanish-American war, his later movie publicity made him out to be a war hero and an adventurer in his own right. According to Hollywood, he'd been a heroic Rough Rider in Cuba, and he'd fought in the Philippine insurrection, the Boer War, and the Mexican War. Mix himself sometimes claimed to have been a Texas Ranger and a U.S. Marshal. In reality, he saw no combat and deserted in 1902 to run off with the first of his five wives. He later observed, "Payin' all them alimonies sorta drowns out the romance."

Mix achieved his boyhood dream when he joined the Miller Brothers' 101 Ranch in 1905. In Oklahoma he learned roping and other cowboy skills, perfecting his riding and his marksmanship. He toured with several Wild West shows and circuses be-

fore he landed a role in a one-reeler silent film in Oklahoma. At first he appeared mainly as a stunt rider or played the villains, but he eventually worked his way up to starring roles.

William S. Hart was the reigning Western screen star, but Mix was more prolific—in 1915 alone he released fifty-one films, mostly one-reelers. Hart made relatively realistic Westerns with adult themes, but though Mix at first wore scruffy range garb, he broke away from Hart's example and began to adopt more flamboyant costumes. His films stressed comedy, and he set the pace with nonstop action. He specialized in daredevil horseback stunts, first with his "Old Blue," then with a sorrel named Tony he'd bought for $17.50.

Hart's popularity declined in the years after World War I as the public lost its taste for his grim morality tales. With his exciting action pictures, the smiling, athletic Mix mirrored the mood of the Roaring Twenties. By 1922 his salary rose to seventeen thousand five hundred dollars per week. He built a splendid mansion, bought a fleet of expensive cars, acquired a magnificent ranch in Arizona and reveled in the lifestyle of Hollywood royalty. Tony the Wonder-Horse shared his master's popularity. A letter addressed: "Just Tony, Somewhere in the U.S.A.," reached Mix's ranch. Horse and rider were so profitable a team that some referred to Twentieth Century Fox as, "The House that Mix Built."

The advent of sound pictures led an aging Mix to tour with John Ringling's Sells-Floto Circus; at twenty thousand dollars per week, he was the show's star attraction from 1929 through 1931. Universal Pictures lured him back to the screen with the promise of his choice of stories and cast, a large budget for each film, and shooting schedules of three to five weeks. Before the end of 1932 the 52-year-old

Tom Mix

star completed nine Westerns. They were appropriately fast-paced, thrilling films, and they were dynamite at the box office—which proved that the most popular star of the silent Western could do just as well in the sound era.

But Mix still handled his own riding and fighting stunts, and his aging body took a beating. He once again left the screen for the less dangerous and less taxing world of the circus. He lensed one more Western in 1935, a popular serial titled *The Miracle Rider;* it was his 307th and last film. He used the proceeds to fund the Tom Mix Circus, but the show folded in 1938.

Even though he couldn't take the stunt work anymore, Mix still craved action. While speeding down the road north of Florence, Arizona, on October 12, 1940, he crashed his custom-built Cord roadster and was killed.

More than five thousand mourners came to the final spectacle of Mix's funeral at the Forest Lawn Memorial Park in Los Angeles. Rudy Vallee crooned "Empty Saddles" as the silver coffin with "TM" engraved on its side was lowered into the tree-shaded grave.

"Movies fault the myth when they dramatize gunfighting, rather than horsemanship, as the dominant skill."

LARRY McMURTRY FROM "TAKE MY SADDLE FROM THE WALL: A VALEDICTION"

Without the need for prairie schooners and the people required to maintain them and the large number of mules and horses, Hart took a smaller company of forty-five to Victorville in September 1919. They established headquarters at the Hotel Stewart, and they soon found they were not alone—the Goldwyn company showed up to do location work for a Mabel Normand film. "It is only a question of little time until Victorville will have a studio or two," predicted the *Victorville News-Herald.* There was a kernel of truth in this claim, since Victorville was fast becoming a supply base for motion picture companies making films with desert scenes.

The plot of *Sand* centered on Hart as Dan Kurrie, a former cowboy turned railroad stationmaster. Unfairly fired from his job, Kurrie returns to cowpunching, foils a train robbery, exposes the real villain, and wins the hand of the leading lady, in this instance played by actress Mary Thurman. It called for badlands and alkali sand, and Hart found plenty of both in the Mojave Desert. The picture also featured the "return" of Hart's famous pinto pony, Fritz, absent from Hart's previous fifteen pictures because of a contractual dispute with Thomas Ince.

SAND COMPLETED, HART BEGAN 1920 WITH A FILM THAT NEARLY ended his life. In *The Toll Gate,* Hart plays an outlaw who rescues the wife of another outlaw who had betrayed him. Hart had developed the plot line as he finished up *Sand* at Victorville. During a visit there, his sister, Mary, offered an ending to a story Hart had written, "By Their Fruits Ye Shall Know Them." Hart liked Mary's ending and promptly adapted it for *The Toll Gate.*

The company went to the town of Sonora in Tuolumne County for location shooting. Hart relates the incident at the Tuolumne River in his autobiography, *My Life East and West:* "About sixteen miles from Sonora we found a swift-running stream which tunneled right through a mountain. It was the most wonderful place in the world for an entrance to our bandit cave." The script called for Hart to ride Fritz into the cave, with cameramen ready to film his emergence at the upstream end of the tunnel. Hart carried a heavy torch to provide enough light to be photographed. Eight men on horseback were to follow him.

It's not clear why Hart was to ride against the current rather than with it. The problem no one wanted to deal with was a stretch of about thirty feet in the tunnel where cameraman Joe August had failed to touch bottom on a preliminary trip. To his horror, Hart rode into a thirty-foot strip that contained a seemingly bottomless whirlpool. Fritz tried mightily to escape the pool, and only the strong current saved Hart and his horse as it finally swept them past the perilous spot and out the entrance.

Hart hadn't even considered using a double for the stunt.

Hart didn't utilize the Mojave region in his next few films. *Cradle of Courage* dealt with the problems of a World War I veteran. For the Western, *The Testing Block,* he took his crew to Ben Lomond, near Santa Cruz. For *O'Malley of the Mounted,* a story set in the Canadian Northwest, he used both the Santa Cruz forests and the hills of Chatsworth. *Whistle* found Hart in the decidedly non-Western role of an embittered factory worker. Then came *White Oak,* a picture that brought Hart back to Victorville and the most hilarious episode that ever occurred during Hart's location work.

The plot called for Indians to attack a wagon train, for a bank robbery, a suicide by drowning and other escapades. Hart filmed the drowning scene in the Sacramento River; he came down with pneumonia, the price he paid for not using a double. He went on to shoot the next scenes in the Mojave Desert, but ended up bedridden with a 103 degree fever in a Victorville hotel. Director Lambert Hillyer, assistant director Steve Roberts, and cameraman Joe August all chose this moment to go duck hunting along the Mojave River.

With time on their hands, the crew members hung around a corral near the railroad tracks that ran right through Victorville. Paul Conlon was sitting on the fence, watching some of the stuntmen in the corral practicing trick riding and roping. A Santa Fe freight train with many oil-tank cars pulled up on the siding next to the corral to allow a passenger train to go through. Two trainmen passed by, both of them in an obvious state of inebriation. One of them said, "Too bad you guys are too dumb to be good trainmen. Lots more fun ridin' trains than trying to stay on them horses."

This was 1921, and Prohibition was in effect. The cowboys grew suspicious of how the train employees got drunk on the job. One of the men, who had experience as a brakeman, ducked under one of the tanker cars, unscrewed a stopcock, and tasted the liquid that came out. It was muscatel wine. Immediately cowboys and crew members scattered, returning in moments with bits of garden hose for siphoning, new garbage cans bought at the Emporium, jugs, buckets, milk pans, canvas horse feed bags, washtubs and even sugar bowls taken from the hotel.

"The muscatel hit the hard-drinking cowboys like a freight coming out of a blind alley," recalled Conlon, who himself joined a circle of people passing around a big jug, "and some of the top rodeo riders mounted their ponies to let off steam. They were not long in the saddle." By the time the train passed on, the cowboys had drained as much as they could of what Hart later claimed was ninety-seven million gallons of, "the finest Mexican wine ever made from grapes."

WITH A HEART OF GOLD: SOILED DOVES ON THE SCREEN

BY LOREN D. ESTLEMAN

Joan Blondell, Julie Christie, Angie Dickinson, Marlene Dietrich, Frances Fisher, Lena Horne, Katy Jurado, Diane Lane, Cloris Leachman, Shirley MacLaine, Marilyn Monroe, Sheree North, Jane Russell, Stella Stevens, Anna Thompson, Claire Trevor, Mae West, Marie Windsor and Shelley Winters.

Linda Darnell, Jo Van Fleet, Faye Dunaway, Joanna Pacula and Isabella Rossellini have all played Doc Holliday's mistress, though not all of them played the role as his real-life mistress, Big Nose Kate.

The era of silent Westerns

Before long riderless horses ran loose in the desert, and drunken wranglers accosted Victorville citizens and danced in the streets. One drunken cowboy's horse tossed him upside down onto a big cactus, where he hung pinned to the plant; no one paid him the slightest attention. Hart's cowboy extras sometimes staged rodeos in the town park and passed the Stetson for voluntary donations, but this time the people of Victorville didn't welcome their unexpected celebration.

The mayor of Victorville tried to restore order, but no one listened. Someone telephoned San Bernardino and asked for a sheriff's posse to come to Victorville and arrest the revelers. Meanwhile, the noise of the merrymakers reached Hart's hotel room. Ignoring the pneumonia, Hart got dressed with the aid of Mary Hart and Lillian Conlon, Paul Conlon's wife. He went outside the hotel in time to witness a street fight between his wranglers and several Victorville men.

Hart lost his temper and quickly began separating men, breaking up fights, and ordering everyone to stop. Finally the combat ended, and an angry Hart—angrier than anyone could recall—fired his entire company on the spot. He turned to go back to the hotel. At that moment, one of the drunken cowboys who had climbed to the roof of Victorville's one-story jail let out a long coyote yell and proclaimed, "I'm a curly bitch wolf and this is my night to howl!"

The cowboy then fell off the roof and knocked himself out. Hart looked at the fallen cowboy and said to the mayor, "Better throw Tex in the jail house. Let him howl there."

The party was over; the sheriff's posse was on its way up from San Bernardino. As it happened, by the time the sheriff and his deputies arrived on the special train, their services were no longer required. "They did not need guns," Hart recalled. "They needed many husky men and many stretchers…every foot of available space outside of Victorville was occupied by a sleeping cowboy. The courthouse was full—the jail was full. Nothing was sacred to those Bacchanalian inebriates."

When his temper subsided, Hart met in his hotel room with the San Bernardino sheriff to settle matters. No damage had been done, and injuries were minimal. Hart and the sheriff smoothed things over with the aid of five gallons of muscatel, thoughtfully supplied by contrite cowboys who attached a note to the bottle—"Have one on us boys, boss."

The sheriff and his deputies returned to San Bernardino and Conlon fabricated a story about how the Indians hired as extras had gotten drunk on firewater, but that the authorities had everything under control. Hart wryly observed that, "there were no 'good Indians.'" Everyone involved, from business manager to wranglers, could share the blame. He called a meeting of the company and said, "Boys, I reckon a little excitement is good for pneumonia. Looks like I'm going to live. Reckon you fellas are goin' to be able to work in the mornin'?"

After he wrapped *White Oak,* Hart made two more Westerns, *Travelin' On* and *Three Word Brand.* Early in 1921 he announced his retirement from motion pictures and closed his studio. Fifty-six years old (he admitted only 49), Hart said he wanted to concentrate on writing novels and operating his recently purchased Horseshoe Ranch in Newhall. Hart had written and published a poem, *Pinto Ben,* in a small collection of short stories he put together with his sister. He'd also written two boys' adventure books and was completing a third while running his studio— more than enough work for any one person—and he wanted vacation and rest time.

After he closed his studio, Hart went to New York for a brief vacation. He also courted Winifred Westover, his co-star in the film *John Petticoats,* and they were married on December 7, 1921, the day after his fifty-seventh birthday. The couple separated after barely five months, a private problem naturally made public by the newspapers. Then an-

NEVER PLAY POKER WITH A MAN NAMED DOC: HOW TO SURVIVE IN A HOLLYWOOD WESTERN

BY LOREN D. ESTLEMAN & DALE L. WALKER

Whatever the *real* Code of the West might have been, Hollywood wrote one of its own in a zillion B-Western movies and television productions. Never mind that the precepts of that code scaled in historical exactitude from faintly laughable to so ridiculous that a youngster who never traveled west of Perth Amboy knew instinctively how stupid it was—if you watched enough, you learned the peculiar set of rules by which you could survive a Hollywood Western.

■ Always avoid the table under the staircase landing during barroom brawls.

■ If you get arrested, see if you can arrange for a cell *without* a view of the carpenters building the gallows.

■ Pass by any town with tumbleweeds blowing down the street; also, avoid towns with names like Hate or Purgatorie or Dogtown.

■ Carefully gauge the distance *between* the horses pulling a runaway stagecoach or wagon so that in leaping between them to save the passengers you do not slip through and end up with horseshoe dents and wheel ruts on your body.

■ Carry an *extra* knife for sagebrush surgery (digging out bullets, performing amputations), in addition to the one you use for skinning animals, slicing chaws from a tobacco plug, and stirring beans.

■ Don't ride with men named Ringo, Reno, Rio, Billy, Bode, Drew, Lomax, Wilson, Lucky, Butch, or Kid; don't dance or drink with women named Gert, Flo, Kitty, Lil, or Lady.

■ When your posse surrounds an outlaw's refuge, don't let them send you "round back," because that's precisely where the outlaws will try to break out.

■ Never play poker with a man named Doc; if you must play poker with him, no matter how much you lose, avoid making comments like, "Mister, you gotta be cheatin.'"

■ Don't get into heated arguments with men who wear one leather glove.

■ Don't herd sheep in cow country; if you must herd sheep, take no public pride in it and bathe often.

■ Never try to bargain with Comancheros.

■ Learn to play "Buffalo Gals" on the piano and you will never go hungry.

■ Be sure you know what time the sun goes down just in case you're invited be out of town by sunset.

■ Remember that the phrase "slap leather" isn't just a kinky proposition in the West.

■ Don't get caught carrying a running iron on property owned by a man named Print; avoid corraling strays that belong to men named Goodnight or Shanghai. Unless you work for them, they will not believe you were "just trying to be helpful."

■ If you toss a glass of bar whiskey into a bad guy's face, try not to miss.

■ It isn't necessary to tip the saloon swamper.

■ If you are an adult male, you'll open yourself up to chiding if you ask the barkeep for, "One sody pop, please!"

THE MOST ENDURING CHARACTERS ON THE SCREEN

Will Kane (Gary Cooper in *High Noon***); Fred C. Dobbs (Humphrey Bogart in** *Treasure of the Sierra Madres***); Kid Sheleen (Lee Marvin in** *Cat Ballou***); Bearclaw Grizzlap (Will Geer in** *Jeremiah Johnson***); the Man With No Name (Clint Eastwood in** *A Fistfull of Dollars* **and sequels); "Chris" (Yul Brynner in** *The Magnificent Seven***); also, John Wayne as the Ringo Kid in** *Stagecoach,* **as Tom Donniphan in** *The Man Who Shot Liberty Valance,* **as Ethan Edwards in** *The Searchers,* **as Rooster Cogburn in** *True Grit,* **and as J. B. Books in** *The Shootist.*

other revelation made front page headlines—a woman accused Hart of fathering her child. The paternity suit received wide-spread coverage, but the outcome didn't get the same publicity. In open court the woman finally confessed that her alleged union with Hart had been a *spiritual* one, and the child wasn't even hers.

These sensational reports shared headline space with such scandals as the death from drugs of actor Wallace Reid, the trial of Fatty Arbuckle for the murder of Virginia Rappe, the mysterious murder of director William Desmond Taylor and a rash of movie star divorces. Hart decided to redeem the reputation that he believed had been tarnished and announced a movie come-back. He negotiated a contract with Famous Players-Lasky for the production of *Wild Bill Hickok,* based on a story Hart himself had written about the famous lawman.

Hart returned to Victorville, where the muscatel escapade had apparently been forgiven. For Wild Bill Hickok, Victorville itself became a stage set. "By building two new streets near the depot, we made Victorville, California, into Dodge City, Kansas," Hart recalled. The set designers hung a sign on the station that said "Dodge City, Kansas," throwing train passengers into confusion as their train stopped at Victorville. "Some of them became quite panic-stricken and acted exactly like a green goods victim when he discovers he has been fleeced," observed Hart. "The train crews all enjoyed the joke." During production, upwards of four hundred people came to Victorville to see the Hickok film through to completion.

During production of Hart's last picture, *Tumbleweeds,* word came from New York that Famous Players-Lasky Corporation was not satisfied with the Hickok picture. Jesse Lasky believed Hart's filmmaking style and variations on the "good-bad man" theme were becoming passe—audiences increasingly preferred the flashier showmanship of Tom Mix. Unless Hart agreed to relinquish control of the stories, their production treatment, and selection of the supporting cast, Lasky would abrogate their contract. Hart stood firm in his demand for complete control of his own films and terminated the contract.

In 1926, Hart permanently retired from the business. He spent the last twenty years of his life on the one location he could truly call home—*La Loma de los Vientos,* "The Hill of the Winds," on his Horseshoe Ranch in Newhall. Upon his death in 1946 he willed the property to the County of Los Angeles, and today William S. Hart County Park provides recreation and a bit of movie history, courtesy of the man who so much enjoyed "the thrill of it all." ∎

Note: An earlier version of this article appeared in the Spring 1992 issue of Southern California Quarterly.

PLAYERS ON HORSEBACK

HERE COMES THE HOOTER!

BY MARYLOIS DUNN

THE TRADITION OF THE STERN-JAWED, STEELY EYED COWBOY HERO faded the first day Hoot Gibson casually strolled onto the screen as a star in 1921, for he was bested at every turn except the last by the villains. He was slugged, shot, roped, tied and dragged in every picture he made. Hoot suffered indignities such as having his gun taken away from him, or having his eye blackened by the frail, pretty heroine. A flapjack he flipped was likely to land in the place hitherto reserved for Keystone comedians rather than the pan for which it was intended. But Hoot always came out smiling.

What happened to Hoot Gibson in his pictures were the things that happened to everyday people. His audiences recognized in his practiced ineptitude their own frailties, and they loved him for it. Like life, Hoot Gibson's epics were completely unpredictable.

Born Edward Gibson at Tekamah, Nebraska, on August 6, 1892, Hoot acquired his nickname as soon as he was old enough to make it stick. Only rarely did anyone use his real name. Although his section of Nebraska was fairly wild, Hoot felt the call of bronco country. He saddled his horse and drifted into the West. By the time he was sixteen, Hoot was known from the Rio Grande to the Canadian border as a top hand. He rode rough strings for bunk and grub and, if he was lucky, ten dollars a month in cash.

Once during a bulldogging contest, his "fun-loving" cowboy friends saddled him up with a hammer-headed outlaw horse who had never been ridden. When Hoot mounted, the hammer-head let out a squall and began sunfishing ten feet in the air. The steer, let out at the same time, understandably made distant tracks.

Hoot busted the outlaw between the ears with fist and hat, scraped him from ear to tail four or five times with his Spanish spurs and lined the surprised horse out after the steer. He fought the reluctant mount within reach of the steer's four-foot horns, made his catch, and threw the steer in time to win the contest—much to the astonishment and delight of his friends.

As good as he was, it was only natural that Hoot would drift into the rodeo circuits. The circuit could bring a good rider six to seven thousand dollars in a season. The rest of the year, rodeo cowboys drifted toward Hollywood and movie-making. Hoot began to double for Harry Carey in 1911, and by 1913 he was playing juvenile leads. Hoot did stunt work and doubled in many pictures.

A fall from a horse brought him fifty cents, and he sometimes made six or seven dollars a day doing falls. Though Hoot and his rodeo *compadres* worked during the winter months as movie extras and stunt men, when summer came they deserted Hollywood for their first love, rodeo.

An overdressed Hoot Gibson puzzles Harry Carey and friends in "The Last Outlaw" (1936 RKO)

Records for 1912 show that the All-Around Championship of the Pendleton Roundup, one of the roughest rodeos in the country, went to Hoot Gibson. Hoot kept his prize, the handsome silver-mounted saddle inscribed with "Champion Cowboy of the World," until the day he died.

After his win at Pendleton, he had offers to join several Wild West shows. For a while, Hoot rode with Art Acord, another old-time movie great, in Dick Stanley's Congress of Rough Riders. Australia was one of the many places the fabulous Western show toured; Hoot was a favorite because he always had time to teach a rider an old trick or learn a new one himself. The tricks he learned in his days with the Wild West shows stood him in good stead when he turned exclusively to movies — he could easily and naturally perform all the dangerous stunts that the pretty faced actors watched their doubles perform. Hoot liked stunt men — they were his kind of people — but he liked them to do other actors' stunts. Hoot Gibson did his own.

Fistfights and gun battles atop moving trains and stagecoaches, jumping horses out of fast-moving boxcars and over cliffs, riding motorcycles into wildly dangerous situations — they were everyday stunts. As a double, Hoot also stunted in cars, but he always preferred horses. Hoot got his first acting job in 1915. As a juvenile lead with Harry Carey in *A Knight of the Range,* he also continued doubling for Harry in the stunt scenes. Carey proved a good friend. He worked Hoot into as many films as he could, and suggested to the studio that Hoot would make good star material.

Just about the time Hoot was ready for his first lead roles, World War I came along. He joined the Tank Corps and was out of pictures for two years, until the fighting was over. When he came back, he returned to the second leads he had left, but with a difference. The audiences had begun to look for Hoot and loudly protested every time he was killed off in the fourth reel. He was, indeed, ready for stardom.

Action, his first starring role in 1921, was a John Ford picture the director subsequently remade twice under the title *Three Godfathers. Action* was an apt name, for Hoot got into every kind of trouble imaginable, and the audience loved him. They worried about him. Like themselves, he wasn't perfect, and they sat tense and excited from scene to scene, wondering what he'd get into next.

In the early days of Westerns, scripts were practically nonexistent. Hoot often said they made them up as they went along, but audiences didn't seem to mind. They wanted action, and with Hoot Gibson, action was what they got. What did it matter if his faithful steed played tricks on him, or he wound up on the floor after a free-for-all? He always won out in the end after plenty of rootin' and shootin.' In one six-year period, he completed forty-eight pictures, some of them two-reelers.

Hoot Gibson decides which trail to take in "The Mounted Stranger" (1930 Universal)

The advent of talkies didn't affect Hoot Gibson's popularity. He just added his easy drawl to his famous smile and his usual hijinks. He became known for the fact that he rarely wore a gun and usually had to borrow one when he needed it. Little gratuitous violence marred his pictures, but there was action a-plenty.

After a while, movie-making became routine and lost some of its old excitement. The studios recycled old clips of dangerous action when the star was far too valuable to live dangerously. As many an old-timer did, Hoot got together a rodeo group and toured the country. He gave a good show, displaying many of the skills that had made him famous. And like many another old-timer who believed in honor and personal integrity, he went broke. The number of ex-wives he had to support didn't help.

When television signaled the death of the B Westerns, Hoot was able to secure rights to about fifty of his old movies, which hit the small screen in the early days of TV. But it wasn't enough. In the 1950s he moved to a small spread in Nevada near Las Vegas, where he worked for years as the genial host and resident celebrity of the Last Frontier Casino.

Hoot Gibson died in 1962 of cancer. When he was buried in his full cowboy regalia, all the Hollywood cowboys came to pay their respects to the man who for years had personified the cowboy-hero to the entire world. ∎

COLONEL TIM McCOY, MORE THAN A COWBOY

BY MARYLOIS DUNN

IT MIGHT HAVE BEEN STRANGE THAT A KID WHOSE BROTHERS WANTED to be doctors, firemen and attorneys just wanted to be a cowboy, but that was his Tim McCoy's soul-deep ambition.

Timothy John Fitzgerald McCoy was born in Saginaw, Michigan, April 10, 1891. After he saw a performance of the famous 101 Wild West Show in Chicago, he drifted to the West to become a cowboy just like the ones in the show. His money ran out in Wyoming.

McCoy had no trouble finding work on various ranches in the territory, and he soon found friends among the Indians who lived there on reservations. He learned their languages, including sign language, and their customs. He became so expert in Indian lifestyle that the U.S. Government used him as an official interpreter.

He bought a small ranch in the Owl Creek Country and had expanded it to over five thousand acres when the Great War came along. McCoy greatly admired Teddy Roosevelt, so he wrote to him and offered to raise a cavalry unit for him composed of Wyoming and Montana cowboys. He raised the unit, but the Army wouldn't allow Teddy to take it abroad. Instead, McCoy applied to Officer Candidate School and gained a commission as a captain in the cavalry. He was among the last of his kind—only three divisions of mounted cavalry survived the war. He could see what the future would bring, so he transferred to artillery before the cavalry was disbanded.

In the Army, he met Major General Hugh Scott, last of the great Indian fighters. The general was impressed with McCoy's homespun knowledge of Indians and his interest in them. He took McCoy under his wing and forced him to read and study until he could say he knew more about the Indians than they knew about themselves.

Along with General Scott, McCoy began to reconstruct the history of the battle at Little Big Horn. The battlefield remained virtually untouched up into the 1920s. The information they gathered at on-site investigations and from talking to Indian survivors of the battle is still a primary source for books on Custer and the fiasco at Little Big Horn.

Although he rose to the post of Adjutant of Wyoming, McCoy resigned his commission when Jesse L. Lasky offered him the job as Technical Adviser on Indian affairs for the moving picture, *The Covered Wagon.*

McCoy was hooked. He loved the picture-making business even though he wasn't actively involved with it. Lasky asked him to prepare a prologue that he would narrate live to audiences about the movie. McCoy brought along some of the Indians he knew from Wyoming, and they brought horses, war paint and actual covered wagons into the larger theaters where the picture played.

The show was such a success that he gathered up more Indians and took the troupe over to Europe, where they stayed mostly in England and Paris for almost a year. When he returned to Hollywood he signed with MGM. They liked him, but since Louis B. Mayer didn't like Westerns, they didn't know what to do with him.

His first picture, *War Paint,* came out in 1926; it was pretty much the product of his own experiences. He put his head together with W. S. Van Dyke to come up with the script. They filmed it in Wyoming and did modest box office business.

Col. Tim McCoy (in the white hat, of course) gets ready for an Indian attack on a wagon train in "The Indians Are Coming" (1930 Universal)

McCoy did many period movies as well as Westerns for MGM. They generally cast him as an officer in some kind of army because he simply didn't look like a baggy-pants cowboy. With his clean-cut features and his ramrod straight back, Tim McCoy was everybody's ideal officer.

When sound came in, the studio dropped the Western series. Although his pictures did well at the box office, they didn't renew McCoy's contract. Disgusted, he took his wife and three children back to the ranch in Wyoming and set about making a life for himself in the country he loved almost as much as he loved making movies.

Carl Laemmle, Uncle Carl as he was called by everyone, had in mind a Western movie called *The Indians are Coming.* He didn't care whether it was a feature or a serial, but it should be called *The Indians are Coming.*

He knew Tim McCoy was the only man who could make the Indians come, and he called him back from Wyoming to star in his first serial. Filmed for both silent and sound distribution, *The Indians are Coming* was so authentic that scenes from it were used in hundreds of movies for years afterward. Remember the village across the river and the Indians in full war paint hitting the water in full cry for whatever fight the plot called for? It came from *The Indians are Coming.* That famous scene and a hundred others were used and reused over the years until color came in and spoiled the profitable resale of footage for Universal.

McCoy made a second serial at Universal, *Heroes of the Flame,* and then he went on to sign a contract at Columbia in 1932. Over the years he made thirty-two features for Columbia, twenty-four of them Westerns. The others were period pieces much like those he'd made in the silents for MGM. His features varied in quality, as did those of most actors and studios of the day, but over all, they set a standard for quality that few Western actors were able to maintain.

FILM COWBOYS AND THEIR HORSES

BY MARYLOIS DUNN

Most everyone remembers the names of the Western stars. Few remember the horses they rode in their motion pictures, even though those horses were an important part of the plot and setting. Kids in the heyday of the Westerns all had their favorite horse as well as their favorite cowboy. Every kid wanted that horse for his special pal and dreamed of riding as well as Ken Maynard, Tom Mix or Tim McCoy. To show no favoritism, even at this late date, we'll list them in alphabetical order:

COWBOYS (and cowgirls)	HORSES	COWBOYS (and cowgirls)	HORSES
Rex Allen	Koko	Alan "Rocky" Lane	Blackjack
Gene Autry	Champion (Lindy), Champion #2 & Champion Jr.	Lash LaRue	Rush
		Little Beaver	Papoose
Johnny Mack Brown	Rebel	the Lone Ranger	Silver
Sunset Carson	Cactus	Tim McCoy	Pal
Hopalong Cassidy	Topper	Ken Maynard	Maizie, Brownie, &Tarzan
the Cisco Kid	Diablo	Tom Mix	Old Blue, Tony & Tony Jr.
Eddie Dean	Flash, Cooper, & White Cloud	Tex Ritter	White Flash
Dale Evans	Buttermilk	Roy Rogers	Trigger (Golden Cloud), Trigger Jr.
Hoot Gibson	Pal (several horses)		
Monte Hale	Partner	Red Ryder	Thunder
William S. Hart	Fritz	Charles Starrett	Raider
Wild Bill Hickok (television)	Buckshot	Bob Steele	Boy
		Fred Thompson	Silver King
Tim Holt	Sheik	Tonto	Scout
Buck Jones	Silver	John Wayne	Duke

McCoy didn't hobnob with the Western set. He'd made his friends when he was at MGM; he was much more at home with Ronald Colman, Warner Baxter and Lionel Barrymore than with Tom Mix and Buck Jones. In fact, he hardly knew the other Western stars in the early thirties. He was definitely on the "A" list.

Two Fisted Lawman was notable among his Western films for Columbia because it was credited to William Colt MacDonald and featured Wallace MacDonald and John Wayne playing McCoy's loyal ranch hands. It was the first of William MacDonald's trio westerns; he went on to write the "Three Mesquiteers" Western novels, which were later made into movies.

McCoy was a fine actor, and he never played the usual easy-going cowboy. He liked to create an unusual role and loved to wear disguises to fool the villains. Twice he masqueraded as a Chinese man, and at least once as a Mexican bandit and a gypsy.

He played in a series of Westerns for Puritan pictures, an independent, and he brought as much to them as he could. They never came up to the quality of his other films.

Monogram's "Rough Riders" series starred Buck Jones, Tim McCoy and Raymond Hatton; the films were typical of the usual run of Monogram pictures. The three stars did the best they could to bring class to the sloppy production values and poor plots and direction, but there was little they could do. The films became vehicles for Buck Jones, and McCoy decided to quit as gracefully as he could. He liked Buck personally very much, but he couldn't see any future for himself in pictures. Besides, he was no longer enjoying the work.

When the second World War started, McCoy worked quietly to have his commission reinstated. He succeeded, packed his bags and took the train to Washington. Tim sent a telegram to Monogram using the words the trio of Rough Riders spoke at the end of each picture, "So long, Rough Riders!"

After the war, McCoy played guest shots in *Around the World in 80 Days* and *Run of the Arrow*—he played, of course, a cavalry officer. He starred in his own television series for a five-year run in prime time on Saturday night. He demonstrated and talked about Indian history, sign language and customs, and he won an Emmy. He was a contestant on the $64,000 Dollar Challenge, and he won the challenge. He toured with several different Wild West shows and circuses, one of which bore his name, until he was eighty-two years old.

When he retired from the last circus Colonel Tim McCoy's blue eyes still sparkled impishly and, though his hair was white, his back was still ramrod straight. ■

Famous horse movie stars without their make up.

BUCK JONES

BY MARYLOIS DUNN

MILLIONS OF KIDS LOVED HIM FOR THE THRILLING ADVENTURES HE brought to the shining screen, but the real life story of Buck Jones was far more exciting than any motion picture he ever made.

He was born in Vincennes, Indiana, on December 12, 1891. His father purchased a three-thousand-acre ranch in Red Rock, Oklahoma, and moved the family out West in three old wagons and a buckboard. Since Charles Frederick Gebhard was a long handle for such a tad of a cowboy, the youngest of the clan quickly became "Buckaroo" Gebhard, shortened to Buck. He took to the saddle like cockleburs to sheep and was a working ranch hand by the time he was ten. He was fascinated by the riding, roping and shooting abilities of the ranch hands, and he soaked up everything he could from them.

A restless teenager, Buck persuaded his mother to lie for him about his age, and in 1907, he enlisted in G Troop, 6th U.S. Cavalry. He began his Army career riding the rough string, and later that same year he saw patrol duty on the Mexican border. The action in those days wasn't tracking dope smugglers but catching cattle rustlers and bandits who came across the border. Buck said that bulldogging bandits was just about as much fun as anything he ever did in his life.

That phase of his Army career was short. Within the year, he found himself on a transport headed for the island of Mindinao, in the Philippines. On that beautiful but treacherous island, Buck made "top sergeant" in spite of his youth. He decided the Army was going to be his career, but the Moros changed his mind. Buck was at the head of his command, a squad of soldiers sent in search of a band of Moro insurgents, when the Moros bushwhacked him and shot him in the thigh. His men carried him back to camp, but his wound became infected. He almost lost the leg, and he carried an ugly six-inch scar for the rest of his life. He couldn't walk for some time, so the Army mustered him out in 1909 with a "Full Disability" at the age of eighteen. He was shipped home to spend the rest of his life as an invalid.

But Buck didn't agree with the diagnosis. Once he was back on his home turf, he decided to do something about the gimpy leg himself. There was no such thing as a physical therapist in those days, so he undertook his own cure. He began exercising the leg daily, increasing the workout until he was able to crawl back in the saddle. Having a bunch of cowhands stand around and laugh every time he fell down did a lot to keep him on his feet and in the saddle. He overcame his disability with willpower and stubborn grit and the constant prodding of a bunch of cowhands who hated a quitter.

When he was twenty-one and sound again, he rejoined the Army, still thinking he wanted to make it his career. This time, Buck joined the 1st Aviation Squadron, where his interest in engines soon got him rated as aviation mechanic first-class. In those early days, you didn't have to be an officer to fly the planes, and Buck found himself flying some of the first planes bought by the U.S. Army. He also took the time to become expert with the rifle, carbine and pistol, and won medals in marksmanship and sharpshooting. When his career seemed like it was going to keep him in grease up to his elbows more than it was in flying, he allowed his enlistment to expire, and he received his second honorable discharge.

As a kid Buck had ridden for a short time with the 101 Ranch Wild West Show, and the call of sawdust had entered his blood. He hired on again as a bronco rider and trick roper as the show began a new tour of the nation. When he saw an equestrienne named Odelle Osborne perform, he told his compadres, "That's the girl I'm gonna marry," before he ever met her. They dated steadily until they both joined the Julia Allen Wild West Show in 1915. They were married on horseback at Lima, Ohio, in the middle of the circus arena between acts in the regular show.

Performing with the Golmer Brothers Wild West Show and Ringling Brothers Circus, and another stint with the famous 101 Ranch Wild West Show occupied Buck and Odelle until World War I came along. The Army career of his youth called out to Buck, and he offered his services to the French Government, which was buying horses in Chicago. He took on the job of breaking their horses, and he soon found himself on a boat bound for France and a remount camp.

TOP: Buck Jones reaches for the sky as a young Ward Bond plays the heavy in "The Crimson Trail" (1935 Universal)

BOTTOM: Tim McCoy (left) and Buck Jones (center) in "Arizona Bound" (1941 Monogram)

Buck soon became the orderly to a French general and an officer-instructor for the French Cavalry. He spent hours in the cockpits of French Spads on reconnaissance duty over the German lines when he could escape his other duties.

A stint as a test driver for the Indianapolis racing cars held Buck's interest until Odelle told him that he was about to become a father. He'd heard from some of his friends that a cowboy could always earn money riding in the moving pictures. Buck hung around the studios daily but he didn't find work immediately. They finally offered him a film role as a sheep herder; the role paid the magnificent sum of five dollars a day, more than a real sheep herder earned in a month. The job lasted for six days, and with thirty dollars in his jeans, Buck's luck changed. The casting directors soon learned of Buck's ability with horse, rope and gun, and he found regular work as an extra at Universal and the old Selig studios.

Eventually Buck doubled for William S. Hart and others in shooting hazardous scenes. He had more work than he could handle as a cowboy and a stuntman by the time he came to the attention of William Fox. The old motion picture pioneer signed Buck to a long-term contract, and Buck changed his name to Jones and got his first starring role in *The Last Straw* (1920), *not* a Western.

Even though she was pregnant, Odelle did some doubling for May McAvoy at Famous Pictures. Dell was slight and her pregnancy didn't show. The work was too strenuous though, and their daughter, Maxine, made her appearance somewhat earlier than was expected. Buck was irritated at Odelle for her recklessness but thrilled with his beautiful little girl. She was their only child.

William Fox was indeed a fox. He was less interested in Buck Jones than he was in keeping his major star, Tom Mix, in line. Tom was angling for a raise to ten thousand dollars per week, and Fox let it be known that Jones was an adequate replacement for Mix—at only $150 per week. Mix was naturally steamed. One day when Buck was shooting a picture on the back lot, he needed an extra gun. Someone sent him over to where Mix was shooting his picture on the front lot, and when Buck asked for the loan of a gun, Mix told him where he could go to get one and where he could put it when he got it. They were never friends after that.

Buck made over one hundred pictures for William Fox. Occasionally he took time out from the Western to play a straight drama. By 1926, Buck was making enough money so that he and Odelle could tour Europe.

There he found that his face was well-known due to the European distribution of his films. Buck was a rich man by the time 1929 rolled around. He owned several valuable pieces of property in and around Los Angeles, a large ranch and some corner lots in Beverly Hills. He did a series for Columbia and another for Universal before he formed his own company. In Buck Jones Productions, Inc., he was the star and sometimes the writer and director as well. Buck liked pictures with light and comic story lines, though he never forgot that action was what the audiences craved. His pictures always contained plenty of action.

Buck and Odelle, with plenty of money to spend, decided to buy their own circus. Buck put his movie career on hold and took Odelle and Maxine on the road. They mounted a fine circus with exciting and authentic acts, so they thought the show was a success. The Joneses even had the luxury of their own car on the circus train. Money was coming in and they thought they were doing well.

One night the roustabouts struck and loaded the tents, and the troupe boarded the train for the next town. The next morning they awoke to find the train hadn't moved. The railroad official Buck approached said their pay was six days overdue. Buck went looking for the manager to straighten out the problem only to find the manager and what cash money they had was long gone. Buck strapped on his guns and went looking for the manager. He said, later, "I'm just as glad I never found him. It's a heap of money. A quarter of a million. But looking back now. I'm glad I never killed a man."

That night while Buck was still looking for the manager, Odelle slipped Buck's four white horses out of the animal tent, stealthed them into a moving van and headed for the state line. Once across, she thought the creditors wouldn't be able to confiscate the horses as they would the rest of the circus property. While a circus friend drove the truck, Odelle rode on the tailgate with a loaded .44 in her hand. Nobody was going to get Buck's horses.

She saved the horses, but they lost everything else. An honest man, Buck Jones wanted every person he owed money to be paid. They sold all the California property, everything they owned except the horses. Buck had to start all over from scratch. He went back to making moving pictures for five hundred dollars per week, quite a comedown from the thirty-five hundred per week he'd been getting when he walked away.

Buck returned to Columbia and worked hard. It didn't take long for him to return to his former place in the Hollywood scene. He bought back his ranch and other property. This time he had not four horses, but nine beautiful milk-white horses, including his favorite, Silver, who had appeared in so many pictures with him.

He made series Westerns for different studios all through the 1930s, but jobs got scarce again around 1938 when the singing cowboy came

FIGHTING WORDS

BY LOREN D. ESTLEMAN

"When you call me that—*smile!*"
Gary Cooper to Walter Huston
The Virginian (1929 Paramount)

"You're a lowdown Yankee liar!"
Alan Ladd to Jack Palance
Shane (1953 Paramount)

"Hey. I got a question. How you gonna get back down that hill?"
Paul Newman to Richard Boone
Hombre (1967 20th Century Fox)

"Fill your hand, you son-of-a-bitch!"
John Wayne to Robert Duvall
True Grit (1969 Paramount)

"For a minute there I thought we were in trouble!"
Paul Newman to Robert Redford
Butch Cassidy and the Sundance Kid (1969 20th Century Fox)

"A'hm yo' huckleberry."
Val Kilmer to Michael Biehn
Tombstone
(1993 Hollywood Pictures)

into vogue. Buck neither sang nor danced, and he was getting a little long in the tooth for the kind of pictures that were becoming popular. He went so far as to play a crooked sheriff in Republic's *Wagons Westward.* Thousands of letters of protest inundated the studio. They wanted action and they wanted Buck the way they loved him. Buck was in demand again. He made two serials, *White Eagle* for Columbia and *Riders of Death Valley* for Universal.

In June of 1941, he signed for a series of action westerns called *The Rough Riders Series,* in which he co-starred with Tim McCoy and Raymond Hatton. At the end of each picture the three stars would bid each other, "So long, Rough Riders," and head out in different directions, Jones for Arizona, McCoy to Wyoming and Hatton to Texas. The "Rough Riders' Song" played over the credits as the three stars gradually disappeared from view. There was always a notice at the end of the credits requesting the viewers to watch until the Rough Riders rode again.

In 1942, Tim McCoy sent the studio a telegram saying he'd accepted a commission in the Army and Jones and Hatton were left without a partner. Monogram planned a series for them together, but Buck made a couple of solo features for the studio. He was set to sign a new contract with the studio, though he was less than happy with the quality of pictures they turned out. Before contract signing time, Buck did what so many stars did during the war—he went on a tour promoting the sale of war bonds. After a successful stop in Washington, the group moved on to Boston. After much persuasion, Buck's friend, Scott Dunlap of Monogram Studios, convinced Buck that he would enjoy an evening at the famous Coconut Grove nightclub. It was Buck's first visit. He'd ceased heavy drinking long before, and the night life didn't impress him. Buck was dancing with one of the ladies in the troupe near a door when the infamous fire started. He pushed the girl outside before he got out safely himself.

He couldn't find Scott Dunlap outside, so Buck went back inside, into the inferno, to find his friend. Dunlap had already escaped with badly burned hands, but he was alive. Four hundred and ninety-one people died that night. When they pulled Buck out of the fire, one of the 181 badly burned survivors, he was barely alive. He died two days later, on November 30, 1942.

Buck Jones rode no more. His warm friendly smile and ready sense of humor, his sense of honor and his courage were missed. Millions of little Buck Jones Rangers mourned the man who meant so much to them, who had urged them to live honorable lives and to value personal integrity above all other virtues. That was the way he'd lived, and that was the way he'd died. ■

PLAYERS ON HORSEBACK

GENE AUTRY

BY ABRAHAM HOFFMAN

FEW PEOPLE IN THE ENTERTAINMENT INDUSTRY CAN EQUAL THE SUC-
cess and influence of Gene Autry. Clint Eastwood won his race for mayor
of Carmel, California, Rex Bell became governor of Nevada, and Ronald
Reagan achieved the political pinnacle of the U.S. presidency. But none
to date have had a town named for them. Gene Autry has. In 1941 the
small town of Berwyn, Oklahoma, changed its name to Gene Autry in
honor of the cowboy star—and Autry at the time had yet to embark upon
his successful business ventures that would make him a millionaire many
times over.

Many Western film stars were enormously popular, but their performances were restricted to B Westerns, and their fortunes never matched
their fame. A few, most notably John Wayne, graduated from the B's to
superstar status. Autry's films would never make a critic's ten best list,
but they provided a springboard for an astonishingly successful career
in movies, radio, television, records, and, ultimately, sports and com-
munications.

Gene Autry was born in Tioga, Texas, in 1907, the son of Delbert and
Elnory Autry. His family moved to Oklahoma and bought a cattle ranch,
giving Gene the experience of a working cowboy—though he candidly
admitted that he never really enjoyed riding a horse. He sang in the
church choir, encouraged by his grandfather, a Baptist minister. After
graduating from high school in 1925, Gene began his working career as
a telegraph operator in Sapulpa, Oklahoma. During that time he practiced singing, playing the guitar, and—in a shrewd and farsighted
move—took a correspondence course in business administration.

Autry began his entertainment career in 1929, achieving success in
a short period of time. While working as a telegraph operator in Chelsea,
Oklahoma, he accepted jobs singing in restaurants and carnivals. This
led to a spot on the Chelsea radio station and local recognition. Before
long Autry faced the decision of continuing with telegraphy or seriously
embarking on a singing career.

When Will Rogers stopped at the Chelsea station, he helped Autry

"I know I'm no great actor, and
I'm not a great rider, and I'm
not a great singer; but what the
hell is my opinion when fifty
million people think I'm pretty
good?"

GENE AUTRY

make his decision by encouraging him to keep up the singing. Shortly afterward, a Columbia Records scout named Jimmy Long, possibly sent by Rogers, signed Autry to a contract. Autry and Long collaborated on "That Silver-Haired Daddy of Mine," a song that won instant success and became the first "gold record." It was only the first in Autry's string of successful hit songs which he composed himself, such as "Rudolph the Red-Nose Reindeer," "Here Comes Peter Cotton-Tail," and "Back in the Saddle Again," his theme song. The songs have sold some forty million records to date and are perennial favorites. Long not only got Autry's career under way but influenced his personal life as well—Autry married Ina Mae Spivey, Long's niece.

In the next four years Autry became known as a singing cowboy, appearing regularly on the "National Barn Dance" radio program. In 1934 he made his film debut in a Ken Maynard film, *In Old Santa Fe,* in which he sang two songs. He took another small part in *Mystery Mountain,* then made his "breakthrough" film, *The Phantom Empire.*

Given Autry's enormous success as a singing cowboy and as the magnate of a sports and entertainment empire, it seems ludicrous that his first major film was one of the most bizarre Westerns ever made. *Phantom Empire* was a twelve-part action serial produced by Mascot Pictures, and its plot owed much to the popularity of Flash Gordon, Buck Rogers, and Ken Maynard in the early 1930s. A blend of the Western and science fiction, the story borrowed heavily from the writings of James Churchward, who in 1926 had published *The Lost Continent of Mu,* a best-selling book that argued for a vanished Atlantis. Autry pretty much played himself in the serial—a ranch owner/cowboy who operated a radio station on the premises so he could sing on his own program—but the story then drew a wildcard: Autry also owned a radium mine, and beneath his ranch lay Murania, a technologically advanced civilization (owing much to Churchward's Mu) whose leaders seemed obsessed with preventing Autry from airing his radio program. Although the mixture of genres proved painfully laughable, the serial, which was later released in two versions as feature films, launched Autry's film career and set a pattern for his future motion pictures. Autry would always essentially play himself, using his own name, and he would make the musical Western into a form all its own.

After *Phantom Empire,* Autry starred in fifty-six films for Republic Studios, the company formed when Mascot and several other studios merged. The films found an enthusiastic audience in rural America, as an exhibitors poll voted Autry the top cowboy star in 1937, 1938, and 1939. In 1940 Autry placed fourth in the top ten box-office stars of the year. That same year, Autry began his long-running radio program, "Gene

"I'm not an actor, I'm a rope thrower."

WILL ROGERS

Autry's Melody Ranch," on CBS. The program featured lots of music, an adventure story, and an exchange of banter between Autry and Pat Buttram. The show provided an audio interpretation of Autry's screen persona.

Autry's musical Westerns set a pattern for the genre that, apart from the challenge of Roy Rogers, was never equaled by its many imitators. Strictly speaking, Autry's films weren't Westerns at all, at least not in the tradition of the films of Bronco Billy Anderson, William S. Hart, or Tom

REMEMBERING AUTRY, LIVE

BY ED GORMAN

I was seven years old the only time I went to see him in person. It was 1949. He came to the Veterans Memorial Coliseum in Cedar Rapids, and I recall my reading in the paper that nobody had ever turned out such a crowd before him.

He was the one and only Gene Autry.

I don't remember if Pat Buttram was with him, but I certainly remember Gene's horse, "Champion." Kids clapped their hands into sores applauding. He dipped, he bowed, he whinnied, he did everything but recite the Gettysburg Address. He was one hell of an animal, let me tell you.

Gene sang all the songs we'd come to hear. He didn't have a crooner's voice but there was real grit to it. We imagined true cowboys probably sounded a lot like him instead of, say, Dick Haymes, when they sat around the campfire every night singing their asses off — at least that was how I figured real cowboys lived.

I never got over that Friday afternoon. No live performance since has given me the same thrill of seeing Gene. By God, but he put on a show! Gene's older now, and so am I. I wish I had a lot of his memories... being a cowboy idol couldn't have

Gene Autry

been all bad...and at least a little bit of his money.

Most of the Western history books claim that Gene never took much pleasure in the gig, that he just did it for the dollars. But I'll tell you something: you sure couldn't have proved that by how his performance made me feel that autumn afternoon back in '49.

Veteran sidekick Smiley Burnette, future Cisco Kid Duncan Renaldo, Gene Autry and Harold Huber practice their knife-throwing on one of the bad guys in "Down Mexico Way" (1941 Republic)

Mix. They didn't recreate the West as much as they created a West without historical precedent. Most of the Autry films were set in the present, using modern technology—radio, automobiles, airplanes, trains, telephones. Despite these present-day conveniences in transportation and communication, the characters packed six-guns, chased each other around on horseback, shot at each other, and made the West of the past live again in an odd and uneasy coexistence with the present. In order to believe, filmgoers had to accept the anachronism, and Autry's mostly rural audience did so. Autry also intended that his audience include children, so the plots never challenged anyone's intellect. They did deal with themes such as floods, drought, cattle diseases, and ecological problems that remain remarkably relevant to modern audiences.

In his films Autry espoused a code of conduct, the "Ten Commands of the Cowboy," which established a code of honor for young fans to emulate. The code emphasized cleanliness in personal habits and actions (never drinking or smoking); observing patrotism and fair play; never telling lies and never going back on one's word; helping children, elderly people, animals, and people in trouble; holding no racial prejudices; showing respect for women, parents, and the law; and the value of hard work. Autry's code did not preclude the hero getting the girl at the end of the film, but he kept the romantic scenes to a bare minimum.

Autry left films and radio in July 1942 to serve in the Army Air Force during World War II. He completed flight training and copiloted C-47s for the Air Transport Command, and after he was discharged as a Flight Officer in September 1945, Autry promptly joined a USO unit and went to the Pacific. By the end of 1946 he had resumed his half-hour radio program, and made five final motion pictures for Republic. Autry had grown tired of his feuds with Republic's Herbert J. Yates, the tight budgets accorded his films, and the studio's backing of rival Roy Rogers as "King of the Cowboys" during his wartime service. In 1947 he formed Gene Autry Productions and began a series of theatrical films for Columbia Pictures, an association that lasted until 1953. Film critics noted a change for the better in the later Autry films—less music and more action, fewer flowery cowboy outfits and better budgets.

As the B Western film cycle drew to a close, Autry was one of the first movie stars to recognize the imminent needs of television for commercial programs. In addition to his own half-hour series of Western adventure stories, Autry also produced several other programs.

Network radio ended in the 1950s, and Autry folded his radio program in 1956. He eventually expanded his business interests to include hotels, radio and television stations, ranches, and the California Angels baseball team. He retained much of his cowboy personality in his folksiness, conversation, and ten-gallon hat—along with a shrewd business acumen that has made him one of the richest men in America. The passing years, however, didn't melt his plainspokenness and sense of humor.

On August 3, 1985, the Platrix Chapter of the Ancient and Noble Order of E Clampus Vitus, a statewide California organization created in gold rush days to mock the serious pretensions of fraternal organizations, honored Anaheim Stadium with its presence. John W. Hays, an executive in Autry's California Angels corporation and a Clamper himself, thought the Clampers might erect a historical marker commemorating the twenty-fifth anniversary of the stadium and Autry's Angels, a quarter century of anything in southern California being worthy of historical consideration. More than 200 Clampers, clad in red shirts and black hats, descended on Anaheim Stadium. A blank wall outside the stadium provided a convenient spot for placing the plaque. The mayor of Anaheim and other public dignitaries gave speeches in which they acknowledged the historical importance of the stadium.

Then it was Autry's turn. Now almost eighty years old, considerably heavier and slower than the graceful cowboy of his movie days, Gene

THE WESTERN BOOK OF LISTS

UNLIKELY WESTERNERS

George Plimpton in *Rio Lobo;* Jerry Lewis in *Partners;* Rick Nelson in *Rio Lobo;* Bob Hope in *Paleface;* Charles Laughton in *Ruggles of Red Gap;* W. C. Fields in *My Little Chickadee;* Humphrey Bogart in *The Oklahoma Kid;* Oliver Reed in *The Great Scout and Cathouse Thursday;* Harry Belafonte in *Buck and the Preacher;* Don Dubbins in *Tribute to a Bad Man.*

Autry gazed at the assembled crowd of Clampers, most of whom were quaffing enormous quantities of beer and interrupting the speeches with raucous cheers and hand clapping. Autry looked at the marker, then at the Clampers again, and said, "I never even heard of you guys before yesterday."

The Clampers voted him an honorary member on the spot. ■

HIGH NOON FOR GARY COOPER

BY BILL O'NEAL

Gary Cooper as Marshal Will Kane, walks down the deserted streets of Hadleyville in "High Noon" (1952 United Artists)

"When you call me that—*smile!*" The most famous line of Western dialogue was first uttered on-screen in the halting but forceful drawl of young Gary Cooper. Born Frank James Cooper in 1901, he got part of his education in England, but spent far more time on his father's Montana ranch. The pain of a broken hip made him sensitive to every move of his mount. He became an expert rider, and in later years he was acknowledged as one of the finest horsemen in the movies.

After a couple of years at Grinnell College in Grinnell, Iowa, Cooper followed his parents to Los Angeles, arriving to live with them on Thanksgiving Day in 1923. After half-hearted attempts to find work produced no promising career possibilities, he encountered a couple of Montana pals in Hollywood in December 1924. That very day he secured employment as a stunt rider in Western movies at five dollars per day, and he soon appeared regularly in bit parts as outlaw, Indian or cowboy.

An agent changed his name to Gary Cooper, and he paid to have a short audition film lensed. In the silent Western, *The Winning of Barbara Worth* (1926), his tall, lanky appearance and subtle appeal to the camera generated great fan response, which lead to meaty roles in silent films.

Owen Wister's landmark 1902 novel, *The Virginian,* had been filmed twice before Cooper took the title role in the first sound version in 1929 (Joel McCrea starred in the 1946 remake). When Cooper delivered Wister's famous line, the villainous Trampas (played by Walter Huston) cracked a sickly smile.

Cooper became a major star and won an Academy Award in 1941 for the title role in *Sergeant York.* His range as an actor was enormous, and even though only one-third of his starring roles were in Westerns, his memorable performances as the quiet-spoken frontier hero of unswerving courage and integrity made him a part of the Western myth.

In more than two dozen sound Westerns Cooper played many notable roles. He starred in *The Spoilers* (1930), Rex Beach's Klondike yarn which was remade in 1942 and 1955, and few Western fans have forgotten Coop's Wild Bill Hickok in Cecil B. DeMille's campy but rousing *The Plainsman* (1936). In *The Westerner* (1940) he brought the understated part of Cole Hardin to equal status with the colorful Judge Roy Bean, played to the hilt by Walter Brennan.

Cooper's career sagged somewhat as he entered middle age, but was resoundingly revived by his Academy Award-winning portrayal of Marshal Will Kane in *High Noon* (1952). His haggard grimace as the beleaguered lawman was intensified by an ulcer, a flare-up of his old hip injury and a back ailment. Later he starred with Susan Hayward in *Garden of Evil* (1954) and with Burt Lancaster in the action-filled *Vera Cruz* (1954). His final three films were Westerns: the sluggish *Man of the West* (1958); *The Hanging Tree* (1959), an underrated film in which he played the tormented Doc Frail; and the slow-moving *They Came to Cordura* (1959).

Although he was dying of cancer in 1961, he narrated a superb NBC television documentary, "The Real West," and for many fans he remains the definitive Western hero.

THE WESTERNERS: RANDOLPH SCOTT AND JOEL MCCREA

BY BILL CRIDER

Randolph Scott, premier Western star, ended his career after Sam Peckinpah's "Ride the High Country"

RANDOLPH SCOTT AND JOEL McCREA WERE BORN ON OPPOSITE SIDES of the continent, Scott in Orange, Virginia, and McCrea in Los Angeles, but though their lives touched from the very beginnings of their movie careers, it was *Ride the High Country* more than thirty years later that proved to be their most memorable appearance together. Neither began in Westerns, but both were working as extras when in 1929 Scott tested for a role in Cecil B. DeMille's *Dynamite,* a role that went instead to McCrea. Scott appeared in the film as an extra.

That same year, Scott served as Gary Cooper's dialogue coach (and did some stunt work) for *The Virginian,* a role for which Scott, with his cultivated Virginia accent, would have been perfect. Ironically, when *The Virginian* was remade in 1946, the lead was played by Joel McCrea, who had coincidentally passed up the lead in DeMille's *Northwest Mounted Police* (1940) because he didn't feel right for the part. The role went to Gary Cooper.

Both McCrea and Scott managed to have successful careers as leading men outside of Westerns, a feat not accomplished by many other Western actors. Scott appeared in such films as *Roberta* (1935), with Fred Astaire and Ginger Rogers; *Go West, Young Man* (1936), with Mae West; and *My Favorite Wife* (1940), with Irene Dunne and Cary Grant. McCrea starred in *Espionage Agent* and Alfred Hitchcock's memorable *Foreign Correspondent* (1940).

But it is for their Western roles that people remember them—McCrea as the great frontiersman reduced to cheap carnival performer in *Buffalo Bill* (1944), Scott playing opposite Robert Young in *Western Union* (1941). After 1950 both men devoted themselves exclusively to Westerns, perhaps having aged a bit beyond romantic leads in drama or light comedy. Their popularity with audiences did not decline; in fact, despite the amazing growth of the television industry, which brought Western programs into American homes on a nightly basis, Scott and McCrea continued to make quality Westerns throughout the decade. Along with Audie Murphy, they were almost entirely responsible for keeping Westerns on the big screens on a regular basis. Six Scott films were released in 1955, four McCrea films in 1957. In contrast, Roy Rogers appeared in only two films between 1951 and 1960, *Son of Paleface* and *Alias Jesse James,* Bob Hope comedy vehicles that were Westerns in only the broadest sense.

Scott's work in the '50s was more interesting than McCrea's, and his

Joel McCrea and Randolph Scott fend off ambushers in "Ride the High Country" (1962 MGM)

films with the Scott-Brown production company and director Budd Boetticher set him apart as the premier Western star of the decade. His rugged face and lanky frame were perfect for outdoor adventure—probably no actor in Westerns has ever been able to convey such steadfast integrity merely by his appearance, and though he always portrayed a man of few words, his wonderful accent further strengthened the impression. Such films as *Hangman's Knot* (1952), *Seven Men from Now* (1955), *The Tall T* (1957), and *Buchanan Rides Alone* (1958) are excellent and unforgettable examples of the B Western at its best, and they raised Scott to almost legendary status. The affection and longing for such films was even expressed in a hit song, the Statler Brothers' "Whatever Happened to Randolph Scott?"

In 1962, Scott and McCrea found their finest hours and their best roles in Sam Peckinpah's *Ride the High Country.* McCrea was originally cast as the semi-villain of the story, but he traded roles with Scott, a brilliant move, since both men not only played their assigned roles but also played on the audience's memories of them in dozens of similar roles. Could any viewer doubt what Scott would do in the film's climactic scene? And could anyone fail to be moved by its inevitability or its outcome? Of course not.

After *Ride the High Country,* Scott retired from moviemaking and never appeared on-screen again. McCrea appeared in two more films and narrated a third, but *Ride the High Country* will always be regarded as a fitting climax to two distinguished Western film careers. ◼

PLAYERS ON HORSEBACK

No Place for a Hero: Audie Murphy in Hollywood

BY THOMAS W. KNOWLES

IT WAS THAT MOMENTARY FLASH IN AUDIE MURPHY'S EYES THAT kept me from changing the channel. As the supposedly mild-mannered, gun-shy novice lawman in *Destry* (1955), he borrowed a tough's guns and coolly blasted the nickel-sized knobs off the saloon's spinning Wheel of Fortune. In that moment he let the rage inside him spill out onto the screen, opened his internal shutters and exposed the thousand-yard stare of the veteran combat infantryman. That's what made me believe that the boyish, not-so-tall Texan was for real.

As a Texan, I grew up with the image of Audie Murphy as the most decorated soldier of World War II. I'd seen his statue dressed in his deco-rated uniform in the State Fair Wax Museum in Dallas. In fact, my father had given me a copy of *To Hell and Back,* the account Murphy had writ-ten (with the help of his friend, David "Spec" McClure) of his wartime experiences.

Murphy slogged through the worst of the war, from North Africa to the deadly beach at Anzio in 1943, through Italy, France and into the heart of Nazi Germany—until the military public relations machine yanked him out at the bitter end, snatching him away from his buddies and their final victory. He served in combat on the front lines for four hundred days—there were no one-year tours for the World War II in-fantryman. He earned thirty-three military awards from several differ-ent countries, including the Congressional Medal of Honor.

I'd never thought much of him as a cowboy actor, even though he made over forty movies, most of them Westerns. I'd enjoyed the Holly-wood version of *To Hell and Back* (1955), but I figured anyone could do a good job of playing himself. I always wondered what led a real-life war hero to play cowboys and gunfighters in Tinsel Town.

After all, Murphy wasn't really a Westerner. He'd been born (June 20, 1924) into a poor tenant farmer's family in rural northeast Texas, more

Audie Murphy on the Hollywood bat-tlefield in "The Red Badge of Cour-age" (1951 MGM) (courtesy of Turner Entertainment Company)

A Selected Audie Murphy Western Filmography

The Kid From Texas
(1950 Universal)

The Red Badge of Courage
(1951 MGM)

The Duel at Silver Creek
(1952 Universal)

Gunsmoke
(1953 Universal)

Drums Across the River
(1954 Universal)

Destry
(1955 Universal)

Walk the Proud Land
(1956 Universal)

Night Passage
(1957 Universal)

No Name on the Bullet
(1959 Universal)

The Unforgiven
(1960 United Artists)

A Bullet for a Badman
(1969 Universal)

A Time for Dying
(1969 Fipco Productions)

a part of the Old South than the West. When Jimmy Cagney first brought him to Hollywood as his protege, Murphy had to take riding lessons as well as acting lessons. Like Sergeant Alvin York, his First World War counterpart, Murphy had learned to shoot for food; as a kid he'd put rabbits and squirrels on his family's table with his .22 rifle. He'd never used a handgun until he joined the Army. He'd never punched cattle or worked on a ranch. He'd been turned down by the Marines because he was only five feet, four inches tall and weighed less than 120 pounds—hardly a threat to John Wayne as a Western icon.

But in battle, Murphy proved an unparalleled warrior in countless tight spots. He fought on even after he was severely wounded at the Battle of the Comar Pocket in Germany, in January of 1945; he stood on a burning tank destroyer, using its machine gun to hold back the German advance while he calmly directed Allied artillery. The TD's magazine and fuel tanks could have exploded at any time, but Murphy stood firm to save his outfit.

Unlike jet-age Vietnam vets, World War II-era vets usually got to decompress before they returned to the civilized world. Not Murphy. He'd intended to make a career of the military, but the Army rejected America's greatest warrior as "unfit for service" because of his wounds. Then they swept him home early after he got his medals, when all he wanted to do was finish the job. The press crowded in on him, a scarred twenty-year-old who had for years seen and experienced about the worst of what human beings could do to each other. They put him in the spotlight, put him on the cover of *Life* magazine and made him a media hero. Then Hollywood put him on the big screen. They didn't let him deal with his nightmares. Heroes aren't supposed to have nightmares.

For some years, he handled the stress of fame and memory, and he kept his life and his movie career together despite failed marriages, bouts of depression and alcohol abuse. He'd pushed the nightmares into a dark well inside himself and welded the cover shut. Ironically, it was his most successful movie, *To Hell and Back,* that ripped the lid off.

Nobody knew about post-traumatic stress syndrome before the Vietnam era—they called it shell-shock or combat fatigue. Re-living even the Hollywood version of his war ten years later put Murphy into a spiral from which he never really recovered. When the movie Western declined and Randolph Scott and the other cowboy heroes retired to the Hollywood hills, Murphy found himself trapped in a series of low-budget oaters. He ended up broke and almost alone.

Murphy was a real-life hero, but I never saw him as a *Western* movie hero...

...until after he died in a light plane crash in May of 1971, and the independent station in Dallas ran a retrospective of his films. I found myself drawn to the tube, and I began to look for the power and the rage I'd seen in his eyes as he played Destry. It was there in his best work and in the standard horse-operas he turned out by the dozen.

In *The Red Badge of Courage* (1951), John Huston's butchered masterpiece of a film based on Stephen Crane's novel, Murphy has to do something he never did in a real life battle—run from a fight. But it's probably his best performance; as Murphy's young soldier wanders the Civil War battlefield, the shock and the confusion of war is plainly written on his face. One look at Murphy in that role, and you can tell he'd been there.

Watch Murphy as the Yuma Kid, Jimmy Stewart's outlaw brother in *Night Passage* (1957), as he taunts his outlaw partner, Dan Duryea, relentlessly pushing him toward a showdown. His polite words and his careless young smile hide the deadly focus of his eyes—most of the time. He reminds you of the Karait in Rudyard Kipling's *Rikki-Tikki-Tavi:* "...something flinched a little in the dust, and a tiny voice said: 'Be careful. I am death!'"

That's what made him different from the other movie cowboy heroes. Murphy's Yuma Kid is the cinematic incarnation of the real Doc Holliday or Billy the Kid, just as his Destry could be the real Wild Bill Hickok or Wyatt Earp. Had Murphy been born in the Old West, his name would be written in the history books beside theirs.

In *The Unforgiven* (1960), Murphy lets his dark side show as the drunken, bigoted brother who abandons his family (Burt Lancaster, Doug McClure, Lillian Gish) because they're willing to defend their adopted Kiowa sibling (Audrey Hepburn). But at the end, when the Kiowa attack, he rides back in to die a hero...

...and in the end, when his career burned out and Hollywood no longer had a place for him, Audie Murphy was still a hero. ■

TOP: Audie Murphy with director John Huston on location for "The Red Badge of Courage" (1951 MGM) (courtesy of Turner Entertainment Company)

BOTTOM: Audie Murphy with Audrey Hepburn in "The Unforgiven" (1960 United Artists)

BUFFALO BILL IN THE MOVIES

BY MARYLOIS DUNN

Though William Frederick Cody's life was a far greater adventure than any motion picture could portray, many have tried. Ned Buntline's dime novels, assisted by Cody's own efforts to publicize his Wild West Show, have intertwined the legends and the facts until they have become inseparable. For the most part, the motion picture industry hasn't attempted to separate them, and that's for the best—Cody the showman would approve of their synthesis of truth and fiction.

Buffalo Bill is one of the few historical Westerners who has received (in most cases) a fair shake from the motion picture industry, and he has probably been represented on-screen more often than any other American hero. Many performers (and a few actors) have portrayed him on the screen, starting with Cody himself in some Thomas Edison silent single-reelers in the late 1890s and early 1900s. The following list is as complete as available research material allows:

PERFORMER	PRODUCTION
William F. Cody	*Seven Acts from the Wild West Show,* Edison 1894
	Buffalo Bill and Escort, Edison 1897
	Parade of Buffalo Bill's Wild West Show, Edison 1898
	Buffalo Bill's Wild West Parade, American Mutoscope & Biograph 1902
	Life of Buffalo Bill, Davis & Harris, 1909 (3-reeler)
	Buffalo Bill's Far West and Pawnee Bill's Far East, Buffalo Bill & Pawnee Bill Film 1910
	The Indian Wars, Essanay & Col. W. F. Cody Historical Pictures 1913
	Sitting Bull—The Hostile Sioux Indian Chief, American Rotograph 1914
	Patsy of the Circus, 1915
	The Adventures of Buffalo Bill, 1917 (the year Cody died)
Art Acord	*In the Days of Buffalo Bill,* Universal 1923
George Waggner	*The Iron Horse,* Fox Film Corp. 1924
John Fox, Jr.	*The Pony Express,* Famous Players/Lasky 1925
Hack Hoxie	*The Last Frontier,* Metro 1926
Roy Stewart	*Buffalo Bill on the U.P. Trail,* Sunset 1926
Wallace MacDonald	*Fighting With Buffalo Bill,* Universal serial 1926 (much footage from this film later used in 1930 serial, *The Indians are Coming*)
Duke R. Lee	*Buffalo Bill's Last Fight,* MGM 1927
William Fairbanks	*Wyoming,* MGM 1928
Tim McCoy	*The Indians are Coming,* Universal serial 1930
Tom Tyler	*Battling With Buffalo Bill,* Universal serial 1931, 12 episodes
Douglass Dumbrille	*The World Changes,* First National 1933
Earle Dwire	*The Miracle Worker,* Mascot serial 1935, 15 episodes

PERFORMER	PRODUCTION
Moroni Olsen	*Annie Oakley,* RKO 1935
Ted Adams	*Custer's Last Stand,* serial 1936, 15 episodes
James Ellison	*The Plainsman,* Paramount 1937
Carlyle Moore	*Outlaw Express,* Universal 1938
John Rutherford	*Flaming Frontiers,* Universal serial 1938, 15 episodes
Roy Rogers	*Young Buffalo Bill,* Republic 1940
Bob Baker	*Overland Mail,* Universal serial 1942
Joel McCrea	*Buffalo Bill,* 20th Century Fox 1944
Richard Arlen	*Buffalo Bill Rides Again,* Schwarz Productions 1947
Monte Hale	*Law of the Golden West,* Republic 1949
Louis Calhern	*Annie Get Your Gun,* MGM musical 1950
Dickie Moore	*Cody of the Pony Express,* Columbia serial 1951, 15 episodes
Tex Cooper	*King of the Bullwhip,* Realart 1951
Clayton Moore	*Buffalo Bill in Tomahawk Territory,* Schwarz Productions 1952
Charlton Heston	*Pony Express,* Paramount 1953
Marshall Reed	*Riding With Buffalo Bill,* Columbia Serial 1954, 15 episodes
Malcom Atterbury	*Badman's Country,* Warner Brothers 1958
James McMullan	*The Raiders,* Revue Studios 1964
Rick Van Nutter	*Seven Hours of Gunfire (Sette Ore di Fuco, Adventuras del Oeste),* Italian/Spanish 1965
Gordon Scott	*Buffalo Bill, Hero of the Far West (Buffalo Bill, L'eroe del Far West)* Italian 1964
Guy Stockwell	*The Plainsman,* Universal 1966
Michel Piccoli	*Don't Touch the White Woman (Touche Pas la Femme Blanche),* Mara Films 1974
Paul Newman	*Buffalo Bill and the Indians, or Sitting Bull's History Lesson,* de Laurentis/Lions Gate Films 1976
Ted Flicker	*The Legend of the Lone Ranger,* Universal 1981

PLAYERS ON HORSEBACK

THE "NEGRO" WESTERN

BY MARYLOIS DUNN

VERY LITTLE EVIDENCE REMAINS OF THE NEGRO WESTERN OF THE late 1930s and early 1940s. As with other motion picture genres, a whole body of Western films were made exclusively to be shown in "colored-only" theaters. They were called "ghetto" films.

Though black Americans played a very real part in the winning of the West, where they were often accepted for their abilities and talents, their part of the story was ignored in the motion pictures produced by and for white Americans. Unfortunately, even Negro Westerns most often ignored the true stories and instead copied the white Westerns, particularly the glitzy white musical horse operas. Their production values were nonexistent, and they used many more racial stereotypes of blacks than any white director or producer would have dared use, even in those times. The sidekick rolled his eyes and trembled at a mention of ghosts, the cooks stole chickens and ate watermelon, and the ranch hands were lazy, gambling buffoons.

This all took place in a totally black West—not a white face showed in the Negro Western. Heroes, heroines, villains, stock players and even the Indians were black. Being derivative, the films failed on a basic level. They lacked the action and excitement of their white counterparts. Their dialogue closely copied the standard Western script, but there was too much of it and that was badly delivered. The producers took their cameras, crews and casts out to the best locations, but they didn't utilize them properly. The chase scenes were inept, and the fights were phony and clumsy.

The plots and stories were sometimes taken directly from white Westerns, about as far from real black interests as it was possible to be. *Harlem Rides the Range* was a copy of a Gene Autry Western in which Autry went after villains who were stealing radium deposits. And yet, it was in *Harlem Rides the Range* that the one true personality emerged from the Negro Western—cabaret singer Herb Jefferies, a singing cowboy after the fashion of Gene Autry (he even wore clothes designed after Autry's outfits). Jefferies was the entrepreneur of black Westerns, some

Danny Glover as the founding member of a cattle and livery company in "Lonesome Dove" (1992 CBS) (courtesy of CBS, photo: Tony Esparza)

of which he produced and directed as well starred in. He played a "light-skinned" hero, as did his comic sidekick, "Dusty," played by Flournoy Miller. His films were designed with supporting players and vicious villains, played by very dark actors, including Lucius Brooks and Spencer Williams. Aside from Jefferies and a few others, the acting level was minimal and the same small company appeared in most of the films.

Some of the Negro Westerns were made by black production companies, but most were made by white companies. Whether white or black, none of them tapped the rich heritage of blacks in the West. The films were made to be shown in separate, inferior theaters, and they sadly reinforced the messages that blacks were somehow less worthy than their white counterparts. Jefferies' *Harlem Rides the Range* and *The Bronze Buckaroo* were two of the better examples, although they were also long on talk and short on the action their audiences wanted to see.

Woody Strode as "Sergeant Rutledge" (1960 Warner Bros.)

Sergeant Rutledge, directed by John Ford and released in 1960, gave black audiences one of the first sympathetic black leads in a major establishment Hollywood Western. Ford supported lead actor Woody Strode with some of the finest of his troupe of white Western actors, including Ben Johnson, Victor McLaglen and Jeffrey Hunter. Strode stood out as the hero of Ford's epic about the Buffalo Soldiers, the black cavalry that served with distinction in the post-Civil War West. Indeed, Strode's brief cameos at the beginning and the end of Mario Van Peebles' 1993 Western about buffalo soldiers, *Posse,* were the best parts of a story otherwise flawed by anachronism and spaghetti-Western sensibilities.

Unfortunately, another genre of film equally bad took the place of the Negro Western and perhaps stifled a trend begun by *Sergeant Rutledge;* these were the "blaxploitation" films of the early 1970s. Blaxploitation films such as *Boss Nigger* with Fred Williamson, and *Buck and the Preacher* with a stellar cast including Sidney Poitier, Harry Belafonte and Ruby Dee, never quite seemed to know where they were going. They struck a stump somewhere between comedy, lighthearted adventure and bloodthirsty spaghetti Westerns. Again, they failed to take into account the real experiences of black Americans in the early West, and copied white Westerns. They aimed to give black people something to be proud of, and when they did not, they failed completely. ∎

PLAYERS ON HORSEBACK

THE DUKE

BY LOREN D. ESTLEMAN

AT THE HEIGHT OF THE DISMAL VIETNAM WAR ERA, IN RESPONSE TO a student challenge, the Duke invaded the Harvard campus aboard a tank to accept the Harvard Lampoon's Hasty Pudding Award. After a day of answering questions about everything from his politics to his hairpiece, this national symbol of monolithic conservativism departed the heartland of radical iconoclasm to an unprecedented ovation.

No one should have been surprised. For four decades, starting with the first nasal honk of a human voice on a Vitaphone sound track and continuing through the splash and thunder of Technicolor and Cinemascope, John Wayne had taken on Indian raiders, Mexican bandits, Nazis, Imperial Japanese, fifth-columnists, and Viet Cong with nothing more than a six gun and a Midwestern drawl as flat as a ricochet. His wrinkled brow and swaggering walk had come to symbolize the way the world viewed Americans: big, strong, short on words but long on action, and aggressively innocent.

In this day of chameleon-like actors, the consistency and timelessness of this image is particularly potent. It's not at all difficult to imagine that Wayne's gangling Ringo Kid of 1939's *Stagecoach* might have crusted over and matured after forty years into the weary, dying J.B. Books of *The Shootist.* Much older and bereft of most of his early ideals, he is basically the same man, quiet and dangerous and confident of himself, if he is confident of little else in a turning world. The Winchester rifle with which Wayne's Oscar-winning character, Rooster Cogburn, charged the desperadoes at the climax of *True Grit* (1969) is the very same customized weapon the Ringo Kid carried out of the desert and into stardom in *Stagecoach.* In fact, if the frames in which Wayne uses the distinctive one-handed levering maneuver are taken from both films and superimposed, they match. The Duke's fans will take this revelation in stride.

Some critics said the Duke merely played himself, but those who said it had never tried to walk across a stage without looking spastic. He was six-four and 250 pounds of meat and muscle, well constructed to carry

John Wayne in "Fort Apache," directed by John Ford (courtesy of CBS)

A Selected John Wayne Western Filmography

BY LOREN D. ESTLEMAN

Stagecoach
(1939 United Artists)

Angel and the Badman
(1947 Republic)

Fort Apache
(1948 RKO)

Red River
(1948 United Artists)

Three Godfathers
(1948 MGM)

She Wore a Yellow Ribbon
(1949 RKO)

Rio Grande
(1950 Republic)

Hondo
(1953 Warner Brothers)

The Searchers
(1956 Warner Brothers)

Rio Bravo
(1959 Warner Brothers)

The Horse Soldiers
(1959 United Artists)

The Alamo
(1960 United Artists)

*The Man Who Shot
Liberty Valance*
(1962 Paramount)

McLintock!
(1963 United Artists)

El Dorado
(1967 Paramount)

True Grit
(1969 Paramount)

The Shootist
(1976 Paramount)

and defend his baptismal name of Marion Michael Morrison when he played football for the University of Southern California. He had a preference for Hispanic wives, drank a quart of gin a day, and read a great deal. He was in his fifties when he lost a lung to cancer; within months he was riding, shooting, and brawling onscreen and off during the filming of *The Sons of Katie Elder.* When he was in his sixties he made the rounds of after-hours bars in New York City until daylight, leaving younger men passed out in his considerable wake; at seventy he was keeping company with a woman young enough to be his granddaughter, and he did so with the intention of marrying her. Everything he did was larger than life and twice as interesting. No wonder the reedy, piping pacifists of the 1960's targeted him for their scorn—until they met him, that is. His personal charm was built on the same scale as the rest of him, so potent that it turned his enemies and detractors into sycophants and fans.

It is appropriate that he's considered the epitome of the cowboy myth, for legends sprang up around him even as they did around Wyatt Earp and Wild Bill Hickok and Billy the Kid. Director John Ford promoted him from grip to superstar because he liked to surround himself with big men on the set. Cameraman had to shoot around Wayne and his equally large friend Victor McLaglen for weeks whenever they appeared in a film together because they fought their fight scenes for real (see their titanic non-Western but typical Irish showdown in *The Quiet Man*) and needed time to heal. Asked if anyone had every called him Marion, the Duke replied, "Once." Some of the stories about Wayne were true, and though some were apocryphal, in true Wild West tradition they will never be proved false. He was and is the stuff of folklore.

When his old nemesis, cancer, returned to claim him in 1979, it was as if a great tree had fallen in another part of the world, a place that few of us had actually visited in person but which affected us all. We were aware of that half-glimpsed tree's existence and continued our own lives secure in that awareness.

Vital windbreaks are instantly missed. It would be naive and simplistic to draw a parallel between the Duke's passing and the almost simultaneous rise of terrorism around the globe, of small bands of murderers set amok for want of an indestructible hero to swat them down. And yet, for all its unrest, the world that John Wayne knew would not have tolerated them. Perhaps the myths of a society are more important than we know to its substance, and when our legends die a part of us dies with them. It is impossible to be an American and to watch *Red River, Fort Apache, Rio Bravo, True Grit,* or *The Shootist* and not feel a sense of irrecoverable loss.

PLAYERS ON HORSEBACK

RIDE A PALE HORSE: CLINT EASTWOOD

BY THOMAS W. KNOWLES

Clint Eastwood (courtesy of CBS)

FOR YEARS HE'S BEEN THE DEADLY STRANGER, THE MAN WITH NO NAME, or the black-clad, gun-toting spectre who rides in on the pale horse. He's been justice, or vengeance, from beyond the grave. And now, Clint Eastwood the director is an honored fellow of the American Academy of Motion Picture Arts and Sciences and the British Royal Film Academy. It's about time.

Clint Eastwood demands respect, whether it's as the critically acclaimed producer-director of such non-Westerns as *Bird* (1988), or as the volatile gunmen he's portrayed in Westerns from *A Fistful of Dollars* (1964) to the Oscar-winning *Unforgiven* (1992). Even though Kevin Costner's *Dances With Wolves* might have opened up the possibility, Eastwood's *Unforgiven* brought the Western back to Hollywood, with an appropriate vengeance.

The only possible comparison to Eastwood's importance in connection to the Western film is that of John Wayne. Both started out in Westerns, and though they worked in other genres, the West is where they felt most at home. Wayne built his Batjac production company on the West, just as Eastwood built Malpaso. Each actor personified the attitudes of his era: Wayne in the '40s and '50s portrayed the exuberant frontiersman and cavalry officer, while Eastwood in the '60s and '70s and played the anti-heroic loner.

But the most important connection is that though they had different visions of the myth of the West, they both believed in the Western story. Since Wayne's passing, Eastwood has done more than any other individual to keep the Western on film, in movie theaters, and in the public eye. He's made no secret of his love for the West, equalled only by his love for jazz, and he's used his own considerable screen presence and his eye for a good story to preserve them both on film.

After his first small roles in movies, Eastwood moved to the small

TOP: Josey Wales (Clint Eastwood) meets soon-to-be-friend Lone Watie (Chief Dan George) in "The Outlaw Josey Wales" (1976 Malpaso)

BOTTOM: Clint Eastwood gets ready to fight in "The Outlaw Josey Wales" (1976 Malpaso)

screen in 1958, where we came to know him as trail drive *segundo* Rowdy Yates to boss Gil Favor (Eric Fleming) on *Rawhide.* One of the most accurate and authentic of the TV Westerns, *Rawhide* filmed location shots in Arizona. Eastwood learned tricks of the trade from the real-life wranglers who handled the cattle; he also honed his acting abilities in the seven years the show stayed on the air. Though the studio frustrated his budding interest in directing, he later said that his stint on *Rawhide* was one of the most rewarding times in his career.

Then, when Richard Harris turned down Italian director Sergio Leone's offer of the role of The Man With No Name, he suggested Eastwood as a candidate. While on break from *Rawhide* in 1964, Eastwood journeyed to Almeria, Spain, to don the infamous poncho for *A Fistful of Dollars,* and the "spaghetti Western" was born. The character he played was a ruthless, stone-cold killer, one who cared nothing for the old-fashioned "Code of the West." To the Man With No Name, life in the West was a game of survival, not a morality play.

As the new genre gained a cult following, Eastwood and Leone followed it up with more roles for The Man With No Name. The critics hated the films and the character, but the public in Europe and America ate 'em up. For a short time, the Man With No Name shored up the film Western's sagging image.

But by the end of the '60s, the nihilism and brutality of the spaghetti Westerns, as well as the overkill of the television Westerns, rode the genre into the ground. For years after Wayne died, Eastwood was about the only actor who could make a success of a Western film. In the first outing for his Malpaso production company, *Hang 'Em High* (1967), he modified his character for his return to American films; the marshal who'd been unjustly hanged might be ruthless, but he had human feelings buried under his badge. He also set the story in a historical location and time, in the Fort Smith, Arkansas court of hanging judge Ike Parker.

Even in his non-Western roles, such as inspector "Dirty" Harry Callahan, he played a lawman who would have been at home in the Old West. Harry's personal code of honor wasn't that much different from Matt Dillon's.

The best example of Eastwood's vision of the Western myth is the excellent version of Forrest Carter's novel, *The Outlaw Josey Wales,* he filmed in 1976. Again, there's a definite sense of time and place. Wales is a Confederate border guerrilla who refuses to surrender at the end of the war and flees to Texas. He's a hunted, haunted man who lost his family and his peaceful life to the Kansas-Missouri border wars; he's been hardened and made ruthless by war. But on his way, he picks up a strange assemblage of folks for whom he finds himself responsible. Despite his nightmares about his first family's tragic end, despite his desire for revenge on those who betrayed him, Wales finds himself drawn back to the new life he can make for himself in the West.

It's the classic pattern of the Western story, similar to, but even more hopeful than the path John Wayne's Ethan Edwards took in *The Searchers*. Though Eastwood's Josey Wales is "greased lightnin'" with a pistol, he's a far more complex character than the enigmatic, cheroot-smoking killing machine in the poncho. Even in Eastwood's homage to Leone, *High Plains Drifter* (1973), his spectral gunfighter has a nobler motive for the violence he creates than does the anti-hero of the spaghetti Western. In *Pale Rider* (1985), he's an instrument of justice that rides in answer to a child's prayer.

In his acclaimed *Unforgiven,* Eastwood uses many of the old Western standards to tell what's essentially an historically revisionist story. Like John Ford, Eastwood uses the land itself as a character—he went to Alberta, Canada, to find sweeping, open fields and prairies over which his characters could ride. He directs his actors so that their characters *feel* as if they've migrated from the *real* West, not the movie West. As the at times genial, at times brutal Sheriff Little Bill Daggett, Gene Hackman could have stepped off the dusty street of any rowdy, dangerous Western cowtown.

Eastwood constantly turns the familiar into the unexpected. In a spectacular scene in the snowy high country, you expect his reformed, widowed killer, Bill Munny, to fall in love with the scarred young prostitute played by Anna Thompson, and provide a happy ending—but he doesn't. The scene is no less touching for it.

In the character of Munny, Eastwood blends all of his experience as an actor to create an authentic Western character. In essence, *Unforgiven* is less a story of revenge than one about Munny's struggle to control the darkness that lies at the bottom of his soul. And so has the fantastic Man With No Name evolved into flawed and complex but very human characters like Josey Wales and Bill Munny. They're not quite the cowboy heroes of the past, but they're no less a part of the Wild West, and they're perhaps closer to its roots. ∎

A Selected Clint Eastwood Western Filmography

A Fistful of Dollars
(1964 Jolly Film/Constantin)

For a Few Dollars More
(1965 P.E.A./Constantin)

The Good, the Bad and the Ugly
(1966 Produzioni Europe Associate)

Hang 'Em High
(1967 Malpaso/Freeman)

Paint Your Wagon
(1969 Paramount)

Two Mules for Sister Sara
(1970 Universal/Malpaso)

High Plains Drifter
(1972 Malpaso)

The Outlaw Josey Wales
(1976 Malpaso)

Pale Rider
(1985 Malpaso)

Unforgiven
(1992 Malpaso)

> "The ancient folk with evil spells, dashed to earth, plowed under!"
>
> NAVAJO WAR CHANT

SUNSET WARRIORS

Get 'em Up Scout! Cinematic Stereotypes of Indians and Their Horses

BY LEE SCHULTZ

THE SCENE FADES IN LONG BEFORE WE HEAR THE CAVALRY BUGLES. Hundreds of Indians ride a dust-choked circle around the settlers' beleaguered wagons in the vicinity of Fort Fetterman, Fort Phil Kearney, or any other place that's good for an ambush along the Bozeman or Mormon-Oregon trails—but probably filmed in Monument Valley, Utah. All of the Indians ride wonderfully decorated paint ponies or Medicine Hat Stallions.

Right? *Wrong!*

As the Indians achieve superhuman feats of warlike equestrianship, not one horse ever stumbles or falters. Each well-trained mount, guided by only a rawhide thong tied to its underjaw and the skilled body and knee language of its expert rider, follows in the perfect circle. Not one shies from the occasional Winchester or Springfield blast over its withers, nor from the fusillade of shots from the circle of wagons. Not one ever breaks that perfect, thundering, dust-generating circle to get back to its comrade ponies who weren't lucky enough to come along. Not one trips in a prairie dog hole, pulls up lame, is kicked by the horse in front of him, or falls and slides on its nose to cough and spit snotty muck at the crippled rider somersaulting over its head.

Right? *Wrong!*

Every single wounded warrior is picked up and returned to his own lines by two bravely charging riders. They carry him off arm-in-arm, swinging between high-stepping, cantering-in-unison chargers a la Barnum & Bailey. If the Indians win, they leave the white man's inferior horses in arrow-punctured, fly-gathering heaps that resemble nothing more than large, saddled porcupines.

Right? *Wrong again!*

At risk of being thought not politically correct (unlike the movie Indians played so well by Native Americans like Jack Palance, Sal Mineo, Chuck Connors, Jeff Chandler and Trevor Howard), let's talk turkey about these cinematic visions of Indians and their horses. We'll hear affirmative whinnies from horse graves everywhere.

First of all, no warrior with any sense would play duck-in-the-shooting gallery by riding in a perfect circle around a defensible position. He'd maybe play merry-go-round only long enough to find the right weak spot to charge. And while some of our warriors would indeed be mounted on exceptional horses, most wouldn't. A good many casualties in cavalry battles were horses—they made big, fine, easy targets—and no Indian would risk his best horse in such a manner.

But, you say, couldn't the warrior merely return to camp after the engagement to draw another war horse from his string of ten or one hundred well-trained mounts?

No!

Out of an Indian's herd, which sometimes numbered as many as two to five hundred horses, only one or two were war or hunting horses—the only ones well trained. To a certain extent, that Indian equalled his special horse. His horse knew him, and everyone knew him by his horse. When his war horse returned unmounted after a battle, it signified the worst.

So every night, he picketed that special war horse by his lodge or camp...

...in case of ambush by the U.S. Cavalry or a marauding band from an enemy tribe?

Wrong again, White Eyes!

Indians didn't have fire and theft coverage. And horse theft, to a plains Indian, translated as Honor, Macho, Wealth, Power and especially Fame. The stereotypical scene of five mounted Indians stampeding a corral of horses out onto the moonlit prairie is only half true. The big prize was a man's war horse or hunting horse. Why? For the horse's skill and the risk, that's why. Stealing him was tantamount to breaking into Fort Knox and making away with a boxcar of bullion. One didn't blunder into such an operation. Most times, a warrior made his stealthy penetration into enemy camp on foot—alone.

Some tribes went to great extremes to protect their special animals. The Pawnee on the lower Platte bedded their special horses and mules in strong log corrals in front of their earth houses.

Needless to say, those corrals were very fine insurance policies, and breaching them was a heroic matter. So it was that a Cheyenne named Bear Feathers decided to risk certain destruction for the chance at the

Native American Actors in Movies, Radio and Television

ACTORS WITH TRIBAL AFFILIATIONS:

John War Eagle, Sioux (dates unknown)

Chief Many Treaties (William Hazlett), Blackfoot, (1875-1948)

Chief John Big Tree, Seneca (1875-1967)

Nipo Strongheart, Yakima (1884-1966)

Jim Thorpe, Sac and Fox (1889-1953)
Olympic gold medalist—played by Burt Lancaster in a biographical motion picture

Monte Blue, Cherokee (1890-1963)

Chief Yowlachie, Yakima (1890-1966)

Charles Stevens, Apache (1893-1964)

Chief Thundercloud (Victor Daniels), Cherokee (1899-1955)
the first movie Tonto

Chief Dan George, Cree (1899-1982)

Chief Thundercloud (Scott Williams), heritage unknown (1901-1967)
Tonto on radio

Rodd Redwing, Chickasaw (1905-1971)

Jay Silverheels, Mohawk (1919-1980)
best known Tonto from movies and television

Dennis Weaver, Cherokee (1924-)

Clu Gulager, Cherokee (1928-)

Will Sampson, Creek (1935-1987)

ACTORS NOT AFFILIATED WITH A TRIBE:

Woody Strode (1914-)

Iron Eyes Cody (1915-)
most famous for his anti-pollution public service video

Michael Ansara (dates unavailable)
portrayed Apache Cochise in television's Broken Arrow

honor. As he sneaked up to the corral one night, Bear Feathers found himself in the grasp of a huge Pawnee who had slipped up behind him.

For some reason—perhaps he felt flattered that his animals had been chosen over those of the rest of the tribe—the Pawnee, who was none other than the chief, welcomed the Cheyenne into his lodge as a guest. In the spirit of comradeship, he gave Bear Feathers his freedom and a fine white mule, complete with silver-mounted Mexican saddle. He wished the Cheyenne well and saw him safely on his way home.

But now Bear Feathers had a problem. How could he confess the evening's happenings and thus tromp all over his own heroic escapade? So he didn't. He lied. He boasted about the risks of his great adventure and his heroic theft of the Pawnee chief's prize mule. He achieved great fame...for a while.

White Thunder, Keeper of the Cheyenne's sacred arrows, chanced to visit the Pawnee village not long after on a peacekeeping mission. The Pawnee chief told him the entire story and inquired about Bear Feathers and his white mule. And so fell the fame and fortune of Bear Feathers. To steal was honorable; to lie about stealing was the ultimate shame.

In fact, stealing horses was the Indian's most popular sport, much more popular and even more dangerous than open warfare. Many engagements between warring tribes resulted in only one or two casualties and several wounded—most warriors preferred to count coup, striking the enemy with a stick, quirt, or open hand to show bravery. But when a man was caught raiding an enemy camp for horses, the epilogue to his death was a contrived gruesomeness beyond description. Wealth, measured in Indian terms, carried a risk far beyond bankruptcy and civil judgment.

And wealth meant horses, which brings us to those beautiful animals ridden by the Indians. Many of the better ones started out belonging to some other tribe, but many had been fed and trained by Anglos or Spanish Americans prior to Indian ownership.

In 1598, Juan de Onate, searching for Coronado's mythical kingdom, moved his few hundred men, along with livestock and a number of horses, to the Santa Fe region of New Mexico. Raiding Apache were wonderfully impressed with the docility of the fine animals. They could be conveniently led from a Spaniard's pen to his own camp—there to be slaughtered and skinned for food.

But on observing how the Spanish handled their horses, the Indian soon found fresh vistas from the back of his new companion. The age of the mounted Plains Indian was born.

The Indian's taste for domesticated horses never abated. For the next two centuries he raided for horses as far south as Chihuahua and Sonora.

For the most part, white men's horses were better trained, fed and behaved than the diminutive range-roaming mustangs. In fact, the breeding stock for many Indian-owned herds came from rustled domestics.

Indians coveted rather than spurned settlers' horses. The pickings were at times so easy that the Plains tribes chose to raid, rather than to round up and train the wild bands that multiplied profusely between 1640 and 1880.

The power and endurance of the tall, long-legged thoroughbred cavalry mounts were not lost on the Plains tribes either. And the Pawnee in particular took special liking to mules provided by farmers or U.S. Cavalry. It was a hardier and more trail-wise mount with a travel gait most times much smoother than the small mustang-type mount. And— sorry about that, movie-goers—lameness was a major problem among unshod Indian ponies. The mule had better hooves than the horse; he went lame much less often.

Could it be that one or more of our Indians circling the wagon train are riding long-eared animals with a "US" brand? Perhaps. But certainly many of our warriors are on taller thoroughbred-type browns and bays rather than flashy paints and pintos.

It was not unheard of for a horse, or a group of horses, to have endured the ownership of a number of tribes. What real estate agents do for the white man's symbols of wealth, horse raiders did for the Indian's. In fact, for many of the tribes, including the Navajo, Comanche, Apache and Kiowa, horse stealing was a sacred commission. The earliest myths and tales of these tribes record the spiritual and economic reason for horse raids. Their gods had given them the sacred animals (sacred "dogs" in one of the Sioux myths), although the white man had received them first. Great magical powers had to be taken on raids, and preparations for some were at times fanatical.

Those whose herds were raided often times retaliated with magical spells. A Chiricuahua Apache band that had taken a herd away from a group of Yaqui fought a spell of severe cramps and leg aches that slowed them down for their pursuers. One of the Chiricuahua counteracted the spell with one of his own. Mixing a concoction of spider's web and cactus, he cast a spell on the pursuers that made their toes cramp so painfully that they fell off their horses. The raid was successful.

An Indian had divine inspiration for horse raiding, for his cultural heroes were horse raiders. One Lipan Apache hero, Killer-of-Enemies, gave specific instructions for his tribe on how to raid. In an inspired example, he himself raided successfully in the Guadalupe Mountains and came back with many horses. Legend says his pursuers' horses turned into the black weeds and bushes (probably creosotes), which can still

Detail from "A Black-foot Indian on Horseback," after Karl Bodmer (courtesy of Joslyn Art Museum, Omaha, NE)

THE WESTERN BOOK OF LISTS

POP QUIZ: WHAT DO THESE ACTORS HAVE IN COMMON?

Victor Mature, Walter Huston, Jason Robards, Kirk Douglas, Stacey Keach, Arthur Kennedy, Caesar Romero, Willie Nelson, Val Kilmer, Dennis Quaid.

They've all played Doc Holliday on the screen.

be seen in that area.

But inspiration being what it may, many horse raids verged on the comical. While Bent's Fort was the major trading junction south of the Arkansas River between the United States and Mexico, a number of enthusiastic raids took place. William Bent, husband of a Cheyenne named Owl Woman, traded among a number of competitive enemy tribes. These tribes, especially the Comanche, Kiowa and Cheyenne were ecstatically fond of each other's horses. In 1826 or 1827, a group of Comanche under Bull Hump arrived at the stockade. Bent hid a band of visiting Cheyenne among his store of goods, then assured the Comanche leader that the Cheyenne had gone north a little while before to a village on the South Platte.

Bull Hump and his band found a Cheyenne and Arapaho village, but thought it too well situated to attack in daylight. Waiting until dark, the Comanche began their horse raid. Bent records that "many of these horses had been stolen from the Comanche by the Cheyennes, and Bull Hump must have felt tickled at getting them back." The chase was on, the Comanche realizing they would soon be followed by the angered Cheyenne and Arapaho.

At the same time, two Cheyenne, Yellow Wolf and his adopted son, Walking Coyote, were running mustangs down near the Arkansas with a big party of warriors. They had been successful, taking about five hundred head. During their return home, at a point some thirty miles north of Arkansas, their scouts reported a strange band with a number of horses.

Walking Coyote, known as a brave warrior, advised the majority of his party to return home with the mustangs. He and a few other men would raid the other camp at dawn and run off with the herd. This they did, except for the horses tethered near the camp.

The chase was on again. The camp they had raided was, of course, Bull Hump's. Although the Comanche outnumbered the Cheyenne, the Cheyenne had superior arms; rifles against mostly lances and bows for the Comanche. After they shot two Comanche from their horses, the Cheyenne relaxed for the trek home...

...and suddenly realized they had stolen their own stolen horses!

Thus, in a short period of time, the herd had been stolen three times: first by the Cheyenne from the Comanche, then by Bull Hump from the Cheyenne, and lastly by Walking Coyote from Bull Hump. Commodity market indeed!

So those horses circling our settlers, although ridden by the Sioux, may at one time have belonged to the Crow, the Ute or the Nez Perce. The last man sitting on a horse owned him.

Which leads to another problem with our attack scenario: our warriors are using only blankets or riding bareback because they disdain the white man's gear, right?

Sorry, pilgrim!

Many of them use Anglo or Spanish-crafted saddles, or at least they rode to the ambush site on them. Though moviemakers like to cover their soft seats with blankets, the Indian prized his captured or traded-for horse tack. Once source witnessed early Lipan Apaches with "good saddles and iron stirrups" in 1724! Another early account of Apache horse trappings places the value of one rider's equipage in the hundreds of dollars. By the later nineteenth century, the Indians had developed metal-working to the point where iron bits with silver and even brass and copper ornaments were not uncommon. The Navajo in particular used recognizable ornaments and amulets on their bridles. They also prized the small silver "hawk bells," much the same as Onate had

HOLLYWOOD INDIAN COUNTRY ETIQUETTE

BY LOREN D. ESTLEMAN & DALE L. WALKER

One would think the heroes of B Westerns and television Westerns would have figured out by now how to deal with Hollywood Indians. Unlike the culturally diverse Native Americans of which movie Indians are caricatures, generic Hollywood Indians operate under a burden of social handicaps as equally ludicrous as the Hollywood cowboy's Code of the West. Here are some suggestions for intrepid explorers in the cinematic West:

When the sage old scout, the obnoxious settler, or the greenhorn West Point officer says, "Shoot, there ain't an Injun within a hunnert miles of these here parts," you can take it to the bank—you're surrounded by every able-bodied warrior in the Comanche, Sioux, Kiowa, Apache, and Cheyenne nations.

■ If you meet a hostile Indian war chief in no man's land for a party, don't offer to become his blood brother unless the chief broaches the subject.

■ Experts in frontier etiquette advise against asking a war chief in full regalia, "Hey, Kawliga, where's your cigars?"

■ Avoid name-related jests when you're visiting Gall, Hump, Roman Nose, or Young-Man-Afraid-of-His-Horses; remember that the chief of the Nez Perce is called "Joseph," not "Joe" or "Joey."

■ If you're visiting a Cheyenne camp, never speak the name Chivington without spitting before and after.

■ When the shaman passes you the medicine pipe at the council fire, don't inhale, don't knock out the dottle and refill the pipe with Bull Durham, and don't hack up phlegm and call the mixture a "lung buster."

■ Don't accept mushroom stew or peyote candy from a strange Indian woman, particularly if she's the war chief's pug-ugly, unmarried sister-in-law or daughter.

■ If it sounds like a coyote, it's probably a Comanche; if it sounds like a Comanche, it's probably a coyote.

■ Always shoot the war chief on the first charge; real Indians would probably just consider you more of a challenge and get down to serious business, but Hollywood Indians will withdraw while they pick a new war chief.

■ Never become overly attached to any dog when you're visiting a Hollywood Indian village.

TOWNS TO AVOID

BY LOREN D. ESTLEMAN

Purgatorio
El Dorado
Warlock
Black Rock
Hell's Hinges
Hard Times
Fort Grant
Rio Bravo
Lordsburg
Hadleyville
Rio Lobo
Lago
Tombstone
Big Whiskey

brought to New Mexico in 1598. And in a pinch, a round cinch ring slipped over the pony's lower jaw would serve as a bit.

Certainly, at our wagon train fight, most of our braves fight bareback, perhaps because our warriors don't want to lose their prize tack in a mishap. Also, clothing and needless decorations are dangerous—a bullet can carry pieces of them into a gunshot wound. No doubt a few of our braves sit on cross-forked cottonwood saddles, and one or two may have spurs strapped over their buffalo hide moccasins.

And if a well-fed domesticated saddle horse survives the attack, old Nellie goes home with the tribe.

THE NATIVE AMERICANS WERE FINE HORSEMEN, BUT THEY weren't perfect. After all, when and how did an Indian break and train horses? A herd-owning tribe constantly sought new pasture for their animals; they didn't have permanent training facilities. A young Indian reared in the presence of horses had time to study each of an elder's herd for long hours day after day. The horses were not, as a civilized owner attempts, taught to behave in certain ways. Rather, a warrior selected his horse from the herd for its natural prowess and athletic abilities—the Indian's was the original "eye for horses." From a herd of two hundred, only one horse could make a war horse; perhaps only one or two became hunters. An Indian's wealth, survival and reputation depended on his choice—rider and animal had to complement each other.

An Indian and his mount were *one*. That an Indian took his exercise on his horse, and that an Indian would rather race his own shadow than sleep are probably truisms. His horse didn't *perform*—it acted while doing something: it escaped; it raced shoulder-to-shoulder with a buffalo; it pulled a travois; it calmly carried its rider while he fired guns and arrows.

Gentling was taking for granted. Young boys swam and jumped from back to back of skittish colts as the animals struggled to keep afloat in a deep river or lake. The horse early on became aware of the smell, sounds and movements of its human masters.

The training process varied from tribe to tribe, but the Crow bargained for horses with the Nez Perce; the Sioux with the Crow (often violently); the Cheyenne with the Sioux. They could also find wonderfully gentle horses at ranches. Kiowa, Apache, Comanche and Cheyenne all raided each other's herds. And the horse trading that went on would make modern stockyard traders blush.

Many tribes merely accustomed horses to being ridden. They spent much time on special horses but little on the many. Cheyenne mustang parties hunted in the early spring when the wild ponies were slow, drawn from the hard winter, their bellies filled with early grass. Hunters carried long poles with nooses, and once they noosed the animal, they choked him down. Then they tied him by a rawhide halter to the tail of another horse, usually an older, gentle mare. The new wild animals soon made friends with the domesticated mares and gave them little trouble.

Upon returning to camp, the Indian hobbled his new horse by all four feet, then picketed him, still "tailed" to the mare. Then he rubbed the horse down, breathed into his nose and mouth, hand fed him and piled heavy buffalo robes on him.

The warrior led the mare and the new horse around the camp until the mustang became used to the weight and smell of the robes, then he mounted him while he was still hobbled. He didn't allow the new horse to jump, kick or buck. Finally, he rode the mustang about the camp while leading the mare along side to keep him quiet.

Special horses chosen for war or the hunt were almost always under four years old, for beyond that age they were virtually impossible to train. Those very special horses were sensitive to every desire of their riders. Courageous pickups of wounded warriors did happen often, and some instances are well-documented. But horses did stumble and shy away from an intended foe or buffalo, and they did spook at gunshots and strange noises and smells. Many more wounded were retrieved on foot after dark than were brazenly swept away between two racing riders. The heroic is always better documented than the mundane.

And so back to the site of our wagon train attack. Yes, some of the Indians are riding horses they've owned for a number of years. Famous warriors such as Crazy Horse and Roman Nose were noted for their special mounts. But the chances are miniscule of assembling a uniform troop of warriors as choreographed by Hollywood directors.

And the way the Indians treated their horses? It varied from tribe to tribe.

Right? *Wrong!*

It varied from individual to individual. Reports are common of ponies with scarred and raw blistered backs, of animals ridden to death and then eaten. But so are those of kindnesses. We can find proof of such kindness in the comments of Captain R. B. Marcy about his Red River trip in 1849. Marcy tried to purchase a favorite horse from a chief of the Southern Comanche. The chief wouldn't be persuaded. The horse, he said, was one of the fastest; his loss would be felt and mourned by the entire tribe. But the final reason the chief gave Marcy was, "I love him very much."

Could this almost filial relationship be the basis for the phenomenal

Detail from "The Modern Comanche," Frederic Remington (*Harper's New Monthly*) (courtesy of Texas A&M University Special Collections and Archives)

communication between rider and horse? Perhaps. N. Scott Momaday tells of an old Kiowa gentleman who preserved the bones of his beloved red horse in a box in the barn. As a child, the author wondered at such an action, especially at the man's grief when someone stole the bones.

By concession, the Kiowa and the Comanche seem to be regarded as the best of our native horsemen. Certainly General Crook's comment that the Sioux were the best light cavalry the world had ever known should merit the tribe the medal for discipline on horseback. Momaday says that the Kiowa were the finest horsemen—of course, since he is Kiowa—and that they had the most horses per person of any Plains tribe.

Stories tell of Comanche warriors returning from campaigns met at their lodges by loving wives whose first duty was the care and feeding of the war horse. Many Nez Perce considered their horses almost family members. The Navajo saw them as supernatural creatures, at times deities, creatures ridden by the sun.

The parts created by the cinema for the Native American's horse forgets or ignores the real relationship between Indian rider and Indian mount. While the movie cowboy says, "G'bye Ma'am," to the schoolmarm, then kisses his horse and rides off into the sunset, the movie Indian is forced to ride a flashy but characterless splotch of colors and handprints in silly, infinite circles. Very seldom do we get to see the Indian's symbiotic, almost religious relationship with his horse.

For example, the elder Crazy Horse, father to the famous warrior, as most men of stature carried a ceremonial pipe in a fine sacramental case. From the case hung four fringes of horsehair from the mane of a fine sorrel mare he'd chased for years. Each time horse hunters went for her, she would lead her band out into the badlands where she would lose her pursuers.

Finally, Crazy Horse followed her and walked her down in the deep snow of a very hard winter. He cut the fringes from the mane over her eyes—the place of the power to see beyond mere sight—and used her hair to decorate his pipe case. Though the red mare never gentled enough to carry a pack nor to pull a travois, in years that were too severe for many of the other mares she bore fine, strong colts to the stallions of Crazy Horse's herd.

At the death of his young wife, mother of his two sons, Crazy Horse took the mare out to his wife's burial scaffold. He knew his wife would need a companion in the next life, and the mare would make a good one. No camera was there to record the tears in his eyes and the tremble in his hand when Crazy Horse shot the mare, but we know the tears were there. ■

THE MYTH AND THE MYTHMAKERS...

PRINT, FILM AND, IN THE END, REALITY

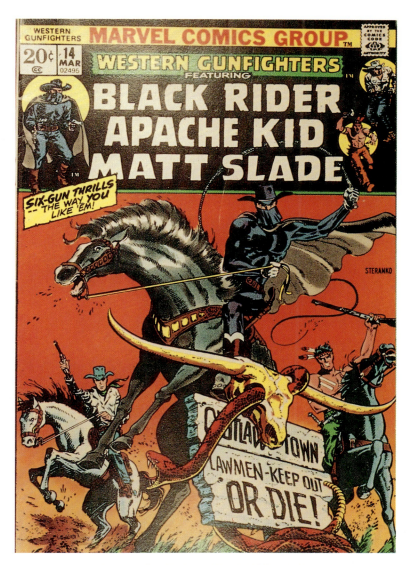

Cover, *Western Gunfighters,* **March 1973, Jim Steranko**
(courtesy of Marvel Comics Group, Inc.)

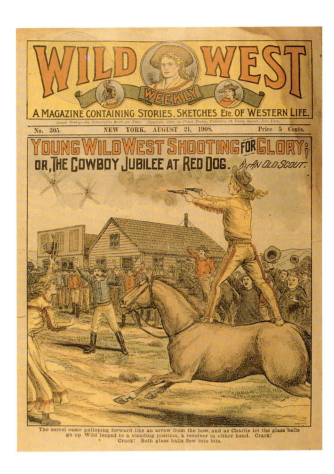

Wild West, old-time pulp (courtesy of Texas A&M University, Special Collections and Archives, Dykes Collection)

OPPOSITE:
Dime Western Magazine rarely featured women (courtesy of Texas A&M University, Special Collections and Archives, Dykes Collection)

Max Brand's Western, from the classic pulp era (courtesy of Texas A&M University, Special Collections and Archives, Dykes Collection)

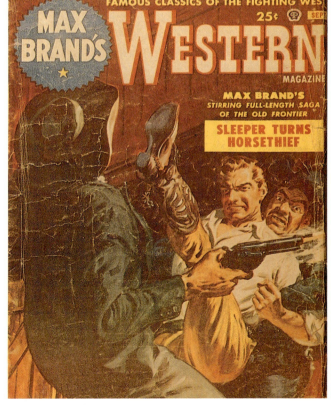

RIGHT: Kevin Costner in *Dances With Wolves* (courtesy of Fotos International/Archive Photos)

BELOW: Clint Eastwood and Gene Hackman face off in *Unforgiven* (courtesy of Fotos International/Archive Photos)

OPPOSITE, TOP: From John Wayne's *The Alamo,* (1960 Batjac) artist's rendition of the final set (donated by John Wayne to Texas A&M University, Special Collections and Archives)

OPPOSITE, BOTTOM: Paul Newman and Robert Redford in *Butch Cassidy and the Sundance Kid* (1969 TCF Productions) (courtesy of Texas Collection/Film Archives)

RIGHT: "The Cisco Kid," Jimmy Smits and Cheech Marin (courtesy of Turner Pictures, photographer: Erik Heinila)

BELOW: "Dr. Quinn, Medicine Woman," Jane Seymour in the title role (courtesy of Fotos International/Archive Photos)

OPPOSITE, TOP: Wes Studi in *Geronimo* (Fotos International/Archive Photos)

OPPOSITE, BOTTOM: *Tombstone,* on the way to a shoot-out (courtesy of Archive Photos)

Taos Business District, c.1919, Oscar E. Berninghaus
(courtesy of Texas A&M Development Foundation,
Bill & Irma Runyon Art Collections)

SUNSET WARRIORS

FROM TONTO TO CRAZY HORSE: THE PATHFINDERS

BY ROBERT J. CONLEY

HOLLYWOOD CAN'T QUITE MAKE UP ITS MIND WHEN IT COMES TO the Indian in the Western, whether he's the bloodthirsty redskin or the noble savage. Both images are equally untrue, two sides of the same old coin. For Native American actors, who only too seldom get to play the roles of Indians in films, it poses something of a cultural dilemma. If the stereotype is changing, modern Indian actors owe their chance to rewrite the false images to those who blazed the trail for them.

Jay Silverheels

If star recognition is the way to measure success in Hollywood, Jay Silverheels is responsible for gaining much of the new recognition for Indian actors in films and on television. Silverheels was probably the first Indian film star, depending on how one chooses to define the word "star." Everyone knows him as Tonto from his work in the Lone Ranger television series (1952-1956); in fact, a generation of American children held him in high esteem second only to the masked man. But he never in his career appeared in a starring role.

A Mohawk, Silverheels was born in 1919 on the Six Nations Indian Reserve in Ontario, Canada. He was a natural athlete and became a professional lacrosse player and champion middleweight boxer. Comedian Joe E. Brown spotted Silverheels at a sporting event and encouraged him to try acting, and so began his long career. He appeared in a great number of films, from *The Prairie* (1947) to *Santee* (1973), which included two Lone Ranger features, *The Lone Ranger* (1955) and *The Lone Ranger and the Lost City of Gold* (1958).

Even though the role of Tonto wasn't the lead, Silverheels was more than a partner to Clayton Moore's Ranger—the masked man just wouldn't have been complete without him. Through the only kind of roles available to him, Silverheels worked hard to improve the image of Indians

"Mako Shika."

SIOUX WORDS FOR THE BADLANDS

GOOD ADVICE

BY LOREN D. ESTLEMAN

"Next time you hang a man, you better make damn sure you get a look at his face!"
—Clint Eastwood, *Hang 'Em High* (United Artists, 1967)

"Manos arriba!"
—Paul Newman, *Butch Cassidy and the Sundance Kid* (20th Century Fox, 1969)

"You skin 'im, pilgrim, and I'll bring you another'n."
—Will Geer, *Jeremiah Johnson* (Warner Brothers, 1972)

"Every day above ground's a good day."
—Bruce Dern, *Posse* (Paramount, 1975)

"Now—spit!"
—Chief Dan George, *The Outlaw Josey Wales* (Warner Brothers, 1976)

in films and television, and he founded the Indian Actors workshop to train Native American actors for the industry. Hollywood must have seen him as a star, for he received his own star in the Walk of Fame shortly before his death in 1980.

Chief Dan George

Chief Dan George, a Canadian Cree, took film audiences by storm when he appeared in the engaging role of Old Lodge Skins in *Little Big Man* in 1970. It was probably the first major Indian role played by an Indian actor in a big-budget Hollywood film. Dan George was in his seventies at the time, and his smile and wit shattered forever the image of the stoic, humorless Indian. He continued to defy stereotypes as he played the wry but dignified Lone Watie to Clint Eastwood's laconic Civil War guerrilla in *The Outlaw Josey Wales* (1976). He made a number of other films, not all of them Westerns.

Though he started his movie career late in life (with *Smith!* in 1969), George made quite an impact on the industry. With the publication of his two books, *My Heart Soars* (1974) and *My Spirit Soars* (1982), he also became popular as a poet and an advocate of Native American values. He was eighty-three years old when he died in 1982.

Will Sampson

It wasn't a Western, but Will Sampson's performance as the enigmatic but compassionate Big Chief Broom in *One Flew Over the Cuckoo's Nest* (1975) threatened to steal the show from star Jack Nicholson. Sampson, born near Okmulgee, Oklahoma, in the heart of the Creek Nation, was a big man who made a big impression. His screen presence won him historical roles in many Westerns; in his cameo as Ten Bears in *The Outlaw Josey Wales,* he brought to the screen a sense of power and ferocity to rival that of Eastwood's vengeful Josey Wales.

Sampson's non-Western roles included his turn as a shaman in the second *Poltergeist,* as well as roles in *Orca* (1977), *Alcatraz: The Whole Shocking Story* and *Insignificance* (1978), and a regular role on the private-eye television series "Vegas" in 1978. No matter how strange the role, no matter how strange the movie, Sampson retained his dignity.

Though *The White Buffalo* (1977) was an otherwise interesting Western flawed by poor special effects and slow direction, Sampson's portrayal of Crazy Horse makes it almost worth watching when he's on the screen. It's said that Crazy Horse could see into the future; if Sampson's performance appeared in one of his visions, the Sioux's mystic warrior might have been proud. And like Crazy Horse, Sampson died too early, not of a bayonet in the back, but of a heart attack in 1987. ∎

THE DIRECTORS

SAM PECKINPAH, CELLULOID OUTLAW

BY MAX EVANS

Katy Haber, Sam Peckinpah's executive secretary on six films, pushes him through the airport in Belgrade as a joke after finishing the violent World War II film "Cross of Iron" (1976)

LEGEND HAS IT THAT SAM WAS BORN ON PECKINPAH MOUNTAIN, BUT the fact is he arrived on this earth in a Fresno, California, hospital. He left us fifty-nine years later after he directed the most profound motion pictures of the transitional West ever put on film. And that's only one of the multitude of contradictions about Sam Peckinpah.

Like so many of the young filmmakers of his time, he found his first idol in John Ford. Not too much later he realized that the great Mr. Ford worked mostly in unlikely melodramatic myths. Sam admitted that Ford's works were important in the sense of telling us what we should be, or what we would like to be, but in most cases weren't. Sam was far more influenced by writings like Robert Ardrey's *The Territorial Imperative*. And long before any of these other influences, there were his childhood hunting trips on horseback with his adored father and his brother, Denny, up into their secret ancestral wilderness spots in the High Sierras. They naturally set him up for the Western.

Before we dive into his fully earned international reputation as a brilliant madman, I'd like to quote from an article that Charles Champlin of the *Los Angeles Times* wrote after Sam's death: "What is easy to forget is that Peckinpah, after graduating from Fresno State, worked toward a masters in theater arts at the University of Southern California and spent two seasons as a director-in-residence at Huntington Park Civic Theater, staging everything from *Our Town* to *South Pacific,* and conducting workshops on Ibsen and Moliere."

He also directed and acted at the Albuquerque Little Theater in New Mexico. Don Siegel hired him as a gofer for five films, and he was a dialogue assistant for others. He wrote episodes for many television shows, including "Gunsmoke," "The Rifleman," and "Wanted: Dead or Alive." Along with Brian Keith, Bruce Geller, Bernie Kawolski, Tom Gries, and a dog named Brown, he made "The Westerner," acclaimed by many as

Slim Pickens (left) and Max Evans acting in Peckinpah's "The Ballad of Cable Hogue," Echo Bay, NV, 1970

the best Western television series ever produced. Unfortunately, it was also the shortest lived of its time, though all the principals went on from there to make heavy and lasting marks on the world.

So Sam had seen the elephant and heard the owl before *Ride the High Country* made him famous. That happened in spite of the studio executives. Though the film provided Randolph Scott and Joel McCrea, two of the most beloved Western actors of all time, with the finest roles of their lives, the studios didn't believe in the film, and just tossed it away like stale beer. It vanished from American movie houses before the critics could give it their rave reviews. Then it was discovered in France, where it ran for over a year in one theater alone.

Suddenly, Sam was *the* new, hot young director, as they like to say in *Follywood*.

We met because he was interested in my book, *The Hi Lo Country*. I didn't even know who he was until my agent told me. To this day I still have moments when I puzzle over the impossibility of our remaining such good friends for twenty-five bloody years. But we did.

We only had a few things in common. First of all, we were both young and full of silly. We liked to drink and raise hell. Second was that we were both interested in transitions. Sam's main drive in film was his interest in the lives of those Western men and women who, around the turn of the century, were squeezed out of their time by the coming of barbed wire and the automobile. My interest was in the next great transition of the West, the one that began just after World War II when the pickup truck altered the working cowboy's chores and attitudes forever. Third was that we both loved the outdoors. Last, we respected individualistic loners who pursued their private dreams all the way to hell if necessary.

Sam was totally unpredictable. Once he invited me to a private story-conference luncheon at the Cock and Bull Restaurant on Sunset Boulevard, and he did the following: He introduced me to his agent, his lawyer, his accountant, a script supervisor, an actress, and two dancing girls. He asked them to our table and invited them to order all the drinks they wanted, the most expensive hor d'oevres available, and graciously offered them their choice from the menu for lunch. He had us all enthusiastically enjoying his generosity, his hunting-knife wit, and his new fame. *Then. Then* the bastard snuck out and left me with a tab so big it broke me.

A week later he had his secretary call me and tell me to wait at my favorite Greek place on Hollywood Boulevard. After I ordered several shots of Metaxa without any means to pay for them or to escape unharmed, the secretary showed up and asked, "Are you Max Evans?"

I answered, "The remains, ma'am, just the remains."

She smiled pleasantly, sat down on a bar stool, then pulled several good-sized bills out of her purse and plopped them down on the bar right in front of my amazed face. In a nonchalant voice she explained, "Sam said for you to have a good time."

Well, bless his ornery bones, I did.

IT ALL HAPPENED TO SAM. ALL OF IT. IT STARTED WITH *MAJOR DUN-dee.* He had gathered together the right talent to make what he expected and believed to be a great epic Western, but a number of people in authority cut up that movie so badly it was unrecognizable to the people who had worked on it. At first Sam fought valiantly to save *Dundee,* and so did others. Charlton Heston even offered to forgo his own salary if they would allow Peckinpah to shoot and edit the picture his own way. He was refused. And that's when Sam started his never-ending, never relenting war with the studios. They would finally win, of course, but before the flame of his rocket died he would burn some permanent history deep into the mountains, deserts, and denizens of the West.

He made many desperate gestures, but when he saw the loss of *Major*

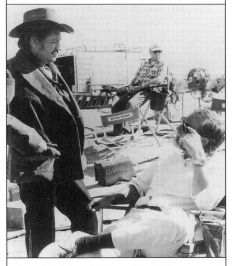

Sam Peckinpah (seated) and Max Evans in the Nevada desert on the set of "The Ballad of Cable Hogue," 1970

THE WESTERN FILMS OF HOWARD HAWKS

BY SCOTT CUPP

Though Howard Hawks directed only five Western films throughout his long Hollywood career, he is generally acknowledged to be one of the two most influential directors (with John Ford) in the shaping of the cinematic West. This is truly astounding when one considers that three of the films—*Rio Bravo, El Dorado,* and *Rio Lobo*—are essentially the same film.

The thing that most distinguished a Howard Hawks film from the mass of competitors was its style—non-traditional and often surprising. Hawks preferred characters who were not mythic or omnipotent, who made mistakes and often acted rashly.

The characters in each Hawks film had major flaws that made them more accessible to the audience. *Red River,* the most famous of the Hawks Westerns, stars John Wayne (who appeared in four of the five Hawks Westerns) as Texas cattleman Tom Dunston, and Montgomery Clift as his adopted son, Garth. It's a classic tale of the conflict involved in growing up—each man is striving for his own goal in their common purpose, the successful completion of a long and arduous cattle drive. Dunston has raised Garth to be more like him than he desires—both men believe that they're right and are a law unto themselves—and their clash of wills leads to a powerful and climactic confrontation.

In *The Big Sky,* Boone, played by Dewey Martin, is a man without a purpose or goal. He can do no more than imitate and anticipate the actions of Jim Deakins, played by Kirk Douglas. Together, they travel up the Mississippi by keelboat looking for adventure and trade. When it becomes obvious that Deakins has fallen in love with an Indian woman, Boone, in turn, "falls" for her, buys her from her people, and "marries" her, even though he has no real love for her. When he'd later discard her, he stays with her because it's what Deakins would have done.

In *Rio Bravo,* John Wayne as John T. Chance doesn't assemble a crew of able deputies to defend his prisoner. Instead, he has a drunk (Dean Martin), an old cripple (Walter Brennan), and a kid (Rick Nelson). Hawks claimed that *Rio Bravo* was his antithesis to *High Noon,* in which Gary Cooper plays a mythic character who spends the entire film trying to get help that he ultimately does not need. In *Rio Bravo,* Wayne spends the entire film turning down assistance that he does need.

Though the stories are compelling, the cinematography is breathtaking. For *Red River,* Hawks achieved the realistic crossing of the Red River by the cattle herd by fording the San Pedro River in Arizona with a camera mounted in one of the wagons. The lurching of camera and wagon gave the crossing a new energy previously absent in the Western film. Rather than simulate the poling of the keelboat up the Mississippi for *The Big Sky,* he filmed the movements of a real keelboat.

Strong cinematography with an emphasis on realism, coupled with realistic yet flawed characters, were the trademarks of a Howard Hawks Western, and with them he helped bring respectability to one of Hollywood's favorite film genres.

Angie Dickinson distracts John Wayne in the 1959 Howard Hawks film, "Rio Bravo."

Dundee coming, Sam resorted to stripping the clothes from one of the producers in the Mexico City airport. He scattered them about so that in gathering them up, the producer would suffer through the maximum visual effect. Word spread fast about his rebellious nature, but he was miraculously offered the *Cincinnati Kid* with Steve McQueen and major supporting actors. He was fired after four days for sneaking a crew into the studio at night to film Ann-Margret nude *under* a fur coat.

After that he was effectively blackballed for years. During that period he wrote under-the-table scripts and took small, foreign acting jobs to stay alive. Even so he optioned *The Hi Lo Country* over and over, and he managed to entertain scores of his friends at his Malibu home. About half of them were from his adopted country to the south—Mexico. My family and I spent what seemed like thousands of years of revelry at his home.

THE GOOD TIMES ROLLED ON. ONE NIGHT WHEN I WAS ENJOYing a drink by the pool with Sam and a Dallas artist named Perry Nichols, Sam pushed me in. He knew damn well I couldn't swim. When I accidentally got my slick, wet hands on the pool's edge, Sam pushed one hand loose and was going for the other when Perry pulled him away, thereby saving my life. About ten hours later— I needed time to replace part of the water in my lungs with air—I picked Sam up and threw him down onto the floor. I was trying to break his neck, but I failed miserably. I only succeeded in snapping his lower leg bone in a cross-hair break. Perry said Sam kicked me in the crotch as I picked him up. That's what probably tilted my aim a bit.

When Dustin Hoffman was in England making *Straw Dogs* for Sam, the *New York Times* quoted him as saying, "Don't ask me what the *real* Sam Peckinpah is like, because I have no idea. It's ironic that he's alive now. He's a gunfighter in an age when we're flying to the moon."

Well spoken, Mr. Hoffman.

I recently sat down with screenwriter David Peckinpah, Sam's nephew, over a cup of coffee, to discuss his late uncle. I asked him how he would describe Sam. David stopped eating, stared off through the wall somewhere, then shook his head, took a deep breath and said, "A man born too late. He was an outlaw in a society of suits and ties."

If someone were to ask a thousand different people about Sam, he'd get a thousand different answers. And yet there seems to be a thread of agreement about his longing for the old ways of, "your word is your bond." He had an attitude toward life that said, "I'll die before I'll let you dig a posthole on my little piece of earth."

It was with *The Wild Bunch* that Sam broke into the mainstream of

BLACK HATS

BY LOREN D. ESTLEMAN
& DALE L. WALKER

Ringo
Stark Wilson
Trampas
El Commandante
Lucky Ned Pepper
Scar
Butch Cavendish
Luke Plummer
Frank Miller
Mongo
Tim Strawn
Liberty Valance
Gold Hat
Blue Duck
Curley Bill

The two great Mexican actors, Emilio (El-Indio) Hernandez (top) and Jorge Russek (bottom) in "The Wild Bunch," Mexico 1968. From the collection of Max Evans

American filmmakers. It just happened to be a Western, but it holds its own with the best of any genre. He was crucified as a worshiper of blood and violence, but he was also highly praised as a brave man who revealed hidden parts of the human soul while showing us how *real* violence destroys and inflicts terrible harm. The slow-motion battle shots that Sam directed through the sharp eye of cinematographer Lucien Ballard obviously revealed that fact, made it clear whether one believed in it or hated it. It changed motion pictures forever, that slow-motion, lonely dying, and sadly enough it instigated so many poor imitations that it helped to doom the successful Western myth as well.

After that he made the soft, lovely, lyrical *The Ballad of Cable Hogue,* which had only enough cursory and justified violence to salt it. It is hard to imagine in any film, much less a Western, a more touching and poetic scene than Jason Robards giving Stella Stevens an outdoor bath and singing the haunting Richard Gillis theme, "Butterfly Morning." The two actors had never been better.

Sam's unusual temperament truly became legendary on that picture. Hounded day after day by ceaseless rain, trapped at a solitary hotel on Lake Mead, many of the crew broke under the strain. Sam fired and rehired eighty people before he completed shooting. The film went way over budget, of course, and it was leaked to the press that a maniac was running amuck in the Nevada desert. In truth, it was the one time for sure that Sam hung tough against all comers and got the picture he wanted. Many critics now consider *The Ballad of Cable Hogue* the equal of *The Wild Bunch* and *Ride the High Country. USA Today* ranked all three in the top twelve Westerns on videocassette. That's one hell of a percentage.

The Getaway was simply a wild modern Western frolic of action with Steve McQueen and Ali McGraw. Slim Pickens, who had a modest part, stole the movie at the end. He once told me, "By golly, that Sam worked Old Steve and Ali around so they'd be together so smooth there wasn't any way they could help uh-fallin' in love." When the picture started, Ali was married to producer Robert Evans, then the head of a major studio. A short time later, McGraw divorced Evans and married McQueen. Once,

John Ford's Mythic West

BY SCOTT CUPP

John Ford, together with Howard Hawks, created a cinematic view of the West that has not yet been equalled by other filmmakers. When people think of the "Classic Western Film," they think of films such as *The Searchers, My Darling Clementine,* or *The Man Who Shot Liberty Valance.*

Throughout his long career in Hollywood, John Ford returned to the Western film again and again. He made more than forty silent Western films in his early days, but he's most remembered for his later sound work, both Western and non-Western. He employed a select handful of actors to help present that vision of the West—stars like John Wayne, Ward Bond, Henry Fonda, James Stewart, and Richard Widmark. Though Ford rarely used them together in any one picture, they star in eleven of the twelve feature Westerns he directed. Only *Sergeant Rutledge,* with Woody Strode in the title role in one of the first establishment Hollywood Westerns with a sympathetic black lead, does not. Ford also supported his fine leads with a strong coterie of character actors, including Ben Johnson and Victor McLaglen.

What is it about the John Ford Westerns that makes people say, "This is what the classic Western is all about?" Ford's films are probably the most romanticized depictions of the West. Unlike the films of Howard Hawks, they emphasize the traditional Western myth and feature heroic (almost mythic) characters. They're infused with a fine sense of action and wonder. Ford's primary theme was the advancement of civilization against the wilderness, and it figured heavily in many of his non-Western films, notably in *The Grapes of Wrath.*

The Searchers is arguably the best Western film ever made, and it features John Wayne in his finest role as the mythic Western loner, Ethan Edwards. The major star isn't John Wayne or Jeffrey Hunter, rather, it's the formidable and striking landscape. John Ford was noted for his early use of Monument Valley, Utah, as the archetypical Western setting. Throughout *The Searchers,* it's this stark, unforgiving, yet hauntingly beautiful land, more than the Indians, that opposes the efforts of the search and emerges as the focus of the film.

John Ford's films are best typified by a line from *The Man Who Shot Liberty Valance:* "When the legend becomes fact, print the legend." More than any previous director, John Ford understood the legend of the mythic West, and brought it to its cinematic pinnacle.

Henry Fonda as Wyatt Earp in "My Darling Clementine" (1946 Fox)

in private and after a few cups of the brown, I asked Sam about it. He turned that pinched-looking face slowly toward me, looked at me out of those dark, mystical Peckinpah eyes, and said, "Yes. It helped the love scenes between them...and...I finally got to shove it to a studio boss."

Junior Bonner flowed more in the line of *Cable Hogue*. Steve McQueen played a slipping rodeo rider returning to his hometown's frontier-days celebration. The casting was wondrous, with Robert Preston as the father, Ida Lupino as the mother, and Joe Don Baker as the safe, stay-at-home brother. Casey Tibbs and Ben Johnson, both world-champion rodeo hands, were also on the picture. Sam was editing *Straw Dogs* while he was shooting Jeb Rosebrook's fine script for *Junior Bonner*. I'm sure the producer, Joe Wizan, was amazed when Sam came in on budget and delivered a top-ranked modern Western as well.

Since I've never seen *Deadly Companions*, Sam's first Western, I will only comment briefly. Brian Keith suggested that Sam be the director because of his work on *The Westerner* series. Sam claimed John Ford recommended him. They probably both did. The film got mixed, mostly poor reviews, but Sam was picked out as a promising new director.

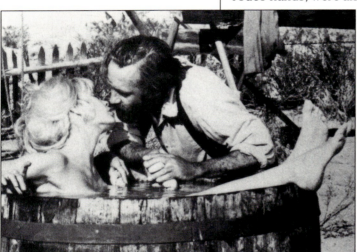

Jason Robards and Stella Stevens in Sam Peckinpah's "The Ballad of Cable Hogue" (1970 Warner Bros.)

There are only two more Peckinpah Westerns worth discussing, one of the Old and the other of the New. *Pat Garrett and Billy the Kid* was almost a good Old Western. It did have some great Peckinpah moments, but it didn't quite make it. The editing was taken out of Sam's hands, so who knows what it might have been.

Sam's worst Western was the modern story of *Bring Me the Head of Alfredo Garcia*. Ironically, it was one of the best concepts he'd ever worked with, from an idea by his long-time, all-around helper, Frank Kawolski. It was also the only film over which Sam had complete control, but by then the man who left us a personal image that will remain as long as there is knowledge or caring for the great American West had mostly burned himself up. The monumental dissipations of both his mind and his body had invaded the camera of his brain.

Whether the man was loved or hated, whether his work was loved or hated, it's for sure that Sam will be missed, for he was an indelible human being as well as a master moviemaker. Toward the end, Sam was like an old cowboy who'd had too many fingers jerked off by the rope—he could still toss the loop, but he was missing the steer's head. I sure wish he'd had a few more loops to toss. ■

SUPPORTING ACTORS

SIDEKICKS

BY ABRAHAM HOFFMAN

EVER SINCE SANCHO PANZA SIGHED IN RESIGNATION AND ACCOMPA-
nied Don Quixote in his quest for hostile windmills, picaresque heroes
have needed someone to offer sage advice or comic relief. No area of
popular entertainment, however, has relied on the loyal friend as much
as the sub-category of Westerns aimed at a young audience, usually male
between the ages of eight and eighty. These loyal friends were called
"sidekicks," and no true Western hero traveled without one. Often
bearded and in nondescript clothing—in contrast to the exaggerated
costumes of some cowboy heroes—sidekicks employed a vast repertoire of euphemistic curses ("Dad-gum it!" seemed to be a favorite exple-
tive), offered conservative and usually unnecessary advice without being
asked for it ("Don't go into the cave, Roy!"), and needed rescuing almost
as often as the school teacher or the rancher's daughter.

Sidekicks became a requisite for Western heroes as a result of their
popularization in B-Western films, radio and television programs and
comic books. Their presence offered a respite from continuous action,
an opportunity for horseplay while the villain put his nefarious plans into
action. Some sidekicks became so popular that they achieved fame in
their own right. There were actors who made careers out of playing sidekicks, providing the comic relief while their knight-errant friends went
about the serious business of righting wrongs. George "Gabby" Hayes,
Fuzzy Knight, Andy Clyde, Smiley Burnette, Pat Buttram, Leo Carillo and
Andy Devine, among others, all enjoyed celebrity sidekick status. they
acted as foils for the likes of Roy Rogers, Gene Autry, William Boyd (as
Hopalong Cassidy), Buster Crabbe and other Western stars, over lengthy
periods of time and in several media.

Take Gabby Hayes, for example, possibly the quintessential sidekick.
He must have looked old when he was young, for he always seemed to
play the same cantankerous old codger from the thirties until his last
roles in the early 1960s. At various times Hayes played Windy Holliday
to Boyd's Hopalong, as Gabby to Roy Rogers and as a pal to John Wayne
in many of Wayne's early Western films. On rare occasions, as in "Man

TOP: Roy Rogers with Pat Brady, his
sidekick for "The Bells of Coronado"
(1950 Republic)

BOTTOM: Hopalong Cassidy (William
Boyd) and Windy (George Hayes).

TOP: Pat Buttram sidekicks for Gene Autry

BOTTOM: In a classic scene from "Stagecoach" (1939 Walter Wanger Productions), veteran sidekick Andy Devine drives hell-bent for leather as the Sheriff (George Bancroft) scans the horizon for renegade Apaches.

of Conquest," the epic story of Sam Houston and the Texas Revolution, Hayes rose above sidekick status, but for most of his career he played the sidekick role. As Hoppy's friend Hayes even earned his own comic book, courtesy of Fawcett Publications, and (at least in the comics) he had a performing trick horse named Corker whose main talent was moving sideways on command. Other actors came to sidekick roles later in their careers. Andy Devine had played a feature role in the classic film "Stagecoach," and his gravelly voice and large belly made him a familiar character actor in the 1940s. In the early days of television Devine took the part of Jingles, a fictional friend to a highly fictionalized Wild Bill Hickok, played by Guy Madison. Devine's face for a time rivaled his handsome friend's on boxes of Kellogg's Sugar Corn Pops, as the cereal was labeled in a less consumer/health-conscious era.

Another character actor who evolved into an ongoing sidekick role was Leo Carrillo. Having played everyone from river pirates to Pancho Villa, Carrillo joined Duncan Renaldo as the hugely successful team of the Cisco Kid and Pancho. Playing to a young audience, Renaldo and Carrillo filmed the "Cisco Kid" television series, appeared in parades, and forever identified Cisco and Pancho as a happy-go-lucky pair of travelers encountering obstacles which they overcame by wit rather than violence. Ironically, the original Cisco Kid, as created by O. Henry in his 1907 short story "The Caballero's Way," was a cold-blooded killer who had no sidekick. It should also be noted that Carrillo's portrayal of Pancho followed an earlier sidekick, "Gordito," played by Chris-Pin Martin so offensively that Latin American film distributors threatened to boycott the Cisco Kid theatrical pictures unless the offending stereotype was changed.

Gene Autry and Roy Rogers, who between them defined a Western hero who appealed to juvenile audiences, followed the formula they had devised faithfully through movies, radio, television and comics. the formula included exaggerated Western clothing, a trick horse, musical ability, avoidance of romance and either companions or sidekicks, sometimes both. Dale Evans was a companion, but Gabby Hayes was a sidekick for Roy.

The distinction between sidekick and companion merits notice. The line was not always clear, but it could be drawn if the relationship was one of dramatic support rather than buffoonery. Noah Beery, Jr., Edgar Buchanan, Dennis Weaver and Buddy Ebsen played loyal companions, but they weren't sidekicks. Their roles were played on a more adult level, as in Weaver's portrayal of Chester in "Gunsmoke" or Ebsen's George Russell in the "Davy Crockett" episodes. Gene Autry often used Johnny Bond as a companion on his radio adventures, but his sidekicks were Smiley Burnette and Pat Buttram. For both Autry and Rogers, as well as the radio version of Red Ryder, radio offered more adult themes than the usual fare found at the Saturday matinees.

Sidekick Fuzzy St. John pals around with Lash LaRue

As to particular characters, Tonto seems an exception to the rule, since the Lone Ranger played to a young audience. Tonto's position was clearly delineated at the beginning of each radio program as the Lone Ranger's "faithful Indian companion." No buffoonery for Tonto, and radio actor John Todd and television's Jay Silverheels, played the role straight. Little Beaver, as a young Indian adopted by Red Ryder, also seemed to be in a class by himself. But Red Ryder did have a sidekick, an old codger named Buckskin Blodgett, featured mainly on the radio series.

Some Western protagonists in their early incarnation had no sidekicks. Hopalong Cassidy, for example, enjoyed the company of his fellow Bar-20 ranch hands, but his rank was first among equals. The original Cisco Kid, as noted, needed no Pancho. But Wild Bill Hickok probably could have used a friend in that Deadwood saloon.

In some cases Western stars went beyond one sidekick to in-

WHY A SIDEKICK?

A hero doesn't brag—so a sidekick does it for him.

A hero never doubts—but a sidekick can point out dangers and show his fears.

A hero is the strong, silent type—so a loquacious sidekick can talk up a storm to fill in the details.

A hero stands alone—but while a sidekick can't be as tough as the hero, he's always there to believe in the hero, to be a loyal friend.

A hero stays focused on his goal—but a sidekick can indulge in gossip, get sidetracked into trouble and provide comic relief.

A hero has no flaws—so the sidekick is there to remind him of human frailties.

A hero needs someone to talk to—so the sidekick is there for company after the hero has kissed his horse and said goodbye to the schoolmarm.

clude a full retinue of friends. Gene Autry's Melody Ranch stands out, with the Cass County Boys providing musical background for his radio show. Artist Fred Harman provided a family of sorts for his Red Ryder comic strip, including Aunt Duchess, owner of the Painted Valley Ranch, plus Little Beaver and Buckskin Blodgett. All of these characters appeared fairly regularly in the comic strip and on the radio, much less so in the movies. The Lone Ranger found his long-lost nephew, Dan Reid, and his horse Silver even obligingly sired a son, Victor, for Dan to ride. Britt Reid, the crime-fighting Green Hornet, was a modern-day descendant of Dan Reid. Tom Mix (actually Curley Bradley) enjoyed repartee with Sheriff Mike Shaw, and he invited every young radio listener to send in Ralston boxtops and become part of his Straight Shooters family. Roy Rogers and Dale Evans, thought married in real life, maintained a platonic if unexplained friendship in films, radio, television and comics. Of course, Roy never explained the incongruity of his elaborate Western wear in the 20th century. The Three Mesquiteers, including at one time or another Ray Corrigan, John Wayne, Raymond Hatton and Max Terhune, enjoyed camaraderie; but no one, excepting possibly Terhune (the leading cowboy ventriloquist, if not the only one) might own up to sidekick rather than companion status.

The era of the sidekick in motion pictures and television ended with the arrival of the so-called "adult Western." Story lines became more complex, and the blurring of the line between good and evil made the traditional white hats vs. black hats obsolete. Western heroes either retired or matured with the changing Western concept. Roy Rogers started a franchise of roast beef sandwich outlets, Gene Autry bought radio and television stations and a baseball team and Randolph Scott retired, as did Duncan Renaldo. Matt Dillon's relationship to Chester was Marshal to deputy, friends to be sure, but not for comic relief. Enter also the era of the "spaghetti" Western, a genre that not only could do without sidekicks, its heroes didn't even need names, as exemplified by Clint Eastwood in his films. Pat Buttram found new work on "Green Acres". John Wayne, in most of the films made during his last decade as a star, made it a point to hire old friends, delighting *aficionados* who could note the presence of Bruce Cabot, Hank Worden and other actors who had devoted their careers to the Western. But they weren't sidekicks.

As a postscript: sidekicks are not extinct. In many ways science-fiction films cater to the same young audience that attended those Saturday matinees; six-guns may have been traded in for ray-guns, but the plots seems suspiciously familiar. And who are C-3PO and R2D2 but Gabby Hayes and Smiley Burnette in a galaxy far away? ■

SUPPORTING ACTORS

YAKIMA CANUTT AND THE GOWER GULCH GANG

BY JAMES M. REASONER & L.J. WASHBURN

Yakima Canutt (courtesy of John Hagner, Hollywood Stuntmen's Hall of Fame, Moab, UT)

ALMOST ANYONE WHO HAS EVER WATCHED A WESTERN MOVIE HAS seen the famous chase scene in John Ford's masterpiece *Stagecoach.* One of the Apache pursuing the coach leaps from his horse onto the team, but before he can do any damage, the Ringo Kid (John Wayne, of course) shoots him. He's knocked from his precarious perch and falls to his death under the hooves of the team and the wheels of the coach. Later, the Ringo Kid makes a similar jump from the box to the team. What many people don't know is that the actor who made *both* leaps was really master stuntman Yakima Canutt. This is only one example of the many times Canutt played more than one part in the same scene; in his day, he doubled for practically every actor who rode a horse or strapped on a six-gun.

And Canutt, probably the greatest stuntman of all time, was only one of an illustrious group called the Gower Gulch Gang.

In the early years of movie-making in Hollywood, the Western was king. Everyone has heard of *The Great Train Robbery,* Bronco Billy Anderson, William S. Hart, Tom Mix, and all the other early cowboy stars. All the studios, small and large, cranked out Westerns along with their other products. The Westerns had to have riding and roping and shooting, so the studios turned to the men who could best handle those chores—the cowboys.

By the early 1900s, civilization had crept in on most of the Old West. Men who had been practically raised on horseback suddenly found themselves unable to get work as ranch hands. Unhappy at other jobs, especially when they couldn't be done from the back of a good horse, some of them found a second home in the movies. It may have been make-believe, but it was as close as they could come to what they had known.

They were called "riding extras." Any time a script called for a posse or an outlaw gang or a cavalry troop or a band of Indians, a casting director would send the word to a small Hollywood speakeasy dubbed "the Waterhole." The cowboys waited there for a call to work, and when the word came, they would appear the next morning, bright and early, at the studio. They came "in costume" as far as the studio was concerned, though the outfits were usually just their own regular clothes and boots and hats. A day's work paid five to ten dollars, plus a box lunch. For those wages, they rode and rode and rode all over Bronson Canyon, Red Rocks, Mixville and the other Western locations around Los Angeles. Many times they rode their own horses, which they stabled at a barn called the Sunset Corral. Some of them became particularly adept at horse falls, and so was born the professional stuntman. Often there was no extra pay for dangerous stunts, and many a cowboy went home from location with bruises and busted bones.

Though the job had its drawbacks, the cowboys loved it. Their camaraderie and rough humor livened up many a location shooting. Their names are for the most part forgotten now, but men like Jack Montgomery, Hank Bell, Bill Gillis, Jack Padjeon, and Neal Hart played a large part in the growth of the Western film. In later years they came to be known as the Gower Gulch Gang, after Gower Avenue, where many of the small movie studios were located. One man who came out of this group to become an Academy Award winner was Enos Edward "Yakima" Canutt.

Yakima Canutt, Rita Cansino (Rita Hayworth) and Tex Ritter make "Trouble in Texas" (1937 Grand National)

Born November 29, 1896 in Colfax, Washington, Canutt picked up his nickname as a teenage rodeo rider. A newspaper reporter called him the "Cowboy from Yakima," and the name stuck. He became a World's Champion Cowboy and gained a deserved reputation as one of the best riders to ever hit the rodeo circuit. During World War I, he worked for the French Army, breaking horses for their cavalrymen. By the 1920s he had moved from rodeos to films and starred in a series of features for various small studios. As a silent star in these action-filled pictures, he was well-nigh perfect.

When his voice proved unsuitable for talkies, he began to specialize in character and villain roles. At the same time, he stood in as a stunt double for John Wayne, Roy Rogers, Gene Autry and many other Western stars. He can be recognized by his distinctive riding style. He was the second-unit director at Republic Pictures for years, and he directed several B Western features. His last major work was staging the chariot race in the film *Ben Hur,* in which his son did many of the stunts. In 1967, after he retired, he received a special Academy Award for his contributions to the art of filmmaking.

Yakima Canutt died May 24, 1986. He may well have been the last of the old Gower Gulch Gang. They brought something very special to decades of Western films—professionalism, realism, and an utter dedication to their work. The movies may have just been a job to them, but they were the kind of men to whom doing the job and doing it well was all that really mattered. There are still stuntmen in Hollywood, but not like the members of the Gower Gulch Gang.

When it came to Westerns, they were the real thing. ■

WAY OUT WESTERNS

The Beast of Hollow Mountain (1956)
Via the stop-action special effects of Willis O'Brien (*King Kong*), Guy Madison and his cowboys try to rope a tyrannosaurus rex that lives in a mountain cavern.

The Black Scorpion (1957)
Willis O'Brien turns his special effects to overgrown arachnids for the cowboys to rope.

Curse of the Undead (1959)
Vampire gunfighter Michael Pate wears black, and preacher Eric Fleming opposes him and his blood-sucking brides to save Kathleen Crowley from undeath.

Billy the Kid vs. Dracula (1965)
William Beaudine directed this low-budget cult film in which John Carradine hams it up as the vampire uncle of the Kid's sweetheart.

Jesse James Meets Frankenstein's Daughter (1966)
William Beaudine's last cult film, in which the Kid defends children in Mexico from the fiendish experiments of the infamous baron's daughter.

Moon Zero Two (1969)
Hammer films transferred the West's tired, poor and huddled masses of cliches to the moon in what they billed as the first space Western.

The Valley of Gwangi (1969)
James Franciscus finds and ropes a tiny prehistoric horse and a very large, very hungry tyrannosaurus rex in a Mexican valley, abetted by Ray Harryhausen's excellent stop-action special effects.

The Beguiled (1971)
In this gothic horror story, Clint Eastwood is a wounded Union soldier trapped in a seminary populated by strange Southern ladies.

High Plains Drifter (1972)
Eastwood's tribute to Leone's spaghetti Westerns, a surreal tale of vengeance from beyond the grave.

The White Buffalo (1977)
Terrible special effects destroy a great idea, in which Charles Bronson as Wild Bill Hickok and Will Sampson as Crazy Horse team up *a la Moby Dick* to destroy a supernatural killer beast.

Shadow of Chakira (1978)
It's all downhill after Slim Pickens dies in a Civil War battle at the beginning and sends his comrade, played by Joe Don Baker, after a diamond mine guarded by vengeful Indian spirits.

Outland (1981)
Sean Connery does a credible job of playing a futuristic version of *High Noon's* Will Kane as a U.S. Marshal against drug dealers in a mining colony on Io; this time, the clock is a digital display.

Timerider, the Adventures of Lyle Swan (1983)
Cross-country motorcyclist Fred Ward accidentally rides his bike through a top-secret time warp and ends up in the Old West; he meets up with Peter Coyote as the black-clad villain who'll stop at nothing to get "that ridin' machine," and with Belinda Bauer as the sexy lady bandit.

Pale Rider (1985)
Clint Eastwood once again assumes the mantle of spectral justice, this time in response to a young girl's prayer. It's a strange but effective blend of *Heaven With a Gun, Shane* and *High Plains Drifter.*

Mad at the Moon (1991)
Rejected by Hart Bochner, the handsome young gunfighter she loves, Mary Stewart Masterson instead marries his farmer half-brother, who has a hairy problem with the full moon.

Veteran actor Jack Elam

SIDEWINDERS

BY LOREN D. ESTLEMAN & DALE L. WALKER

SOMEWHERE BETWEEN THE SOCIOPATH AND THE GILA MONSTER, AT an evolutionary level somewhat higher than the common cockroach but significantly lower than the jackal, there is the sidewinder. Vaguely human in shape, he combines the conscience and morality of a lesser invertebrate with the table manners of a bilge pump, and he lays a trail of slime and treachery from the Kansas buffalo camps to the California gold towns. Unlike the villain, who is a recognizable specimen of *homo sapiens* who merely does evil in the pursuit of money or power, the sidewinder metes out pain and grief for the pure joy of watching his (and sometimes *her*) victims suffer.

And yet, the screen Western owes the breed a nod of thanks. How far would the Zachary Scotts and the James Gregorys get in their perfidy without the rattlesnake tactics of an Anthony Zerbe or a Harris Yulin? Without sidewinders like Victor French or Eli Wallach or Dan Duryea to give them reasonable cause, why would the John Waynes and the Clint Eastwoods and the Randolph Scotts take to the vengeance trail? And how entertaining would the Western films be without them?

Many actors (Christopher George, for example) who exhibit panache in portraying the true Western sidewinder, genus scumbag, are also quite adept at playing other, more sympathetic Western characters, and can even carry the starring role in Westerns and other genres. Possibly the lowest (and therefore most successful) of the frontier sidewinders was Strother Martin, he of the straggly, winter-killed hair and the guilty possum's eyeteeth grin. He is probably best known as the farm warden ("What we have here is a failure to communicate.") in the post-modern Western prison story, *Cool Hand Luke.* It's true that he could play sympathetic roles, such as the horse trader hopelessly outclassed by Kim Darby's plucky precociousness in *True Grit,* and he could even manage to be lovable, as with the ill-fated mine owner ("That's what you get when you've been living in Bolivia for fifteen years; you get colorful.") in *Butch Cassidy and the Sundance Kid.*

But dedicated Strother-watchers recognize these as rare deviations;

we know and love him best as the lowlife who, with that other prototypic human coyote portrayed by L. Q. Jones, scavenged the corpses for gold teeth and other valuables after the shoot-out that opened *The Wild Bunch.* Nor will his fans forget the way he blew Raquel Welch's screen husband in two with a shotgun from ambush in *Hannie Caulder,* then strutted in front of his equally benightedbrothers and boasted, "Did I *git* him?"

A word about those brothers, Jack Elam and Ernest Borgnine. Multi-talented former studio accountant Elam, gosh-eyed and bitten-bearded, could play endearing town drunks and desert-crazed old-timers with the same ease as he played sidewinders and hardcases. Borgnine won an Oscar for playing the nice guy in the non-Western, *Marty,* but as the simian sergeant who beat Frank Sinatra to death in *From Here to Eternity* he proved that the sidewinder species wasn't confined to the Great Plains. As fraternal bandits in *Hannie Caulder,* Martin, Elam, and Borgnine were the perfect argument for family necktie parties in extreme cases.

In the pantheon of the celluloid West, that family is matched only by the clan of the Lincolnesque John Anderson, the snake-lidded John Davis Chandler, the wooden-faced L. Q. Jones (again!), the neanderthalic Warren Oates, and their family pride, James Drury (better and more respectably known as television's "Virginian"). They assayed to welcome Mariette Hartley into the brood with a down-home gang rape in *Ride the High Country.*

A logical runner-up family of sidewinders would be Donald Pleasance, the demented preacher who, along with his troglodytic sons (including the inimitable Bruce Dern), hounded Charlton Heston and Joan Hackett in *Will Penny.* Fans may remember that Dern first attracted attention on the small screen in "Gunsmoke" as the scummy kin of Dodge City gunsmith Newly O'Brien's hillbilly girlfriend. No true Dern aficionado could forget his performance as the gaunt, horse-toothed rustler who backshot John Wayne in *The Cowboys.* It's a rare sidewinder who can get the best of the Duke, even with downright treachery.

R. G. Armstrong, Robert Middleton, Geoffrey Lewis, John Vernon—the appalling role call goes on. Morgan Woodward, Matt Dillon's prow-nosed, pockmarked, gravel-voiced nemesis from the mountains in episode after episode, wasn't always quite as lowdown and dirty as the typical sidewinder, but he made up for it in sheer ferocity and persistence. Bill McKinney's excesses as Missouri redleg Captain Terrill in *The Outlaw Josey Wales* earned him every inch of the broken saber Clint Eastwood drove up into his rotten heart. Neville Brand—Al Capone to a generation of fans of "The Untouchables"—looked equally at home as the Duke's merciless but likeable Indian companion in *Cahill, U.S. Mar-*

Randy rides alone, but only because he's too cheap to hire a sidekick.

Gregory Peck outdraws Richard Jaeckel in "The Gunfighter."
(1950 Fox)

shal, and as the evil, obsessed one-handed posseman in the otherwise unwatchable *Deadly Trackers.*

Their names don't ring with the instant recognition of Gable, Cooper, or Wayne, but they'd be sorely missed if they were absent. Dub Taylor and Edgar Buchanan are not as well known as the scores of stubble-faced, derby-hatted prairie rats they've played onscreen. Millions of moviegoers familiar with the hollow-cheeked, burning-eyed religious fanaticism of Royal Dano, and the tobacco-drooling brutishness of Albert Salmi couldn't pick them out of the credits. But they and their multitudinous sidewinder brethren have enlivened many an otherwise forgettable oater. Hollywood would be in their debt if they hadn't already stolen so many scenes along with everything else but the cameras. ◼

ACT V: THE BIG SKY ON THE SMALL SCREEN

FADE OUT SLICKS—FADE IN TV

BY THOMAS THOMPSON

IN THE VERY LATE 1950s AND THE EARLY 1960s, TELEVISION IN HOLLY-wood was like a newborn colt. It knew by instinct that it had the potential to become a triple-crown winner, but its legs were still wobbly. It sought the security of its mother, and in Hollywood, that mother was film—the motion picture. And what, in the history of Hollywood, had never failed? The Western. Some wise man in Hollywood said, "Let's do a TV West-ern." The TV community was highly imitative even then, so every other wise man in Hollywood said, "What a splendid idea! Let us, too, do a Western."

And so it came to pass that in those glorious days there was little else on the small screen but Westerns. A Western story writer who had a bit of a track record and could adapt to the film media had to beat back the offers with a club. I had the uncanny luck of being in the right place at the right time, and I found myself in Hollywood. There may have been a bit more to it than that, for I saw writers of much more stature than I fall flat on their faces under the demands of the newly created electronic monster.

In the first place, you had to *tell* a story. I mean verbally. Some of the best darned writers in the business stood before a menial story editor, who was probably in awe of the writer, and mumbled a bunch of gibber-

"Never borrow trouble, or cross a river before you reach it."

OLIVER LOVING, CATTLEMAN

ish that didn't get them the assignment. That same writer, alone in his room, would have made a small masterpiece of the story he had in mind. Sadly, he didn't survive in Hollywood. It was my luck to have been a saloon singer in my past, so talking didn't bother me. It was said that given two people on a street corner, I would either organize a club or give a speech. I met some nice people, some of whom were even kind enough to say they had read my published stories.

Within a short time I found myself swept up in what was to me a glamorous business. I got to visit sets, I met stars—let's face it, I loved the whole crazy mess, and they paid me more than I'd seen since the days of the serial in the *Saturday Evening Post.* Since the *Post* and the other slick magazine markets were no more, I thought, "What the heck?"

For about a year June and I tried commuting between Santa Rosa, California, and L.A. It's approximately six hundred miles one way, rather a long commute. We had an apartment in West Los Angeles, but our home was in Santa Rosa. I'd go to L.A. to tell my story and get an assignment, then I'd go home to Santa Rosa to write the outline, and then I'd go back to L.A. and talk to the story editor and he'd say O.K., and then I'd go back to Santa Rosa and write the first draft and mail it in, and then they would sometimes notify me they were against a deadline so they were hiring a local writer to re-write me—and share *my* rerun money— and I got to thinking that was a bum deal, so we sold the house and moved to Hollywood. Whew!

The only lesson here is, you gotta move to the studios, because the studios ain't gonna move to you.

I ACTUALLY HAD A BIT OF A BREAK. MGM, WHICH WAS BIG AT THE time, owned a story by John Cunningham. This was shortly after his *Tin Star* became *High Noon.* The story was *The Return of Johnny Burro,* and I thought it was one of the best short stories I'd ever read. My New York agents, Brandt & Brandt, used Famous Artists as their Hollywood representatives. Ben Benjamin at Famous Artists knew of my interest in that particular story. When MGM decided to activate it, Ben got me the job of doing a "treatment" on it—a few pages that showed how the short story could be turned into a full-length movie.

I soon found that it couldn't be done because of the vast difference between the printed page and what you see on the screen. But in the process I made friends with the producer, Armand Deutch, and MGM had a writer under contract named Rod Serling, and I came up with a completely new idea and they had Robert Taylor under contract and they could get Julie London and there was this new actor by the name of John Cassavetes...

And that's how things happen in Hollywood. I was writing a novel at the time with a working title of *Saddle the Wind.* The folks at MGM thought that was a right fine title. They offered me $500 for it and since that was a pretty good rate for three words, I sold it to them. That's how I got my first screen credit. I did the story; Rod Serling did the screenplay.

There I was in Hollywood. The studio was paying for a rather sumptuous apartment, and I had a $500 a week salary and all expenses...I was very careful about the expenses. The apartment had a Pullman kitchen; June cooked our meals and we kept the receipts from the market. The first week I timidly submitted our expenses and...gosh! They were almost $50 and I was prepared to cut that down some. The man looked at me in amazement and said, "Where do you eat?" I said, "In the apartment." He said, "For godsakes take your wife out to dinner and dancing at Ciro's or someplace..." Shortly after that A.B. Guthrie, Jr., who was working at

James Arness and Amanda Blake in "Gunsmoke" (courtesy of CBS)

Fox, came over, and we all went out on the town. Bud set me straight — Hollywood people look with awe on people who spend money.

We had lived in Portland, Oregon, for several years during the time when it seemed to be the writing capitol of America. When the editors came to the West Coast, they came to Portland first. We had Ernest Haycox, Robert and Victoria Case, John and Ward Hawkins, Steve McNeil, N. B. Stone, Jr., and Giff Cheshire. At the same time Richard Neuberger and Al Stump were writing articles, and nearby were Dwight Newton and Bill Gulick and Wayne Overholser, and on and on. Shortly after I went to Hollywood, we had what was known as "The Oregon Invasion."

Some of the Oregon writers had been writing for the *Post* and *Colliers,* the slicks, et al, and since those magazines were defunct, they, like I,

figured they were too old to suffer the indignity of poverty. So they tried their luck with television. Some made it, some did not. Dick Neuberger became a U.S. Senator—a sensible decision. Bob Case did some TV work but was never entirely comfortable in his new surroundings. Ernie Haycox had sold some big movies from his *Post* and *Colliers* serials and didn't have to go through the hassle. Steve McNeil did some work here, some there, but he always yearned for the Oregon coast, for the glory days when he sold more than one hundred stories to the *Post*—I think that's close to a record. Bo Stone did quite well with television and also turned out a story for the fine motion picture, *Ride The High Country*. I took to the crazy business like a duck to water, and so did John and Ward Hawkins. I wound up running the story end of "Bonanza" with John as my assistant, while right down the hall Ward was ramrodding "High Chaparral." Those were hectic but happy days.

The first TV show I ever tried after I finished the MGM picture was "Wagon Train." John Hawkins, Steve McNeil and I sat down and went over my story. They had me tell it to them. I rehearsed that telling as if I were rehearsing a play. Then my agent got me an appointment with Howard Christie, the producer of the show at Revue, the big production company located at the old Republic studios.

The writer is the low man on the totem pole in Hollywood. There was no reserved parking spot for me, no red carpet. I parked on the street and showed my one-visit-only pass to the guard at the gate. I was admitted under what seemed to me suspicious scrutiny, and in time I was ushered into the presence of that highest of all beings, the producer.

Howard "Red" Christie didn't look like a producer. A former All-American lineman from the University of California, he was still robust and fit and had a booming, genial voice that matched his bulk. Dwight Newton had worked as a story editor on "Wagon Train," so I had an opening wedge for conversation. I also knew Frank Gruber who, teamed with Nat Holt, was doing "Tales of Wells Fargo" at the same studio. After five minutes with Howard Christie I felt I had known him all my life. He's retired now and lives not too far from me. I still consider him my "father" insofar as television writing is concerned.

At any rate, I *told* my story as I'd rehearsed it with Steve and John, and I added a few fillips of my own. I paced...I waved my arms...I slapped leather...I suffered in the desert heat...and Red Christie nodded. He could *see* my story, and that was the whole point. I got the assignment to go ahead with the story outline, for which I would be paid. You put not one word on paper in Hollywood unless you are paid for it.

Since I'd rehearsed my story so thoroughly, the little six-page outline was a cinch. Within two days I was given the word to go into first draft.

HOW OKLAHOMA! WON THE WAR AND OTHER MUSICAL LEGENDS OF THE WEST

The Broadway cast of "Oklahoma!" (left of surrey) Lee Dixon as Will Parker and Celeste Holm as Ado Annie; (in surrey) Alfred Drake as Curley and Joan Roberts as Laurey (courtesy of Special Collections Photo Archives)

If there's one piece of music that instantly brings to mind the legendary West, it's Gioacchino Rossini's overture to *William Tell*. Originally designed to characterize a straight-shooter of European legend, for the past fifty years it has heralded the arrival of the inimitable Lone Ranger on radio, screen and television.

But Rossini's stirring overture is by no means the West's only legendary theme song, any more than it's the only such piece related to a classical source. It was Western and American folk music, as well as the majestic land itself, that inspired Czech composer Antonin Dvorak to incorporate the rhythms and themes of the West in his "New World Symphony" in 1882.

Aaron Copland, a kid from Billy Bonney's hometown of Brooklyn, followed Dvorak's lead and used melodies from traditional cowboy songs in his score for his folk ballets, *Appalachian Spring, Billy the Kid,* and *Rodeo*. Copland's tunes are probably familiar to many a fan of Westerns who doesn't know their source — they've been used as background for Western documentaries, movies and television shows, and even news programs. And *Rodeo*, originally commissioned by Agnes de Mille for the Ballet Russe de Monte Carlo, heavily influenced de Mille's choreography and Richard Rodgers' score for Laurey's "dream ballet" in *Oklahoma!*

That Rodgers and Hammerstein musical became a legend in its own right, and not just because it ran on Broadway from 1943 through 1948, 2202 performances in all. It was the first Broadway musical to use songs to advance the storyline rather than as set pieces. It eloquently expressed simple truths and hopes, often with humor, in songs like "Oh, What a Beautiful Morning," "Surrey With the Fringe on Top" and "I'm Just a Gal Who Cain't Say No." It contained all the basic Western story elements: the battle between good and evil, a love for the land and one's neighbors, the endurance of hope and the value of courage and honor. They were important messages in the dark days of the Second World War, especially for the young men and women who got a chance to see the musical in New York before they left for duty overseas. A Western distillation of all that was important to the American character, *Oklahoma!* reminded America's young warriors what it was they were fighting for.

Composers who score motion pictures and television programs have carried on the tradition of basing their work on classical and folk music. Dimitri Tiomkin in particular wrote some of the finest Western movie scores — for John Wayne's *The Alamo* (1960), he also conducted the orchestra. He won two Oscars for the score of *High Noon* (1952 United Artists), and Tex Ritter's recording of Ned

Washington's lyrics to "Do Not Forsake Me Oh My Darling," became a popular hit. Frankie Laine, who later recorded a cover version of that song, sang Washington's lyrics to Tiomkin's scores for Paramount's *Gunfight at the O.K. Corral* (1957) and the CBS television series, "Rawhide."

Much like Dvorak (and director John Ford), Elmer Bernstein used the land as a character to evoke the legendary magic of the West in his rousing theme for *The Magnificent Seven* (1960 United Artists), which is popularly known as "the Marlboro song." The classical and traditional sounds of the West are there if you listen for them — echoes of Dvorak, Copland and Rossini, of "Turkey in the Straw," "The Old Chisholm Trail" and "The Streets of Laredo" — in Alfred Newman's score for the epic *How the West Was Won* (1962 MGM), in Franz Waxman's suite for *The Furies* (1950 Paramount), in Jerome Moross's score for *The Big Country* (1958 United Artists), and in themes for dozens of Western television shows. Ry Cooder's erie instrumentals for *The Long Riders* (Huka 1980) relies heavily on traditional mountain music, and Bob Dylan's hit, "Knockin' on Heaven's Door," from *Pat Garrett and Billy the Kid* (1973 MGM) could be an unsentimental version of a Ned Washington song. Thanks to these composers, the music of the West survives in an unbroken line from the open prairie to the concert hall to the small screen.

THE WEST'S BESTS

BEST DRESSED: In cavalry uniform or bib-front shirt, campaign hat or Stetson, frock coat or duster, John Wayne heads the list of the fashionably authentic. No real-life cowboy ever looked more at home in a kerchief.

BEST BREAKTHROUGH: Gary Cooper forever disproved the snide comments about his acting range when he wept in *High Noon* (United Artists 1952), anticipating gender liberation by two decades without sacrificing one iota of Marshal Will Kane's manhood.

BEST SIDEKICK: Can anyone match the depth and humor of Ken Curtis as Festus Haggen on "Gunsmoke" (CBS 1955-1975)?

BEST VILLAIN: By far and away, the most menacing villain is Jack Palance as gunfighter Jack Wilson in *Shane* (Paramount 1953).

BEST INDIAN: In anything he does, in particular the famous public service announcement decrying pollution, Iron Eyes Cody is the best Indian actor on the screen. Chief Dan George and Will Sampson are close runners-up.

BEST HEROINE: It's hard to beat Jean Arthur struggling with divided loyalties and affections between her husband (Van Heflin) and the gunfighter (Alan Ladd) in *Shane* (Paramount 1953).

BEST DOC HOLLIDAY: From an impressive field that includes Walter Huston, Jason Robards, and Caesar Romero, we pick Kirk Douglas for his haunted and homicidal performance in *Gunfight at the O.K. Corral* (Paramount 1957).

BEST GUNFIGHT: John Wayne's Ringo Kid versus Tom Tyler's Luke Plummer in *Stagecoach* (United Artists 1939), even though we never get to see it.

Along the way I had picked up a "Wagon Train" script. I'd also had long sessions with Bill Cox and his wife, Lee—she was a top-flight script clerk and probably knew as much about Hollywood as anyone I've ever known. Also, Dwight Newton was still around and John Hawkins had sold a few scripts…I did my homework on script structure and in about four days turned in the finished product. I got a phone call from Howard Christie the next day. He said, and I quote—for the words are engraved in my memory—"This is not only the best "Wagon Train" script I've had, it's one of the best scripts I've ever read." He wanted me to come see him the next day.

The guard at the gate seemed a bit more friendly. I was ushered in with pomp and ceremony to Mr. Christie's inner sanctum. We sat down and went through the script, line for line. It was a story about an Army deserter, and having never been in the army, I had made a few technical mistakes. It was seventy-two pages long; it had been a struggle to get it there, but since the sample script was that long, that's how long I thought it had to be. We cut it to sixty-five pages by cutting the exact words I'd padded in. Howard called his secretary. "Send it to mimeo," he said, "and put through a voucher for final draft."

Her mouth fell open. "Final?" she gasped. "No rewrite?"

"Final," said Howard.

Their short exchange was lost on me. I thought that was how it was supposed to be. I had about a week's work invested and I had a check for $2,500 coming. I was mentally figuring that $2,500 a week was not too bad a salary…then came the dawn.

It seemed I'd become an overnight genius on the Revue lot. They had several shows going—all Westerns—and each one wanted me. One show, with George Montgomery, was in bad shape. The show was "Cimarron City" and they had a sick script that needed a quick fix. Call in the new genius. Watch the new genius fall flat on his face. I rewrote that thing three or four times and couldn't please anyone. The producer was a Hungarian—as nice a man as you'd ever meet—but he didn't understand me and I didn't understand him. I tried to explain *Comancheros* to him. He puzzled for a long time, and then his face erupted in a big grin. "Ah ha!" he said. "Zay are gypsies!" What the hell. Close enough.

They called in Dwight Newton to try to save me; they called in several others. I did end up with my name on the script—heaven knows why—but much more important, I started to learn just a little bit about television. You don't write. You rewrite. That first script of mine had been an out-and-out fluke. In the some 100 scripts I was to write, perhaps no more than three were shot first draft.

Rewrites are not just a perversion of producers and story editors.

Making a filmed television show is a complex business and it's a day by day adjustment until that film is safely in the can. Even then I've seen one of my finished products on the screen and wished to the devil I could change it. It all depends on how the director sees it, on casting, available sets, the weather, and cost. Always the cost. The production manager is watching every penny even though to the layman it seems the studios throw money away by the millions. And sometimes they do. No one ever said the picture business isn't one hell of a gamble.

There's an apocryphal story in Hollywood (it could certainly be true) about an eager young writer who does a fine script on the Custer massacre. An independent producer buys it and his eyes fall on that figure of five thousand Indians. "No matter," he thinks to himself. "We'll get five hundred extras and shoot 'em so they look like five thousand."

Then comes the art director. "There isn't enough money to go on location, so since this will all have to fit on the back lot could we cut down those Indians a bit?"

"No problem," says the producer. "We'll hire a hundred and run 'em from left to right and back. It'll look like five thousand."

The script is rewritten a few times and finally the assistant director breaks it down and puts it on the board.

And here comes the production manager. He's been sharpening pencils and burning midnight oil and he doesn't much care what the story is about, anyway. But the star costs much more than they planned and the cameraman they want is now getting paid twice what he used to get paid, so the above the line (talent) costs are so out of line that the below the line (production) costs have to give a bit. He faces the producer and says, "Would you believe two feathers projecting over a log?"

Those are the problems of Hollywood, and that's why many of our best writers couldn't adapt to the media. In television, and even in full-length features, the original writer has little control over his material. It is writing by committee. It has been cussed and discussed by the six thousand-plus members of the Writers Guild of America, East and West, but they've never reached a solution. Unless a writer can adjust to this basic fact of life, he had better stay out of Hollywood.

I long ago looked at my belt and saw no Pulitzer Prizes dangling there, no Nobels. I asked myself if I wasn't just a commercial writer—an entertainer—and if there was any great disgrace in that as long as I did the best I could do. Not courting comparisons, it seemed to me that old Bill Shakespeare and Charlie Dickens were pretty darned good entertainers. My conclusion was that it wasn't a bad way to go. So I became a commercial writer. And commercial, to me, meant money. After the slicks folded the obvious money was in Hollywood.

THE WEST'S WORSTS

WORST HAT: Richard Harris, in _The Deadly Trackers_ (Warner Brothers 1973)—picture the gaunt actor sporting a ten-gallon lid with a two-inch brim like Hoss Cartwright's tall, bullet-shaped crown.

WORST LINE: Marlon Brando to Ben Johnson in _One-Eyed Jacks_ (Paramount 1960)—"You scum-suckin' pig!"

MOST EMBARRASSING PORTRAYAL OF AN AMERICAN INDIAN: Edward Everett Horton as "Screaming Chicken" in an episode of TV's "F-Troop" (ABC 1965-67).

WORST PROSTHETIC DEVICE: Again in _The Deadly Trackers_, Neville Brand made not very convincing use of a length of railroad rail in place of a missing hand.

WORST PORTRAYAL OF TRAMPAS FROM OWEN WISTER'S NOVEL, _The Virginian_: Doug McClure, the blond, all-American beach boy, inexplicably cast as Wister's dark-visaged Evil Incarnate, portrayed Trampas as the Virginian's best friend for nine years opposite James Drury as the laconic hero.

LEAST TASTEFUL SCENE: Bill Bixby hulking out and disemboweling himself with Chuck Connor's red-hot branding iron in _Ride Beyond Vengeance_ (Columbia 1966).

"East is East, and West is San Francisco, according to Californians."

O. HENRY

When I went to work as a story editor for David Dortort on an NBC show called "Bonanza," my salary was $650 a week. I learned later that the four stars weren't getting a lot more, but that didn't last long. Even though through the years my salary rose again and again, it never quite matched the forty to fifty thousand a week the stars made. Writers just don't get that kind of money, even in Hollywood.

In addition to writing my own scripts for the show, I served from time to time as story editor, story consultant, associate producer, and executive consultant. They all mean about the same thing. You interview writers, try to guide them into the sort of stories that will fit the series, work with them and then, in the end, generally wind up doing a major rewrite yourself to fit the demands of the director and the production department. Sometimes I was rewriting right up to the last day of shooting. I'm not saying all this rewriting helped the story in every case. I'm just saying that's the way it's done.

I'VE BEEN WITH THE BRANDT & BRANDT AGENCY FOR MANY YEARS. I considered the late Carl Brandt, Sr., one of the most astute men I ever knew. But he had a real fear of TV, I think. His comments, generally veiled, were to the effect that TV writing would ruin you for any other kind of writing. For once, I have to disagree with him. Writing for television teaches you a structure and a discipline that even the pulps couldn't teach. It teaches you to think a story through, to put it down in outline form before you ever tackle that final draft. Above all it teaches you humility—you realize that not each and every one of your words is engraved on gold with a diamond stylus. The story is still the thing and a deadline is a deadline.

Things change. As the pulps went away, the slicks went away. The television Westerns, too, went away. What happened? Where did they go? Will they ever come back?

I have a theory.

They'll come back when we get the David Dortorts and the Howard Christies and the John Mantleys and the Charles Marquis Warrens and the Andy Fenadays back to running things. Those men were Westerners. I don't mean they were born in the West, I mean they thought West. They had a feel for the Western that came through—you saw it there on the screen.

I remember a series called "Shane." David Susskind was executive producer and David Snow was head writer. Some mighty big talent there, but they thought New York, and they cast David Carradine as Shane and gave him psychological problems until they ran out his ears...and the show fell on its rear end.

More recently the networks tried "The Yellow Rose." The original premise was fine, and the casting was out of this world. Paul Savage was ramrodding the scripts, and he's a damn good Western writer. It should have worked. But the twenty-year-old geniuses on Madison Avenue decided they should goose the old Western up, so they had the little girl kidnapped by a child prostitution ring in Hollywood, and the good ranch people went to Hollywood to rescue her—and I said to June, "There goes 'The Yellow Rose.'"

And sure enough, a few weeks later it went off the air.

It's a damn shame. The fault didn't lie with Paul Savage, heaven knows.

The Western will come back to television and the screen when somebody stops to think about what brought it all about in the first place, and what made it fade in the end. Television was standing on its wobbly legs looking for security, when it realized that the most secure thing on the screen was the Western. So they went that-a-way. They overdid it, of course, and that was one reason it faded. But "Gunsmoke" lasted a hell of a long time, as did "Bonanza" and "Wagon Train" and "Rawhide" and the little "Rifleman." And people are still watching the reruns. Why?

Do any of the network people ever stop to analyze what it was that made it work, that it was the real, deep-down respect for the Western and the West itself held by the men who wrote and ran those shows?

I doubt it. With some exceptions, I don't think many of them think that deep. ◾

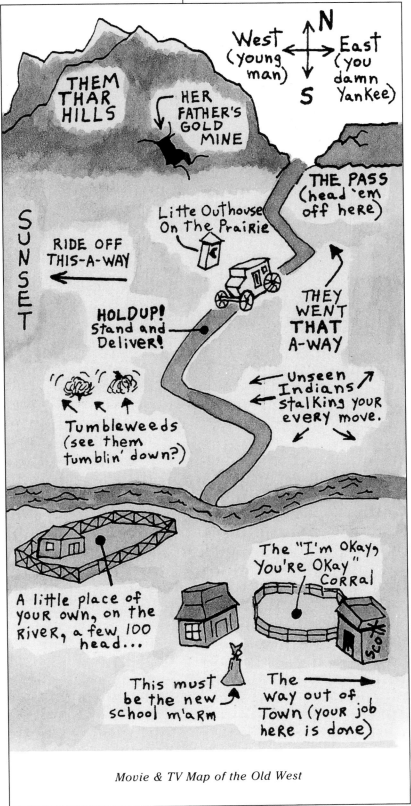

Movie & TV Map of the Old West

WESTERN TV TRIVIA

BY LOREN D. ESTLEMAN
& DALE L. WALKER

Which U.S. President had a TV Western series? Ronald Reagan hosted "Death Valley Days" 1965-66. His predecessor was Stanley Andres (1952-65), and his successors were Robert Taylor (1966-68), and Dale Robertson (1968-70).

Who was the only U.S. Ambassador to Mexico to have a TV Western series? John Gavin starred as Destry in the series of the same name (1964) that was based on the Max Brand character.

How did television prevent the Custer massacre? The series "Custer" (1967) with Wayne Maunder and Slim Pickens was canceled before the 7th Cavalry got to the Little Big Horn.

Who'd you say? There were so many TV series about famous Westerners that not all of the actors that portrayed them had names to conjure with—like Gail Davis as "Annie Oakley" (1952-56), Chris Jones in "The Legend of Jesse James" (1965-66), Don Durant as "Johnny Ringo" (1959-60), Bill Williams as "Kit Carson" (1951), and Keith Larsen as "Brave Eagle" (1955-56).

What was the dumbest name for a TV Western series? "Cowboy G-Men" (1952) with Russell Hayden and Jackie Coogan is a good contender for that honor. Runner up is "Frontier Circus" (1961-62) with Chill Wills, John Derek, and Richard Jaeckel.

Which were the most humiliating portrayals of American Indians in TV Westerns? Of course, Edward Everett Horton as "Screaming Chicken" in *F-Troop* (1965-67) takes the prize. Runners up are Lon Chaney, Jr. as "Chief Eagle Shadow" of Wretched, Colorado, in "Pistols N' Petticoats" (1966-67), Guy Marks as "Pink Cloud" in "Rango" (1967), and X. Brands as "Pahoo" the Pawnee in "Yancy Derringer" (1958-59).

"Stardust" memories in Wyoming: Hoagy Carmichael, famous composer and pianist, had a continuing role as ranch hand "Jonesy" in "Laramie" (1959-63).

Thank you, Doug McClure: For retiring from Westerns, that is. Not only was he incredibly miscast as Trampas in "The Virginian" and its later incarnation, "The Men From Shiloh" (1962-71), McClure also played Cash Conover in "Barbary Coast" (1975-76), and dazzled us as Flip Flippen, William Bendix's sidekick in "Overland Trail" (1960).

Bad Western TV series made from good Western movies: "Butch Cassidy and the Sundance Kid" (1974-75), a cartoon series, turned the free-spirited outlaws into young government agents posing as rock 'n' roll musicians. "Hondo" (1967) starred a wooden Ralph Taeger as Hondo Lane, with Noah Beery, Jr. playing Noah Beery, Jr. In "Shane" (1966), David Carradine was preparing for his starring role as Caine in "Kung Fu" (1972-75).

Who was the first black actor to have a continuing role in a TV Western? Raymond St. Jacques played Simon Blake in "Rawhide" (1959-66).

Who were the best sidekicks? Our favorite will always be former Tommy Dorsey singer Ken Curtis as Festus Haggen in "Gunsmoke" (he played the role 1964-75), along with Paul Brinegar as Wishbone in "Rawhide," and Frank McGrath as Charlie Wooster in "Wagon Train."

Big movie stars who have appeared as regular characters in TV Westerns: Henry Fonda as Marshal Simon Fry in "The Deputy" (1959-61); Ryan O'Neal as Tal Garrett in "Empire" (1962-64); Burt Reynolds as pilot Ben Frazer in "Riverboat" (1959-61) and as halfbreed blacksmith Quint Asper (1962-65) in "Gunsmoke;" John Mills as British barrister Dundee in "Dundee and the Culhane" (1967), with Sean Garrison as Culhane; James Coburn as Jeff Durain in "Klondike" (1960-61); Bruce Dern as E. J. Stocker in "Stoney Burke" (1962-63); and of course, Clint Eastwood as Rowdy Yates in "Rawhide" (1959-66).

Movie Tarzans in TV Westerns: Denny Miller of *Tarzan the Ape Man* (1959), played scout Duke Shannon on "Wagon Train" in the 1961-63 era. Jock Mahoney

An early photo of veteran character actor Chill Wills

of TV's "Yancy Derringer" (1958-59) played the ape man in *Tarzan Goes to India* (1962) and *Tarzan's Three Challenges* (1963).

The denizens of Dodge City: We all know who played Matt Dillon (James Arness), Chester (Dennis Weaver), Festus (Ken Curtis), Doc (Milburne Stone), Miss Kitty (Amanda Blake), and Newly (Buck Taylor) on *Gunsmoke,* but who were all the rest of those folks? James Nusser played Louie Pheeters, Dodge City's most persistent drunk; Ted Jordan played Nathan Burke, the nosy and insufferable freight agent whose office was always the target of bandits; John Harper was Percy Crump, the undertaker who owed his thriving business to the stupidity of the hardcases who messed with the marshal; Woody Chambliss played Lathrop, the storekeeper; Roy Roberts was Mr. Bodkin, the banker; Sarah Selby was boarding house proprietor Ma Smalley; and last but not least was Glenn Strange as the enigmatic Sam, who tended a spotless bar and protected the Longbranch and its mistress with a sawed-off shotgun.

Most true-to-life portrayal of a real Western character: Edgar Buchanan even looked like "Judge Roy Bean" (1956), the self-styled "Law West of the Pecos."

Least true-to-life portrayal of a real Western character: Gene Barry was just a bit too thin and dapper as "Bat Masterson" (1958-61); Hugh O'Brian was just too craggy and even-tempered for "Wyatt Earp" (1955-61); and Guy Madison was way too clean-cut and sober and sedate to be a really "Wild Bill Hickok" (1951-56).

THE TRANSFORMATION OF THE CISCO KID

BY ABRAHAM HOFFMAN

TO ANYONE WHO KNOWS THE CISCO KID ONLY BY MEDIA PORTRAY-als—almost two dozen motion pictures from 1929 to 1950, a long-run-ning radio series, 176 television episodes, and comic strips and comic books—it may come as a bit of a surprise to learn that the original Cisco Kid bore virtually no resemblance to his later characterizations. The Cisco Kid appeared in just one story, "The Caballero's Way," written by O. Henry and published in the July 1907 issue of *Everybody's Magazine*. Later in the year O. Henry anthologized the story in his book *Heart of the West*.

O. Henry died in 1910, and so he never saw what movies, radio, tele-vision, and, most of all, Duncan Renaldo did to his Cisco character. Of all the Western heroes whose personalities were enhanced and devel-oped through various media presentations—"From Hopalong to Hud," to borrow C. L. Sonnichsen's title—none was more greatly transformed than the Cisco Kid. To read the way O. Henry introduced him in "The Caballero's Way" and to see an episode of the television series starring Duncan Renaldo is to witness an extreme mutation in philosophy and personality.

In the beginning of his story, O. Henry wrote, "The Cisco Kid has killed six men in more or less fair scrimmages, had murdered twice as many (mostly Mexicans), and had winged a large number whom he modestly forbore to count. Therefore a woman loved him." As was characteris-tic of his stories, O. Henry created a sharp dramatic conflict and resolved it with a surprise ending. The Cisco Kid loved Tonia Perez, described as "half-Mexican, half-Madonna, and half-hummingbird."

When Lieutenant Sandridge, a Texas Ranger, is sent out looking for the Kid, he meets Tonia and falls in love with her. Tonia reciprocates with her own heart. After some time the Cisco Kid pays a visit to his erstwhile lady love, but in coming up to her house he realizes she has company. Cisco overhears Tonia tell Sandridge of her willingness to

Cesar Romero as the Cisco Kid in "The Gay Caballero" (1940 Fox)

betray the Kid by sending Sandridge a note when the Kid returns. After Sandridge leaves, the Cisco Kid shows up and pretends nothing is amiss. Later on Sandridge receives a note telling him that Cisco feels unsafe and will leave at dawn, but to make sure that no lawmen are around, and to test Tonia's love, he is going to wear one of her dresses while she puts on his clothes.

At dawn Sandridge is in position. The figure wearing Cisco's clothes rides out. When the one wearing the dress appears, Sandridge puts five shots into his target. Sandridge then learns very quickly that the note was forged by Cisco, that no one switched clothes, and that Cisco, by now safe and far away, had successfully plotted a suitable retribution for Tonia's unfaithfulness.

Sandridge is grief-stricken over the error as he stands over Tonia's body; but then, as O. Henry observes, Sandridge "was not a *caballero* by instinct, and he could not understand the niceties of revenge."

This was the simple story that would spawn the movies, radio programs, and the television series that would delight several generations of young and not so young people. If we discount the silent film versions (*The Caballero's Way,* a 1914 one-reeler, and *The Border Terror,* made in

"SEE THEM TUMBLING DOWN..."

BY MARYLOIS DUNN

Remember all those television and movie Westerns in which tumbleweeds spooked the herd or rolled fetchingly around the campfire while Gene or Roy and the boys were singing charming paeans to the ubiquitous weed?

Well, folks, if the movie they rolled around in was set before 1885, those symbolic tumbleweeds took a big chunk out of its authenticity. Tumbleweeds are *not* a native American plant. The seeds of the *salsola kali*, or Russian thistle, a member of the goosefoot family, came to North America around 1885 in a shipment of Russian wheat or flax. Some seeds may even have sneaked in inside the pockets of Ukrainian immigrants who settled in the Dakotas in the late 1800s.

When the Russian thistle matures, the dry plant breaks loose and rolls with the wind to spread its seeds across the range. The wind witch (a folk name for tumbleweed) soon rolled from the Dakotas into Canada and over most of the western United States, scattering seeds as it tumbled. The Big Spring, Texas, weekly newspaper noted its presence around 1910, calling it both "prickly" and "pretty."

Prickly it is, but few westerners who have dealings with the superabundance of tumbleweeds think it pretty. It's a genuine nuisance that loves drought, the drier the better, and finds root easily in any soil that has been disturbed by man. Ranchers say it will grow in the dust on a pickup's bumper.

Though the tumbleweed was romanticized in TV and movie Westerns, even Hollywood's science fiction and horror directors came to recognize the scare value in being pursued by a slithery, skittery, stickery pack of tumbleweeds. Today, tumbleweeds grow everywhere in the modern West,

but when you see them in a Western set prior to 1885, you can be certain that somebody didn't do his homework, or just didn't care to challenge the myth.

1919 by Universal), Cisco received his first major media attention in 1929 with the film *In Old Arizona*.

The movie was a landmark effort, the first sound Western that proved Westerns could talk and have sound effects. Warner Baxter, who played the Cisco Kid, won an Oscar for his portrayal. O. Henry's version was followed fairly well, but there were a few differences in the Hollywood treatment.

First of all, O. Henry had placed his characters in south Texas. Hollywood, for whatever reasons Hollywood has for such things, chose to stage the action in Arizona, hence the title. Second, Baxter chose to play his part by speaking broken English, making the Cisco Kid a Mexican *bandido*. And third, Lieutenant Sandridge became Sergeant Mickey Dunn. The story was stretched out with additional scenes to make it into a feature-length film. Nowhere in O. Henry's short story is the Cisco Kid described as a Mexican. In fact, one of the characters, a storekeeper named Fink, says, "This *hombre* they call the kid—Goodall is his name, ain't it? He's been in my store once or twice." So here we have the first major transformation of the Cisco Kid, from Anglo to Hispanic.

More changes were to come.

Just as we live today with film titles like *Superman* I, II, III, *Rocky* I, II, III, and so forth, Hollywood has always made it a point to squeeze as many golden eggs out of the goose as possible before the old bird dies of exhaustion. The Cisco Kid offered no exception. Baxter returned to the role in 1930 with *The Arizona Kid*, again with *The Cisco Kid* in 1931, and, seven years later, *Return of the Cisco Kid* in 1939, all of these films made by the Fox Film Corporation.

In these sequels we find another addition to O. Henry's story, a Mexican comic relief character—a sidekick named Gordito—played by Chris-Pin Martin, who in the late 1930s made his career by playing buffoon characters in a string of films with Latin American themes. Gordito

TOP: The bad guys get the drop on Leo Carillo as Pancho and Duncan Renaldo as Cisco in "The Girl From San Lorenzo" (1950 United Artists)

BOTTOM: Warner Baxter took the best actor Oscar for his portrayal of the Cisco Kid in "In Old Arizona" (1929 Fox), an adaptation of the original O. Henry story; Edmund Lowe plays the Texas Ranger who competes with him for the hand of his lady love.

TELEVISION SIDEKICKS

BY LOREN D. ESTLEMAN

Tonto

Chester Goode

Festus Haggen

Artemus Gordon

Sergeant Garcia

Hey Boy

Mingo

Jingles

Bernardo

Pancho

Pat Brady

made his first appearance in *The Cisco Kid,* third in the series, and did this role throughout the rest of the Warner Baxter films and through six more films in which Cesar Romero played Cisco. Baxter's salary was getting too high, and Fox wanted someone younger and more Latin-looking to play the part.

And play it Romero did: Romero, who had appeared in *Return of the Cisco Kid* as a secondary character, chose to play him as a foppish character with fancy clothing and a wicked trigger finger. Between 1939 and 1941 Romero appeared in *Cisco Kid and the Lady, Viva Cisco Kid, Lucky Cisco Kid, Gay Caballero, Romance of the Rio Grande,* and *Ride On, Vaquero.*

By this point the series had long run out of intelligent story lines. As the review of *Ride On, Vaquero* in the *New York Times* stated, "The Kid has been around for quite some little time now, and he's done all right for his sponsors, 20th Century-Fox. To be sure, he isn't doing any better in this current episode; he's still just righting wrong at the point of his trusted six-gun, dawdling gallantly with a pretty lady and then disappearing into the night."

But there was a problem much more serious than a stale plot line in which Cisco had evolved from a villain to a perpetually wronged bad man who never got the girl. Many Latin American countries were protesting to the U.S. State Department over the stereotypical and degrading portrayals of Latins in Hollywood films, especially the Cisco Kid series and the Gordito character. Threats were made to boycott Hollywood films if this stereotyping continued.

Fox avoided the problem by selling the story rights to independent producers who hired Duncan Renaldo, best known for his role in the film *Trader Horn,* and Renaldo thoroughly revamped the character. To appease the Latin American market, Renaldo demanded the right to change the Cisco Kid from a cold-blooded killer into a Robin Hood of the West, a picaresque character in the tradition of Cervantes' *Don Quixote.* No more Gordito; Cisco's partner would be Pancho, modeled on Sancho Panza. The Rockefeller-financed Inter-American Relationship Committee, set up to smooth over hemispheric diplomatic problems, approved the changes. Renaldo made three films that were successful on both sides of the border.

When Renaldo stepped down from the role near the end of World War II to work for the U.S. Government on inter-American friendship programs, Monogram Studies hired actor Gilbert Roland to take over the role. Renaldo had cleaned up Cisco's act considerably, but Roland smoked, drank, and chased senoritas in a throwback to the Cesar Romero films. Chris-Pin Martin returned as a buffoon character as well.

Latin America rejected these films, and production of the Cisco series stopped in 1947. To restore the image, Monogram brought Renaldo back for five more films, once again in the Don Quixote tradition.

And then Renaldo made the big decision to move to television. In the early 1950s he made 176 half-hour Cisco Kid television episodes (the first syndicated series on television, and shot in color, though color TV sets were still ten years away), and in not one of them did he kill a single person. Toy manufacturers were dismayed to find that Renaldo refused to endorse toy guns. He played Cisco with a touch of comedy and an ounce of philosophy.

This Renaldo characterization achieved positive results. Cisco became popular throughout the world, and Renaldo and Leo Carrillo, who played Pancho, made many personal appearances, handed out thousands of free autographed pictures, and made Cisco into an international, nonviolent children's hero.

Meanwhile, the Cisco Kid was also acquiring fame in other media. A radio version of the Cisco Kid went on the air in 1943 and lasted for a decade, played most of that time by Jack Mather. Scripted in the Don Quixote tradition, the radio series depicted an intelligent Cisco, while Pancho provided comic relief.

Dell Comics published a Cisco Kid comic book, and from 1951 to 1968 the Cisco Kid appeared as a daily comic strip, drawn extremely well by a talented Argentine artist, Jose-Luis Salinas.

By the mid-1960s the Cisco Kid appeared finally to have ridden into his last sunset. Renaldo had retired, Carrillo was dead, the radio series long gone, and science-fantasy was about to create new heroes for youngsters to emulate. Renaldo could look back on a job well done. He had taken a murderous villain and transformed him into a symbol of international good will, intelligence, and satirical wit. O. Henry may have turned over in his grave a few times because of what Renaldo did to his Cisco character, but that character had taken on a life of his own.

The old television episodes still run on local stations, and some radio stations feature "old-time" radio programs, occasionally bringing back Cisco and Pancho. In 1994, their latest incarnation returned to television via the first of a proposed series of original TV films by Turner's TNT network; the film chronicled the pair's historic meeting during the Juarez rebellion against Emperor Maximilian in Mexico. The popular TV actor Jimmy Smits starred as a reluctantly heroic Cisco, with veteran comedian Cheech Marin as a more serious and *married* Pancho. Though O. Henry is best remembered by modern readers for his stories like "The Gift of the Magi," his creations, the Cisco Kid and Pancho, have secured their own niche in the popular mythology of the fictional West. ∎

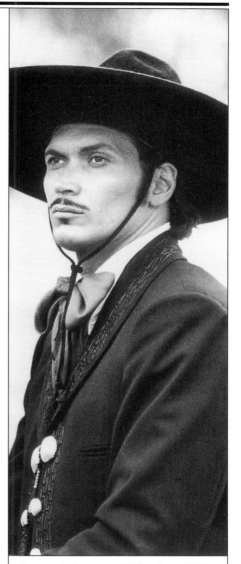

Jimmy Smits, star of "The Cisco Kid" (1993 TNT) (courtesy of Turner Pictures, photo: Erik Heinila)

ZORRO, THE ULTIMATE SWASHBUCKLER

BY ABRAHAM HOFFMAN

ZORRO IS ONE OF THE MOST EASILY RECOGNIZABLE HEROES OF THE fictional Old West—his black costume and mask, his expert swordsmanship, the familiar "Z" his rapier carved on walls, trees, furniture, and villains—and he's been that way for more than sixty years. Since the first publication of Johnston McCulley's *The Curse of Capistrano* in 1919, Zorro has appealed to successive generations of children and many adults who crave a simple story with a lot of action. We all know the basic framework of the Zorro story, but the original version offers some distinctions from later treatments.

The original story has no defined stage-setting, but it begins in a tavern in the small settlement of Los Angeles sometime around 1820. Sergeant Gonzales boasts to his companions about his vow to capture Zorro, then Zorro himself suddenly appears to confront him. Following this introduction, which is played for humor, the author establishes the relationship between Gonzales and wealthy but effete Diego Vega. Don Diego, scion of a wealthy pioneer California family, is a languid, timid fellow, easily bored yet hesitant to take part in any activity that promises adventure or danger. It's a masquerade that conceals his alter ego—*el Zorro,* the Fox, a hero dedicated to fighting the wrongs perpetrated upon the province of California by a dictatorial regime. Don Diego courts Lolita Pulido, daughter of Don Carlos, whose fortune has been ruined by the rapacious governor.

Captain Ramon, the villain of the story, meets Lolita and makes improper advances. Lolita, who rejects Diego for his overly languid personality, falls in love with the dashing Zorro, and spurns Captain Ramon. Sergeant Gonzales vainly pursues Zorro as Ramon plots the further downfall of the Pulido family. The governor visits Los Angeles and orders the Pulidos incarcerated. Learning of this injustice, Zorro recruits a band of young caballeros who rescue the Pulidos from the jail. After several more pursuits and escapes, Zorro vanquishes the villainous

Captain Ramon but is then surrounded by soldiers. With him is his lady love, Senorita Pulido. At the last moment Zorro is rescued by the caballeros who have taken Zorro's pledge to end injustice in California. The governor accepts a truce with the unhappy caballeros and promises to leave them alone so long as they promise not to plot against him.

With the villains out of the way, Zorro doffs his mask to reveal his true face, that of Diego Vega. In the original version, Vega explains that he became Zorro after deciding ten years earlier, at age fifteen, to right the wrongs being done to helpless people. He practiced horsemanship and swordsmanship in secret until he was expert at both. Perhaps recognizing the implausibility of having his hero practice in secret, author McCulley rewrote this explanation so that Vega learned his talents while a student in Spain.

McCulley made some rather careless errors in the first version of his Zorro story, such as locating a presidio in the pueblo of Los Angeles and describing horseback rides through eucalyptus groves that didn't exist in California until half a century later. McCulley also tinged his story with racism, referring constantly to the quality of everyone's blood. The Vega family had the "best blood" in California; the Pulido family was runner-up with "high blood," and other families were ranked according to their "blood" content.

Meanwhile, he reduced California's Indians and working-class Mexicans to unimportant servile status as servants and tavern-keepers. McCulley was also uncertain about his geography. The action centered around Los Angeles, yet Zorro was nicknamed "The Curse of Capistrano." Even the language the characters used was archaic and trite to the point of embarrassment, the characters themselves hopelessly stereotypical.

The Curse of Capistrano was a second-rate story that might have been mercifully forgotten after its initial publication. Hollywood, however, decreed otherwise, and found visual appeal in a masked hero adept with sword and horse. The motion picture industry soon translated McCulley's story into film as *The Mark of Zorro,* a star vehicle in which Douglas Fairbanks, Sr. could display his acrobatic skills. A succession of motion pictures followed: *Don Q, Son of Zorro* (1925), in which Fairbanks played both father and son, with the action set in Spain; *The Bold Caballero* (1937); and two Zorro movie serials in the 1930s—*Zorro Rides Again,* which featured Noah Beery, Sr., who played Sergeant Gonzales in the Douglas Fairbanks silent, and included Duncan Renaldo, who would later become the best-known Cisco Kid in films and television; and *Zorro's Fighting Legion.* The remake of *The Mark of Zorro* (1940), a lavish production starring Tyrone Power, is reckoned by many as the best of the Zorro films. It was followed by two more serials, *Zorro's Black Whip*

Tyrone Power plays the masked hero of Old California with style and rapier wit in "The Mark of Zorro." (1940 Fox)

(1944) and *Ghost of Zorro* (1949), in which Clayton Moore donned an earlier version of his more famous Lone Ranger mask. Some of these versions changed the time of the action to the 1870s to allow the characters to pack holsters and six-guns in the mold of the B Western formula, and even carried the Zorro idea down to the twentieth century.

Who Was That Masked Man?

BY JEFF BANKS

"The Lone Ranger," radio's first really successful and long-running network series Western (1933-35), was also the first to make the transition from radio to movies (1938) and TV (1949). A few other shows and heroes followed the trail blazed by the Ranger, but the usual crossover was from the opposite direction (*Hopalong Cassidy* and *Have Gun, Will Travel,* for example).

There was a series of eighteen novels based on the radio show, a newspaper comic strip that lasted well over a decade and ran at its peak in almost three hundred papers, and a series of 145 monthly Dell comic books with peak sales above two million copies. Practically all this material, including the radio and TV scripts, was written by Fran Striker, surely one of the world's most prolific writers. Tonto and Silver had their own comic books with respectable runs and circulation.

On television, Clayton Moore and Jay Silverheels made the masked man and his faithful Indian companion the most recognizable and beloved Western heroes for a generation of children. Reprints of the comics had reasonable later success, and several years after the end of the live TV series (still a favorite in syndication) an animated Saturday morning TV show enjoyed a three-year run.

Nor does this tell the whole story. There were the Ranger's personal appearances, the first of which (at the mid-point intermission of a circus) caused such a sensation that the entertainment scheduled to follow was canceled. The "entire cast" of the radio show presented twenty-eight performances of a Lone Ranger skit at a leading Detroit movie theater in 1933. There was even a Lone Ranger pulp magazine, though it saw only a single issue.

The world's best-known fictional heroes—Sherlock Holmes, Superman, Tarzan, the Shadow, and the Lone Ranger—are all multi-media heroes. The last two were created first on radio, all but Tarzan had exceptionally long radio lives, and all of them have been adapted for motion pictures. Some outdid the Ranger in one medium or another, but few did so more than once—the Lone Ranger blazed a unique and enduring trail.

As Tonto, Jay Silverheels points out trouble to his kemosabe, *Clayton Moore, in "The Lone Ranger" (1956 Warner Bros.)*

Bob Kane, creator of Batman, admitted that Zorro was his inspiration for the Dark Knight of Gotham City. He transformed Zorro's black mask and cape into Batman's trademark black cowl and batwing cape, the secret cave where Zorro stabled his horse into the Batcave, and Zorro's sleek, black stallion, Diablo, into the atomic-powered Batmobile.

By returning to the original concept, Walt Disney produced a very successful television series in the late 1950s (starring Guy Williams), parts of which Disney adapted for a feature film, *The Sign of Zorro.* Disney also published a Zorro comic book.

Johnston McCulley worked on many of the Zorro screenplays, as well as the first of the Disney television episodes. He also wrote several Zorro sequel novels in which he tinkered with the names of most of the characters at one time or another—he made the Vega family name sound more aristocratic by changing it to "de la Vega." He never made a serious effort, however, to establish a realistic historical context for his masked hero. Zorro sought justice for all and fought tyranny in Old California, but McCulley kept the exact place and time deliberately vague.

McCulley died in 1958, but the Zorro story mill continued to grind out its product as foreign filmmakers got into the act. The years 1962 and 1963 witnessed a flood of Zorro films: besides *The Sign of Zorro,* there was also *The Shadow of Zorro, Zorro vs. Machiste, Zorro at the Court of Spain, Zorro and the Three Musketeers,* and *Zorro, the Avenger,* most of them made (with execrable plots) in foreign countries.

In the 1970s, the television movie of the week continued the Zorro tradition with "The Mark of Zorro" (1974) in which Frank Langella starred as Zorro. Former guest-star villains in the Disney Zorro series, Ricardo Montalban played Captain Esteban and Gilbert Roland (who played the Cisco Kid briefly in film in the 1940s) took a turn as Don Allejandro de la Vega. Yet another theatrical film, *Zorro* (1975), was set somewhere in Latin America rather than California, and starred Alain Delon as the hero, the son of the original Zorro. CBS even added a Saturday morning cartoon show to the legend of Zorro.

Despite modern cynicism, the masked hero's appeal persists. The debutof the Disney Channel on cable television brought back the 1950s Zorro television series to delight a whole new generation of children. In a 1983 television comedy miniseries, "Zorro and Son," Henry Darrow (Manolito in "High Chaparral") starred as the elder Zorro, and in a new Zorro series filmed in Spain for Cable's Family Channel, starring Duncan Regehr as Zorro, Darrow plays the role of Don Allejandro Vega. *El Zorro,* the fox, lives on in the hearts of children, writers and actors—and he will do so as long as Hollywood executives have faith in the box-office draw of a masked avenger who may well be the ultimate swashbuckler. ■

VASQUEZ ROCKS, FROM OUTLAW HIDEOUT TO HOLLYWOOD HAVEN

BY ABRAHAM HOFFMAN

ANYONE WHO HAS ENJOYED ACTION-ADVENTURE FILMS, FROM B WEST-erns to television series, is familiar with Vasquez Rocks. Did you see Zorro, or the Lone Ranger and Tonto, ride to rescue some rancher's daughter? They probably rode past Vasquez Rocks. Kane, the enigmatic hero of "Kung Fu," helped Chinese laborers build the Central Pacific Rail-road—not through Nevada or the Sierras, but through Vasquez Rocks.

Captain Kirk, valiant leader of the starship Enterprise, fought aliens in Vasquez Rocks as the location became different planets for several "Star Trek" episodes, as they did for Captain Picard and "Star Trek: The Next Generation." For years after the "77th Bengal Lancers" became a TV trivia footnote, the fort built for the series remained mute testimony that Vasquez Rocks could serve as Imperial India, as they also had for Tyrone Power in *King of the Khyber Rifles.* For low-budget Westerns and Western television series, "Head 'em off at the pass!" probably meant, "at Vasquez Rocks." From automobile commercials to shoot-em-ups, or for any script that called for an exotic setting not too far from Hollywood, Vasquez Rocks has served as the location of choice since silent movie days.

Vasquez Rocks, a Los Angeles County Park since 1969, is located some twenty miles north of Hollywood, easily accessible by modern free-way, but not a difficult trip even a century ago, as the site isn't far off the inland route from Los Angeles to Sacramento. The unusual rock for-mations, huge boulders and rock scarps that earthquakes thrust upward from the earth at odd angles, create an eerie landscape.

As befits a Hollywood legend, the rocks got their name from Cali-fornia's second-most notorious outlaw, Tiburcio Vasquez. Unlike Juaquin Murietta, whose apocryphal exploits became the stuff of legend, history knows Vasquez as a stagecoach robber, horse thief, and outlaw gang leader. Taken alive after his last hold-up attempt, Vasquez dictated a statement to a newspaper reporter while he awaited execution.

Vasquez Rocks, 1994 (photo: Abe Hoffman)

Vasquez claimed that he took to a life of banditry because he resented the Anglo takeover of his homeland. A native-born Californio, Vasquez decided to avenge the wrongs done to his people's land, women, and pride. He and his gang roamed through central and southern California, robbing stores and holding up stagecoaches. In the process of robbing a store at Tres Pinos, the Vasquez gang shot and killed several people. Several sheriffs pursued Vasquez, which made him the most famous outlaw in the region. They finally trapped him at the home of Greek George, near what is now Hollywood, wounded him and took him prisoner. During his incarceration in the Los Angeles County Jail every prominent citizen who could pay him a visit did so, and he even received flowers from Los Angeles women who thought his career picturesque.

But murder was murder, and as soon as his wounds were healed Vasquez was taken to Tres Pinos, and then to San Jose, where he was tried, found guilty, and hanged in March 1875. By then the stories about Vasquez were already circulating—it was even said that he could tell a native-born Californio by the way he rolled his cigarette.

But it was "the rocks" that became the most enduring memorial to the *bandido,* Vasquez. It was said that Vasquez and his gang had sought refuge in the Rocks from pursuing sheriffs. It was also said that the remains of campfires, indeed the very soot on the boulders by those campfires, were the legacy of Vasquez's outlaw days. It may be that Vasquez did indeed hole up in the Antelope Valley, north of the San

Gabriel Mountains for a while. But it's obvious that the remains of any campfires made by Vasquez more than a century ago have long since been outnumbered by more recent encampments, as evidenced by the innumerable beer cans of recent vintage left to rust around the alleged campfire sites. Fortunately, since the area is now a county park, modern outlaws are discouraged from dumping.

Vasquez Rocks County Park welcomes visitors, but anyone touring the area should be forewarned that appearances may deceive. Many times studios have left set decorations behind after a film or commercial was completed. One visitor was almost injured when the tree he leaned against toppled over; it was held in place by roots made of wooden slats. Occasionally, one will find a papier-mache boulder. Somehow it all ties together: Vasquez was captured at a ranch near what is now Hollywood, and in turn Vasquez's hideout captured Hollywood—at least those budget-minded producers who prefer to keep expenses down rather than to send film crews to more isolated locations. ■

WESTERN THEME MUSIC

BY ABRAHAM HOFFMAN

Children who grew up as radio or television Western fans learned immediately to recognize their favorite shows by the program's theme music. The granddaddy of them all, the Lone Ranger, alerted his radio audience with the electrifying last movement of "The William Tell Overture." This association is so fixed in the minds of the American public that to this day, concerts at which the overture is played always elicit a gasp of recognition as children of all ages exclaim, "Hey! That's the Lone Ranger music!"

Actually, the producers of the Lone Ranger show at station WXYZ in Detroit didn't limit the repertoire to Rossini's most famous overture. The program always featured snippets of classical music to set mood and accentuate action. Liszt's "Les Preludes" signaled the mid-program commercial break, and the second half of the program began with a continuation of the music. "Les Preludes" also became a major theme in the Flash Gordon movie serial.

Other WXYZ-originated shows also featured classical music. Of only slightly lesser fame than "William Tell," the "Dona Diana Overture" by Reznicek announced the arrival of Sergeant Preston and his dog, Yukon King. Fans of the Green Hornet, the fictional lineal descendant of the Lone Ranger's nephew, instantly recognized Rimsky-Korsakov's "Flight of the Bumble Bee."

In January 1940 Western film star Gene Autry took to the air waves and let listeners know he was "Back in the Saddle Again." At about the same time the Tom Mix radio show, without Tom Mix (other actors, chiefly Curly Bradley, portrayed the radio Mix), made "Roundup Time in Texas" its ongoing theme. Red Ryder began with a rendition of "Bury Me Not on the Lone Prairie," while the Cisco Kid stuck pretty much to Khatchaturian's "Saber Dance."

Roy Rogers went through several themes, depending on who was sponsoring his radio or television shows. Perhaps best known is "Happy Trails," when Dodge was the radio sponsor; but Roy also used "Smiles are Made Out of Sunshine" for Quaker Oats, and "It's Roundup Time at the Double R Bar" for Post Sugar Crisp. "Happy Trails," also used on his television series, is his best-remembered theme.

The heyday of television Westerns was in the 1950s, and almost all of the programs commissioned original theme music without lyrics. "Maverick," starring James Garner, was an exception, as were "Rawhide," "Lawman," and "Wyatt Earp." Singer Frankie Laine, who sang the theme from *Rawhide* over the show's credits, enjoyed a last hit record as rock 'n' roll took over popular music. The long-running "Gunsmoke," a success on both radio and television, used as its theme a melody titled "The Old Trail," a familiar tune but with a title virtually no one knew. "Bonanza" also featured catchy theme music, but it was an instrumental piece--though at the end of the unaired pilot episode, the Cartwrights saddled up while singing the never-used lyrics to the music. The themes of other Western programs, like the titles of the shows, are pretty much forgotten today. It would take a true Western trivia buff to whistle the theme from "Sugarfoot," "Trackdown," or "Wanted—Dead or Alive."

RIN TIN TIN

BY MARYLOIS DUNN

HE MAY HAVE BEEN A DOG, BUT HE WAS THE BEST OF THE FOUR-LEG-ged actors, and in many ways, better than some of the two-legged stars of his day. When Rin Tin Tin was found in an abandoned German dug-out in the Chateau Thierry sector of France in 1918, he was so young his eyes weren't yet open. His first memories were of listening to the heart-beat of his rescuer, trainer and friend, Lee Duncan. Although he was Ger-man-born and bred, he grew up to understand English with an uncanny canine intelligence. Because he'd spent the first two months of his life under almost constant bombardment by the German Army, he became so accustomed to it that in later years he became irritated if it got too quiet.

Duncan soon recognized the superiority of his adopted pal and began to teach him some tricks. He met Jack Warner, and convinced him he could guide the dog to super stardom. Warner saw some of Rinty's tricks and agreed to produce a picture. A young Darryl Zanuck wrote the script for *Where the North Begins*.

Rinty was small for a German Shepherd, about ninety pounds, and he was dark, almost black. Duncan said, "When he was making movies back in the 'Twenties, we didn't have the lighting equipment and sen-sitive film we have today. Sometimes he'd look more like a shadow than a dog. When Jack Warner saw the first rushes, he almost had a fit. He was afraid we'd have a dog picture in which no one could see the dog. After that I sprinkled Rinty with talcum powder to make him a little lighter."

Rin Tin Tin became the recognized king of the Canine Cowboys. Many studios had their own dog stars: Strongheart, Peter the Great, Napoleon Bonaparte, and Universal's rip-off Rinty, Dynamite, but Rinty was the original.

He may not have exactly been a beautiful animal, but Rinty was a born actor. In the first movies you can see him looking at the camera for instructions from Duncan, but in his later pictures, he knew exactly what he was expected to do, and did it flawlessly. Duncan said that Rinty

The original Rin-Tin-Tin

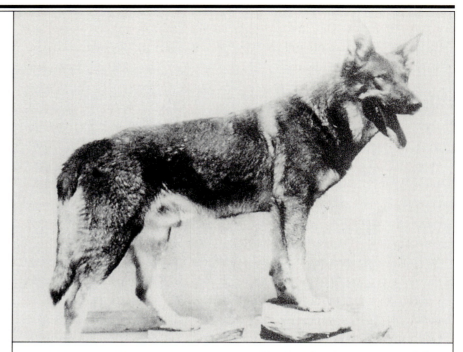

would become disgusted when an actor flubbed his lines or missed his mark. He laughed as he told how Rinty would step behind the offender and express his irritation wetly against the actor's leg. Rinty never did such a thing with the ladies; he'd just hang his head and walk to his trailer to wait until the scene was reset and ready to shoot again.

Rinty's facial expressions are what won him most of his fans, for he was capable of displaying an amazing range of emotions. In *The Night Cry* (with John Harron and June Marlowe), Rinty returns to his master's cabin under suspicion of sheepicide. In one take, he manages to convey hope, grief, tolerance and finally joy when the couple's infant proves to be his steadfast friend. His writers always put one emotional scene in each of his pictures—and the audience needed no subtitles to understand what Rinty meant.

Rin Tin Tin had no doubles, and neither did his grandsons when they took over the starring role. He performed his own stunts, which included climbing cliffs and trees and leaping into canyons and rivers. He could use a telephone, work a lever, turn a wheel, open a door, unlock a gate, untie ropes, unfasten chains and recognize important clues. He was the outstanding doggie detective of his day. Even Lassie, in later days, never matched the cleverness of the original Rin Tin Tin.

Lee Duncan raised Rin Tin Tin's descendants over the years, and they also made movies, but the most famous was Rin Tin Tin IV. The handsome television star was larger than his Granddad and lighter in color; he was the only one to match his ancestor's acting talent. Duncan always called Rinty IV "The Pup," and said of him, "Old Rin knew he was acting, and the Pup does too. In almost every one of our pictures, Rin has got to attack guys. Like his predecessor, the Pup can play around with the actors, but once the cameras start rolling, he goes after them tooth and nail. The second the director yells 'cut,' he's back to licking the actors' faces."

Even Duncan admitted that the other two Rin Tin Tins were not as smart. When Rinty I died in 1932, Rin Tin Tin, Jr. made *Tough Guy* with Jackie Cooper. Rinty III made *The Return of Rin Tin Tin* in 1947. Duncan said, "I couldn't let them get friendly with the stunt man before the cameras rolled. They'd jump on 'em alright when I gave the command, but if they knew the actors, they'd start licking their faces right before the cameras. They just didn't know when to act and when to play."

Rinty IV starred with Jim Brown, Joe Sawyer and Lee Aaker in his television series, "The Adventures of Rin Tin Tin" in over a hundred episodes. Like many modern television stars, Rinty IV loved to meet people and gave interviews happily with a paw-shake and a couple of husky barks. Although he was rich enough and probably smart enough to be either, he never aspired to be a director or producer, as did so many of his human counterparts. He did his job and proudly carried on the tradition of Rin Tin Tin.

Jim Brown, who played Lieutenant Rip Masters, was a handsome six-footer from Texas. He'd made his way to Hollywood by way of a tennis tournament where he was spotted by scouts. Warner Brothers signed him, and he made many films before he turned to television. He employed his fine singing voice on "The Adventures of Rin Tin Tin," introducing several songs into the action in the tradition of the old-time singing cowboys.

Joe Sawyer, who played Sergeant Biff O'Hara, spent thirty successful years as a character actor, but through all of his roles, his favorite was the part he played in *The Informer* with Victor McLaglen. After his stint on "The Adventures of Rin Tin Tin," Joe hung up his spurs and retired to attend to his successful contracting business.

Young Lee Aaker came to his role in the series with the experience of having played Geraldine Page's son in the John Wayne film, *Hondo.* Playing the part of the young "soldier" in the Rin Tin Tin series was more like play than work and the youngster took to the part naturally. His fellow actors liked him and found him easy to work with, but the one who liked him the most was Rinty IV. They became true companions, and they were often off playing together and had to be found when time came to shoot their scenes.

Lee Duncan laughed and said, "Lee came to my whistle as fast as Rinty did." ∎

SUNG HEROES

BY LOREN D. ESTLEMAN

What TV Westerners belong to these lyrics?

1. "A knight without armor in a savage land."
2. "One man stood out above the rest."
3. "He was panther quick and leather tough."
4. "Brave, courageous, and bold."
5. "_____ is the legend of the West."
6. "Straightened out Congress, so we hear tell."
7. "_____ _____ was a man."
8. "He was cursed with a quick and restless gun."
9. "Out of the night, when the moon is bright."
10. *"Thwack!"*

Answers:

1. Paladin from "Have Gun, Will Travel"
2. "Bat Masterson"
3. Johnny Yuma from "The Rebel"
4. Wyatt Earp from "The Life and Legend of Wyatt Earp"
5. "Maverick"
6. Davy Crockett from "The Adventures of Davy Crockett"
7. "Daniel Boone"
8. Jesse James from "The Legend of Jesse James"
9. "Zorro"
10. Jim Bowie from "The Adventures of Jim Bowie"

"Gunsmoke," the Greatest of Them All

BY KRISTINE FREDRIKSSON

WHEN JOHN WAYNE INTRODUCED "GUNSMOKE" AS A HALF-HOUR television series on Saturday evening, September 10, 1955, many in the audience were already familiar with the show. The thirty-minute weekly radio version of the popular Western was a staple of the CBS Radio Network lineup from April of 1952, to June 18, 1961. Producer Norman Macdonnell and writer John Meston, who were responsible for the radio show, developed the television concept with director Charles Marquis Warren, who became the series producer for its first season. Macdonnell and Meston originally wanted merely to transpose the radio actors to television, but with the director's prerogative, Warren preferred to begin with a brand-new cast.

The image the actors projected became all important in the relatively new visual medium. For the role of Matt Dillon, U.S. Marshal, Warren envisioned someone on the order of John Wayne. Macdonnell claimed that the idea of casting Wayne was a publicity ploy, although the actor went on record as saying he was offered "the world" to take on the role. But Wayne was a major star in motion pictures, and unlike today, a role in a television series would have been considered a step down in status for a film star.

No less than twenty-six actors auditioned for the part, among them William Conrad (radio's Matt Dillon), Raymond Burr, and a young man named James Arness. A World War II veteran, Arness had appeared in a few motion pictures: as Loretta Young's brother in *The Farmer's Daughter* (David O. Selznick, 1947); in the title role of the science-fiction thriller, *The Thing From Another World* (RKO/Winchester, 1951); and the John Wayne production of *Big Jim McLain* (Wayne/Fellows, 1952). At the time of the search for the "Gunsmoke" lead, he was under contract to Wayne's Batjac Productions. It's reported that Arness hesitated, believing that a television role would impede his chances for motion picture stardom. However, Wayne persuaded his protege to accept the assignment as it was likely instead to accelerate his rather stagnant acting career.

Traditionally, the hero in a Western tale is a lineal descendant of James Fenimore Cooper's Leatherstocking character. He evolved through dime novels, silent motion pictures and the serials into the hero of the television screen. With one foot in established society, the other in a less-civilized world, he is, in essence, an antihero who can readily identify with the evil forces he is nevertheless duty-bound to pursue. Marshal Matt Dillon was a composite of a number of earlier, historical frontier lawmen, none of whom he really resembled. Though larger than life, he was perceived as authentic by the viewing public. Tourists visiting Dodge City, Kansas, only a few years after the TV series premiere, went in search of Matt Dillon's grave on Boot Hill. In 1959, U.S. Senator Andrew F. Schoeppel (R-Kansas) tried to get Congress to build three markers to commemorate Wyatt Earp (assistant marshal of Dodge City 1876 and 1878-79), Ben Masterson (deputy marshal of Dodge City 1876) and the fictional Matt Dillon.

Although "Gunsmoke" is a Western in the true sense about the most publicized railhead of all, cowboys were never regular characters. Only occasionally did they figure in the plots, and then very rarely in leading roles. The Marshal was surrounded by folks who might be found in any ranching/farming town: the local tradesmen, the banker, the freight agent, the farmers of the surrounding countryside and the inevitable saloon girls. This was the mainstay that enabled the stories to move forward and the series to survive. The characters formed an extended family, against which was mirrored the growth and maturing of a community that could have been located anywhere on the westward-moving frontier.

When the Western, as a genre, came of age in literature and film, the traditional cowboy hero was transformed into a man with a gun. This increased the plot possibilities, making the stories more acceptable to a wider range of readers and viewers. This metamorphosis also opened the way for the hero to engage in a greater number of activities and confrontations than if he had remained just a hired man on horseback. More important for the sake of audience identification, in this new persona the cowboy myth was allowed to continue, represented by the character of a lawman. The combination, achieved through clever casting, worked to the advantage of the series.

Three other regulars made the series debut. Only one of them was to remain, along with Arness, for the twenty-year run. Character actor Milburn Stone was cast in the role of Dr. Galen Adams, popularly known as Doc. Early on, Mr. Stone had launched his show business career as one half of the vaudeville team of Stone and Strain. For a time the pair

Amanda Blake as Miss Kitty and Milburne Stone as Doc Galen Adams in "Gunsmoke" (courtesy of CBS)

THE WEST'S BESTS

BEST SINGLE FRAME: It's a three-way tie between the comic and the deadly serious: John Wayne emerging god-like from the Western desert as the Ringo Kid in *Stagecoach* (United Artists 1939); Lee Marvin as Kid Sheleen leaning drunkenly astride his drunkenly leaning horse in *Cat Ballou* (pictured above) (Columbia 1965); and the Duke, again, as Marshal Rooster Cogburn in *True Grit* (Paramount 1969) he puts the reins in his teeth, levers his Winchester one-handed, and charges Lucky Ned Pepper's gang. A close runner-up is the last scene of *The Searchers,* when John Wayne as Ethan Edwards turns his back on the happy family reunion and, framed by the doorway of the house, stares out into the empty plains into the West.

BEST LINE: Joel McCrea, as Steve Judd in Sam Peckinpah's *Ride the High Country* (MGM 1962), said, "All I want is to enter my house justified."

SECOND BEST LINE: Two decades later, Sam Peckinpah would have shown us the corpse and lost the effect. Under Howard Hawks's direction in *Red River* (United Artists 1948), John Wayne had only to raise his lantern over the unseen remains of a cowhand missing after a stampede and say, "Was Curly wearing checkered pants?"

was featured on the CBS radio network. In 1932 he made his dramatic bow on Broadway and in 1934 began appearing in motion pictures, 150 in all.

The original concept of Doc Adams appears to have been on the order of the legendary frontier dentist Doc Holliday. In the early years of the series, the characters were delineated in a rawer yet more theatrical fashion. Later on, as the TV medium grew up, they took on varying degrees of refinement and a wider spectrum of qualities and attributes. Kathleen Hite, writer of numerous radio and television episodes, has said she believed Doc had "a terrible booze problem." Macdonnell perceived that Dr. Adams had to have performed illegal operations in the back room of Long Branch. Doc of the radio show (Howard McNear) did, in fact, have a shady professional past and had come West after service on the Mississippi River boat, "The Tennessee Belle." Stone softened the character for TV, making him more like what one would expect a crusty old frontier doctor to be.

Amanda Blake, cast in the role of Miss Kitty Russell, had been groomed at MGM Studios to follow in the footsteps of Greer Garson. She had also been under contract to Columbia Pictures. Although she had numerous motion-picture and television roles in both the dramatic and comedy fields to her credit, her career had not yet taken on star proportions. In the early shows, she wasn't the owner of the Long Branch Saloon, but rather one of the working girls at the Texas Trail and Alafraganza saloons, and she appeared in low-cut, bare-shouldered gowns. Her styles took on a tailored, elegant look once she became a businesswoman in her own right.

New Orleans was Miss Kitty's original home. In episodes that aired between 1957 and 1959, she was visited in Dodge City not only by her father, Wayne Russell (John Dehner), but also by a younger brother (Barry McGuire, later one of the folk-singing group The New Christy Minstrels), neither of whom were ever referred to again. The mission of both their visits was to persuade Kitty to give up her profession and move back to New Orleans. Television never overtly dealt with her advancement to ownership of the Long Branch, although in radio she first became co-owner with Sam, former sole owner (the original owner of the Long Branch Saloon in Dodge City, Kansas, was Fred Beeson). Sam was later relegated to bartender when Kitty took over the establishment.

As she grew in stature as a lady of enterprise, so did her importance as a character on the series. She was originally considered as just someone for Matt to talk to and against whom light-hearted scenes could be played. A hint of romantic relationship with Matt Dillon evolved, and there's no doubt that, over the years, their affection grew, keeping the viewers constantly speculating. Miss Blake was given greater challenges in her role as Kitty, and, in the process, her talent as a dramatic actress became apparent. One of the most poignant episodes dealt with her inability to cope with yet another vigil after Marshal Dillon was gravely wounded. She sold the Long Branch and moved away from Dodge City, but in the end returned and resumed life as usual.

When Blake left the series after its 19th season, Fran Ryan came in as Hannah to take over the Long Branch. She played the role in a more matronly and bucolic fashion, and created a likable character that fit well in Dodge City. However, the sophistication that Blake had brought to her part—and to Dodge City—was missing in "Gunsmoke"'s 20th and final season.

The first actor to leave the series (in April, 1964) was Dennis Weaver, who played Matt Dillon's limping deputy, Chester Goode. During the first nine years, he and the Marshal had become more or less of a team who together set out on investigations and manhunts. For his replacement the producers searched for someone with whom Matt could interact with the same effective results.

Burt Reynolds, at the time virtually unknown, played the part of the halfbreed blacksmith Quint Asper for two seasons, 1962-64. In that role he created the first in a series of characters who hadn't been represented in the radio version of the show.

Another actor, Ken Curtis, had been featured in various guest-starring roles since the 1958-59 season. Beginning in 1963-64, he assumed the regular role of Festus Haggen, continuing through the 20th season. He came to the series with experience in numerous screen and television roles, including *The Searchers* (Warner/C.V. Whitney, 1956), *How the West Was Won* (MGM/Cinerama, 1962), *Cheyenne Autumn* (Warner/Ford-Smith, 1964), and as one of the leads in the syndicated series "Ripcord" (1961-63).

Festus was a former drifter, the only honest member of an outlaw family. On occasion, his relations came to visit and to cause trouble, but they always came across as loveable, small-time crooks, kept from pursuing a life of crime by their own stupidity and ineptness. These shows were highlights among the rare comedic episodes of "Gunsmoke."

Mr. Curtis soon gathered as loyal a following as Festus. His character was more broadly drawn than that of Chester, but many viewers seem to have confused the two, possibly more by the similarity of their names than by the characters themselves. Festus was illiterate, but he had compassion, warmth and a deep sense of justice. On occasion his illiteracy was made an issue—for comic relief—and he would simply justify his inability to read by saying he had forgotten to bring his "readin'

THE WEST'S WORSTS

WORST PORTRAYAL OF A MEXICAN BANDIT: A tie between Humphrey Bogart, sounding like the infamous Frito Bandito imitating Humphrey Bogart, in *Virginia City* (Warner Brothers 1940), and Dirk Bogarde, mouthing allegorical crypticisms with a decidedly British accent, in *The Singer Not The Song* (Warner Brothers 1961).

MOST GLARING ANACHRONISM: A jet aircraft bisecting with its afterburners the supposedly 1700's sky as Roger Miller sang and sowed his way down a frontier Kentucky road as Johnny Appleseed in an episode of "Daniel Boone" (NBC 1964-1970).

MOST OVERRATED WESTERN: Another tie, between Marlon Brando's bloated and boring retelling of the Billy the Kid story in *One-Eyed Jacks;* and *A Man Called Horse* (National General Pictures 1969), in which Richard Harris shamelessly chewed every tipi in sight, but at least didn't wear his *Deadly Trackers* hat.

WORST PORTRAYAL OF A SOUTHERN BELLE: A flawlessly lovely Gene Tierney lamenting her losses in "the wowuh" in the role of the rather horse-faced female outlaw, *Belle Starr* (Twentieth Century Fox 1941).

WORST IMITATION OF A GUNFIGHTER AS A MARTYR: Paul Newman as Billy the Kid goes for a holster he knows is empty when he draws on Pat Garrett (John Dehner) in *The Left-Handed Gun* (Warner Brothers 1958).

"THE PRETENDER"

AN EXCERPT FROM "THE PRETENDER"—A "GUNSMOKE" SCRIPT, STORY AND TELEPLAY BY CALVIN CLEMENTS, SR.
ORIGINAL AIR DATE NOVEMBER 20, 1965

ACT ONE

REV. 9/21/65

FADE IN: 26. I

NT. DELMONICO'S—DAY   26.

Doc and Festus are seated at a table near the window waiting for their breakfast and engaged in their customary barbed exchanges. Festus studies Doc, shakes his head.

FESTUS: I jest hope the word never sifts back to any of my kinfolk.

Doc fixes him with a gaze.

DOC: Now what are you talking about...?

FESTUS: You.

DOC: Well you've stumbled onto one of my favorite subjects.

FESTUS: I think they'd pack me in ice.

DOC: I thought you were talking about me.

FESTUS (nods): If any Haggen—old enough to set up by hisself—had any notion I'd take a meal with a store doctor, they'd fetch me clean away from here.

DOC: Well how do we get word to them?

FESTUS: Yessir—pack me in ice—and feed me cricket powder till my brain fever give—that's what they'd do.

At this point, the WAITER brings two plates and sets them before each of them and goes away. Festus regards his plate—catfish, but the head isn't on it.

FESTUS (cont'd): Now what we got here?

Doc has begun to eat; he regards Festus' plate.

DOC: Catfish—it's what you ordered.

FESTUS: Nothing says that's catfish.

DOC: Well sure it is—take a bite.

Festus pushes away from the table.

FESTUS: Oh no. I ain't a fool.

DOC: You're a fool and—that's a catfish.

FESTUS: Where's its head?

DOC: Well, it's not there, but—

FESTUS: Then how do I know it's catfish-?

DOC: Ohforheavensakes.

FESTUS: Might be it's a mermaid.

Doc drops his fork and stares at Festus.

DOC: Somebody better pack you in ice!

FESTUS: Haggens only eat fish who's got their heads on—or how do you know it ain't a mermaid????

DOC: Ohh Festus—that's the wildest superstition you've ever come up with.

FESTUS: That's di-rect from the Louseeanna Haggens.

DOC You don't really believe that.

FESTUS (indignantly): Well of course I believe it!...anybody that don't believe in mermaids is tetched in the haid.

DOC (pointing to the fish): Mermaids...that size?!

FESTUS: Well you don't think they're born full grown do you?

DOC (acidly): I see...that's a baby mermaid.

FESTUS: Never said it was...only said it could be.

DOC (nodding): Without the head you can't tell.

FESTUS: That's right...I jist won't eat no fish less'n it's got its head on.

He pushes his plate away, stands up and points to Doc's plate.

FESTUS (CONT'D): But don't let that bother you...you jist go right ahead...probably wouldn't bother an ol scudder like you a bit...t' know he's practically a cannibal.

He waits, but Doc does nothing

9/20/65 — Rev.

FESTUS: Well, what are you waiting for...She can't bite you when she's had her head lopped off.

Doc does a slow burn, then:

DOC: Oh get out...get out of here! Before I do something I'll regret.

Festus nods gravely, trying very hard to conceal his triumph, and starts toward the door. The CAMERA TIGHTENS on Doc as he shakes his head, and then looks down at his catfish dinner.

27. EXT. ANGLE ON DELMONICO DOOR   27.

As Festus exits, crosses the window, nods at Doc who scowls back at him, and then the CAMERA TIGHTENS as Festus, after passing the window, flattens himself against the wall, turns and peers back in.

28. POV SHOT—THROUGH WINDOW   28.

As Doc moves his plate a little closer and picks up his knife and fork. He poises the fork over the catfish and hesitates.

28A. CLOSE ON FESTUS   28A.

As he grins.

28B. CLOSE ON DOC   28B.

As he swallows, sets his jaw, and tries again. He knows it' ridiculous, but he can't cut into that catfish. He puts down the knife and fork and stares at the fish. CAMERA PULLS BACK as the waiter approaches.

WAITER: What's the matter, Doc?...Somthin' wrong with the lunch?

He looks from Festus' untouched plate to Doc's.

DOC: No...no, it's just that...I seem to have lost my taste for fish.

WAITER: But Doc, that fish is good...I had it for breakfast myself...it was fresh this morning.

DOC: Yeah...well just take it away and bring me a couple of soft boiled eggs.

The waiter looks at Doc as if he were slightly demented, but shrugs and removes the two plates. Doc looks after him and sighs.

28C. ANGLE ON FESTUS   28C.

As he straightens up, sticks his hands in his pockets and starts toward Matt's office, CAMERA TRACKS with him and holds on the street until Festus leaves shot by entering the office.

specs." Audiences came to love his many endless, usually unresolved arguments with Stone's Doc. The two actors often ad-libbed their verbal sparring matches — they'd come to know the characters they played far better than any writer. In the process, Curtis coined some very colorful phrases that will always be attributed to Festus Haggen.

As a Saturday night television institution, "Gunsmoke" was number one from its second season through 1960-61. That fall it expanded to sixty minutes and continued to stay high in the ratings for a few years. At the beginning of the 1966-67 season, a new character, Clayton Thaddeus Greenwood (played by Roger Ewing) was introduced in an effort to attract viewers of a younger generation. At best he could be described as a young, pretty face, as was the vogue in both period and contemporary films and TV shows of the time.

That season, too, "Gunsmoke" was for the first time filmed in color, the last CBS series to switch from the black-and-white format. Neither of these changes helped, and by the end of its twelfth season, it had slipped to 34th place in the Nielsen Ratings. As a result, the program was canceled early in 1967. The Kansas state legislature censored CBS for having taken this step. U.S. Senator Robert C. Byrd (D-West Virginia) brought the issue up before Congress on March 2, 1967, asking that an editorial on the subject from the *Farimont* (West Virginia) *Times* be reprinted in The Congressional Record, a request that was granted.

At the insistence of CBS president William S. Paley, "Gunsmoke" was quickly reinstated in early March. By that time, however, its old Saturday evening slot (10-11 p.m.) was already occupied by another program for the coming fall season. This, as it turned out, was a stroke of good fortune. Instead, it was assigned the 7:30-8:30 period on Monday nights, exposing the series to a younger audience unsuccessfully solicited before. In its first year in this new time slot, "Gunsmoke" climbed to number four.

The producers introduced several innovations, like creating a younger character, Newly O'Brien, played by Buck Taylor from 1967 through the twentieth season. Born into a show business family, Mr. Taylor had over a hundred film and television credits in addition to stunt-work experience. In the role of Newly, a former medical student from Pennsylvania turned gunsmith, he was a great deal more refined, without the Western speech patterns that had characterized his predecessors in secondary roles. He fit well in Dodge City, the characters and the viewers readily accepted him. His background also made it possible to place him in a greater variety of dramatic situations, in which he was often the featured player.

Certainly by the time "Gunsmoke" was expanded to an hour (1961-62), it had emerged as the prototype for the adult Western. Many of the artists who had guest-starred during the first six half-hour seasons returned. The show also introduced new faces and talents, among them Katherine Ross, Dyan Cannon and James Stacy. Big-name actors were

Milburne Stone, Amanda Blake, James Arness, Dennis Weaver on parade for "Gunsmoke" (courtesy of CBS)

THE MOST ENDURING CHARACTERS ON TELEVISION

James Arness as Matt Dillon, Amanda Blake as Kitty and Ken Curtis as Festus Haggen on "Gunsmoke," Lorne Green as Ben Cartwright on "Bonanza," James Garner as "Maverick," Richard Boone as Paladin on "Have Gun, Will Travel," Clayton Moore as the Lone Ranger and Jay Silverheels as Tonto.

drawn by the prestige of a guest role in the famous Western. Bette Davis appeared in "The Jailer" (1966-67). James Whitmore and Warren Oates played various lead roles over the years. While the 1968-69 season was being prepared, Faye Dunaway requested, after her success with the motion picture *Bonnie and Clyde,* that an episode be written for her. Calvin Clements, Sr., who later became executive story consultant, created the character Abelia, a young woman whose husband had deserted her and two young children to join an outlaw gang. His activity later widowed her. Miss Dunaway was unable to appear, and the role was instead played very ably by Jacqueline Scott, who returned to the character in the 1969-70 episode "A Man Called Smith."

Location filming had been restricted to that which could be done on day-trips from Los Angeles. In the spring of 1970, "Gunsmoke" undertook its first long-distance location jaunt to the Black Hills of South Dakota, with the historic town of Custer as its headquarters. In the years that followed, "Gunsmoke" traveled to the canyonlands of Utah, the Arizona desert, and the lush forests of Oregon. This, in turn, made more diversified and elaborate plots possible, allowing for an interesting array of guest characters. The 1970-71 two-parter "Snow Train" was an early vehicle for Loretta Swit, who went on to a lead in "M*A*S*H" (CBS 1972-83). In another two-parter that year, Jeanette Nolan and Dack Rambo co-starred in "Pike," which became the springboard for the Western comedy series "Dirty Sally." Rambo later went on to a featured role in the long-running CBS series "Dallas." The following year, Ruth Roman, a leading lady from the 1950s, appeared as a crusty madam in "Waste," filmed in Utah.

As the result of a conscious consolidation of writers and directors working in close collaboration with the production staff, other episodes were planned in which characters sometimes were brought back in different stories. The so-called "Gunsmoke family" had grown, as had the population of the fictitious Dodge City in the 1870s. The team of creative people who guided the series in its last several seasons has been referred to by one of its most ingenious writers as "a gentlemen's club." By another, the series was termed "a calling card," whereby doors were opened to show-business careers.

In this atmosphere were conceived Festus Haggen's hapless hillfolk family members, first introduced in the 1967-68 comedy "Hard Luck Henry," later returning in "Hill Girl" that same season, and "Uncle Finney" and "Gold Town" (1968-69). John Astin, Lou Antonio, Royal Dano, Victor French, Lane Bradbury, Anthony James and Burt Mustin were some of the actors who brought laughter to Dodge City.

Statistics show that Victor French was one of the most frequently seen guests on the series, usually in dramatic parts. In the show's last season he directed five of that year's 24 episodes. Later he went on to prominent regular roles on the NBC programs "Little House on the Prairie" and "Highway to Heaven."

The long list of writers, directors and actors associated with "Gunsmoke" over the years proves that the series served as a training ground and a springboard for many talented individuals and significant professional careers. The early TV half-hour years introduced a number of artists who later starred in various series of their own, among them Angie Dickinson, Carl Betz, Barbara Eden and James Drury; others, such as Charles Bronson, achieved motion picture fame or became successful in related entertainment careers.

Aaron Spelling has created and produced several popular network programs: "Burke's Law" (ABC 1963-65), retitled "Amos Burke, Secret Agent" (ABC 1965-66): "Charlie's Angels" (ABC 1976-81); "The Love Boat" (ABC 1977-86); "Hart to Hart" (ABC 1979-84); and Fox's "Beverly Hills 90210," to name just a few. Director Mark Rydell "toiled in the "Gunsmoke" vineyards," as executive producer John Mantley liked to call it, and later directed such memorable motion pictures as *The Reivers* (National General, 1969), *The Cowboys* (Warner Bros., 1972, *Cinderella Liberty* (20th Century Fox, 1973), *The Rose* (20th Century Fox, 1979) and *On Golden Pond* (Universal, 1981). Writers William Kelley and Earl Wallace won Academy Awards for their screenplay for the 1985 Paramount film, *Witness*. The basic story was originally assigned as a "Gunsmoke" episode but later abandoned, and was then developed for "The Macahans" (ABC, 1978-79), a series on which many former "Gunsmoke" personnel worked.

The series also developed its stock company of actors, those who played recurring roles as the citizens of Dodge City. Among these were Sam, the bartender (Glenn Strange), Louie Pheeters, the town drunk (James Nusser), Burke, the freight agent and town gossip (Ted Jordan), Hank, the stableman (Hank Patterson) and many others who became familiar faces over the years. It was through these and the principals, the plots and production values that "Gunsmoke" demonstrated more than "skill and attention to detail," as an early review commented.

The series left the air after its twentieth season, with the last of 636 episodes shown on March 31, 1975. To this day it holds the record as the longest-running network dramatic series. It is still airing in a number of markets and continues to be a favorite among the viewers who watched it the first time around, as well as by a new generation, too young to have seen it in the first-run broadcasts. The nostalgia is kept alive by a company called Radio Yesteryear in Sandy Hook, Connecti-

cut, which offers cassettes of the radio "Gunsmoke," and by Columbia House Video Library, which sells videocassette of a Collector's Edition of early half-hour, black-and-white episodes. In the late 1980s, CBS began filming a new series of made-for-television "Gunsmoke" movies, once more calling James Arness back to the saddle as a retired but still forceful Matt Dillon, ably sidekicked by Bruce Boxleitner.

"Gunsmoke" helped remind more than one generation of twentieth-century Americans that the real Old West was populated by real people with timeless problems, concerns, joys and sorrows. Its extended family of characters put human faces to the Westering experience and the mandate of Manifest Destiny, and to the flow of life as it was lived on the 1870s Kansas frontier. ■

THE GREAT "GUNSMOKE" QUIZ

BY LOREN D. ESTLEMAN

1. What was Doc Adams' first name?

a. Columbo   b. Abraham
c. Galen

2. The Long Branch was a safe place to drink, possibly because Matt Dillon spent so much time there. Most of the brawls took place in another Dodge City Saloon. Its name?

a. The Alhambra   b. The Bull's Head
c. Gilley's

3. Who ran the general store?

a. Ann Page   b. Judge Garth
c. Mr. Lathrop

4. Where did Matt spend most of his time when not in Dodge?

a. Abilene   b. Hays
c. Plato's Retreat

5. In a famous episode, which particular portion of Festus Haggen's anatomy was in danger of being shot off by his feuding kin?

a. Earlobe   b. His "I ♥ the Sons of
c. Nose   the Pioneers" tattoo

6. What Hollywood star turned down the role of Marshall Dillon but introduced the first episode?

a. Dan Dureya   b. John Wayne
c. Rory Calhoun

7. Who played Dillon in the radio version of "Gunsmoke"?

a. Lyle Talbot   b. William Conrad
c. Conrad Hilton

8. What part did Burt Reynolds play for four seasons?

a. Thad Greenwood
b. Kitty Russell   c. Quint Asper

9. What was Chester's last name?

a. Goode   b. Linguini
c. Pheeters

10. How may years was the show on the air?

a. Fifteen   b. Twenty
c. Twenty-five

11. Who owned the boardinghouse?

a. Johnson Howard
b. Ms. Hanna   c. Ma Smolley

12. Recommended restaurant.

a. Delmonico's   b. Hop Sing's
c. The Palmer House

13. Matt's favorite expression.

a. "Not tonight, Kitty! I have a
headache."
b. "Throw up your hands!"
c. "Hold it!"

14. Who ran the express office?

a. Nathan Burke   b. Percy Crump

c. Hiram Zippy

15. Name Matt's horse.

a. Fritz   b. Paint
c. It didn't have one.

16. Where was Matt wounded most often?

a. Cleveland   b. Left shoulder
c. Right leg

17. On what night of the week did "Gunsmoke" air for its first thirteen seasons?

a. Sunday   b. Monday
c. Saturday

18. What actor holds the record for being killed the most times by Matt?

a. John Wayne   b. Victor French
c. Morgan Woodward

19. What actor holds the distinction of playing the last man to loose a gunfight to Matt?

a. Tom Selleck   b. Gerald McRaney
c. Ronald Reagan

20. What was the major significance of "Gunsmoke" in television history?

a. It kept Peter Graves off the air until 1968.
b. It was the first dramatic program to feature a handicapped character in a continuing role.
c. It was the longest-running series with continuing characters.

Answers: 1-c, 2-b, 3-c, 4-b, 5-a, 6-b, 7-b, 8-c, 9-a, 10-b, 11-c, 12-a, 13-c, 14-a, 15-c, 16-b, 17-c, 18-b, 19-b, 20-c

THE CURTAIN

DREAMS WEST, REVISITED

BY THOMAS W. KNOWLES

TOGETHER WE'VE RIDDEN THE LONG, TANGLED TRAIL OF THE MYTH OF the Wild West, from the early Wild West shows to the modern cinematic Western and beyond. Despite the gulf that lies between the real West and Western fiction, we've traced the connection between them. We've seen how the Western in film and literature is an indelible component of the American character and culture, as much a part of our history as is the real West.

And yet, for more than a decade in recent history, American popular culture did its best to ignore the Western. If the Western myth is so central to the American character, why did Western fiction almost fade away during the late 1970s and the early 1980s? How and why did it survive? And why has it returned with such force in the 1990s?

First of all, television rode the Western to death in the '50s and '60s, when the majority of television dramas were Westerns. Story lines got stale or far-fetched, past the point to which viewers were willing to suspend their disbelief—the point at which any fiction loses its audience. In its search for newer, more relevant material, the television Western lost its connection to the roots of the Western myth.

The American character itself underwent serious stress in the late '60s and early '70s. Television Westerns became more violent in response to cultural changes, and movie Westerns countered with even more violence to attract audiences jaded by TV overexposure. That triggered a backlash. Body counts and battlefield scenes televised from the very real carnage of Vietnam made the fictional violence of Westerns less palatable. Also, for many Americans, it was a time for questioning old values and old myths, not for revering them. The traditional white hat/black hat conflicts of the Western faded into the grays of historical ambiguity.

Even the great "Gunsmoke" left the air in 1975. Television turned to family-oriented series with minor, less violent frontier themes, like "Little House on the Prairie," "Father Murphy" and "The Life and Times of Grizzly Adams." Motion pictures turned to ultra-violence.

Then the Western lost its greatest living icon, the powerful screen personality who could draw audiences even from among those who rejected the Western myth as a whole. In John Wayne's last film, *The Shootist* (1976 De Laurentis), he played gunfighter J.B. Books, victim of an enemy (cancer) he couldn't beat with his gun skills. It was an elegy not only for Wayne but for his era. When the Duke himself died on June 13, 1979, he took a substantial chunk of the old-fashioned Western's soul with him.

Only Clint Eastwood came close to matching the Duke's drawing power, perhaps because Eastwood's films appealed to the morally ambiguous times. Though his best '70s Westerns (*High Plains Drifter* and *The Outlaw Josey Wales*) ran along traditional themes, they still carried a touch of nihilism from the spaghetti Westerns that had launched his movie career.

The '70s was a decade for iconoclasts, and only non-traditional historical Westerns like *Jeremiah Johnson* (1972 Warner Brothers) and historically revisionist Westerns like *Little Big Man* (1970 Stockbridge/Hiller) did well at the box office. Despite a hit song by Bob Dylan, outlaw director Sam Peckinpah's mangled masterpiece, *Pat Garrett and Billy the Kid* (1973 MGM), didn't draw big audiences.

Though the Western had built Hollywood, in the '70s it became not only culturally *passe* but no longer a sure thing economically. After the film establishment orphaned the butchered version of Michael Cimino's *Heaven's Gate* (1980 Partisan) because it went far over budget, the critics incorrectly labeled it as historically inaccurate. The picture died at the box office. Suddenly, no studio wanted to sink money into another Western.

The low point came not long after the great Jay Silverheels died. The producers of *The Legend of the Lone Ranger* (1981 ITC), sued Clayton Moore to force a halt to his public appearances as the masked man. Instead of asking Moore to make a cameo appearance, they told America to forget the actor who had personified the Ranger for two generations. The script, which portrayed the Ranger as a campy superhero, reflected modern contempt for the traditional Western.

It was a sign of neglect, a long and subtle process by which most American moviemakers, writers and audiences had lost touch with the core Western myth. A host of blurred second- and third-generation copies had obscured the myth, and a new historical perspective, particularly in regard to past treatment of Native Americans in film, had called into question some of its traditional themes.

Traditional Western novels also declined in popularity. Conversely, only a Louis L'Amour byline guaranteed good sales and acceptance for a Western novel. Like John Wayne, L'Amour's popularity made him bankable even though he was a traditionalist.

L'Amour's popularity carried over into television, ably assisted by Sam Elliot, an actor born to play a L'Amour hero. Elliot stood out in "The Sacketts," a 1979 miniseries based on L'Amour's novels *The Daybreakers* and *Sackett,* and in the television adaptation of L'Amour's *The Shadow Riders.* In 1987, Elliot brought a L'Amour hero to cable television (HBO) in the author's own adaptation of *The Quick and the Dead.*

In the early '80s, small, independent companies kept the movie Western going with low budgets, new locations, quirky heroes and atypical stories: country singer Willie Nelson's *Barbarosa;* Canadian productions of *The Grey Fox* with veteran stuntman Richard Farnsworth, and *Harry Tracy* with Bruce Dern. Larger scale efforts fell short of the mark: Steve McQueen's realistic, downbeat *Tom Horn* was before its time; Walter Hill's *The Long Riders* concentrated more on cinematography than story.

The most popular "Western" of the early '80s wasn't about the American West at all—it was Australian director George Miller's *The Man From Snowy River.* Miller took a page from John Ford's book and used the magnificent Australian scenery as if it were the main character, a trick of the trade most American filmmakers had either forgotten or discarded.

The Western weathered the lean years in out-of-the-way places, preserved by those few actors, directors, writers and fans who still believed in the power of the Western myth. It took a resurgence in the Western novel to turn the tide—in particular, two books by authors not afraid to go back to the well for their inspiration.

The first was Evan S. Connell's *Son of the Morning Star* (1984), a revealing look at the life of George Armstrong Custer through his relationship with his wife, Libby. Connell approached the oft-told tale with a true sense of historical accuracy, one that matched human faces and human desires to the forces that drove two cultures into conflict.

The second breakthrough novel, Larry McMurtry's *Lonesome Dove,* was a surprise package considering the source. McMurtry usually wrote bleak, character-driven stories of the modern and post-modern West (*Hud, The Last Picture Show, Terms of Endearment*), many of which were made into Hollywood movies. In 1985, he turned an old screenplay he'd written with Jimmy Stewart, Henry Fonda and John Wayne in mind into an epic novel—*Lonesome Dove.* McMurtry skillfully blended the power

Robert Duvall and Tommy Lee Jones star in "Lonesome Dove" based on the Pulitzer Prize-winning novel by Larry McMurtry. (courtesy of CBS)

Jane Seymour stars as "Dr. Quinn, Medicine Woman" (1993 CBS) (courtesy of CBS, photo: Peter Kredenser)

of the Western myth with his own views of history to revive the timeless story of the great trail drives. True to his own style, he built his story around strong but fallible human characters. Augustus McCrae and Woodrow Call drove McMurtry's readers willingly to suspend disbelief as competently as they drove their herd to Montana.

At the same time, two American-made Western films pushed the envelope of resistance. Lawrence Kasdan (*Raiders of the Lost Ark*) wrote and directed *Silverado* (1985 Columbia), a big budget, big-hearted, old-fashioned action-adventure Western. Though the film didn't quite revive the Western, it gave Kevin Costner a chance to stand out as Scott Glenn's fast-gun kid brother in a fine ensemble cast.

In *Pale Rider* (1985 Malpaso), Clint Eastwood's confident performance invoked strong resonances of the mythic gunfighter turned savior in *Shane* (1953 Paramount), antithesis to his killer ghost in his cynical *High Plains Drifter.* With its rich historical look, attention to detail and modern production values, *Pale Rider* was an old-fashioned morality tale made the way they all *should* have been made.

Still, most of the '80s Western televison series ("Wildside," "Paradise," "The Young Riders") failed to find a large enough audience to satisfy marketing demographics. In 1987, CBS brought Matt Dillon back to television and reunited James Arness and Amanda Blake for the last time in the first "Gunsmoke" special, "Return to Dodge." CBS followed it with a series of specials starring Arness as a retired Matt Dillon, including "The Last Apache" (1989), "To the Last Man" (1991), "The Long Ride" (1993) and "One Man's Justice" (1994). Matt Dillon appeared to be impervious to age and time, as did "Gunsmoke" itself. The CBS movies proved that the Western could work on television in specials, if not in a series.

But it was the 1988 CBS television miniseries of McMurtry's *Lonesome Dove* that thrust the Western once more into its deserved prominence. Robert Duvall and Tommy Lee Jones proved more than equal to the task of portraying McMurtry's two old Texas Rangers, Augustus McCrae and Woodrow Call. Along with Danny Glover, Robert Urich, Rick Schroder, Anjelica Huston, Diane Lane and Frederic Forrest, they brought the strong, character-driven Western drama to the small screen. The success of "Lonesome Dove" no doubt prompted CBS to continue the series of "Gunsmoke" specials and to develop "Dr. Quinn, Medicine Woman" (premiered 1993), their critically acclaimed series starring Jane Seymour as a frontier physician.

On cable, Turner began a series of TNT Originals with a remake of Gore Vidal's version of *Billy the Kid* (1989), with Val Kilmer as the Kid and Duncan Regehr as Pat Garrett. Sam Elliot and Katharine Ross returned as characters from L'Amour country in the TNT Original of *Conagher* (1993); Elliot and Ross co-wrote the script. *Conagher* not only renewed Elliot's connection to L'Amour's works, it gave the late, great Ken Curtis a chance for a last Western role.

The new breakthrough for Westerns on the big screen came with *Dances With Wolves* (1990 Tig/Orion), based on Michael Blake's novel. Kevin Costner not only directed the visually rich three-hour epic but took the starring role as John Dunbar, the lost young cavalry officer befriended by the Sioux. Even though *Dances With Wolves* sometimes sacrificed historical accuracy for political correctness (the Sioux weren't *always* such sensitive, New Age guys), it did give Native American actors (Rodney Grant, Graham Greene) a chance to play the Indians for a change. Not only did it tell a hell of a good story, using the sweep and character of the land, it also swept the Academy Awards.

If anyone doubted that the Western had returned, Clint Eastwood's *Unforgiven* (also in 1992) convinced them otherwise. *Unforgiven* was the perfectly evolved Western, a revisionist blending of the original Western myths with a 1990's historical perspective. Essentially another old-fashioned morality play, it contained all of the character elements of the classic Western, from Eastwood's own performance as the redeemed sinner (William Munny) who falls from grace, to that of Anna Thompson as Delilah, the innocent prostitute. But though he worked from a classic pattern, Eastwood didn't allow *Unforgiven* to take the expected fictional turns; instead, he surprised the audience at each turn by adhering to an uncompromising and grim reality. In skillfully blending the classic myth with stark realism, Eastwood proved he was at the peak of his style as both an actor and a director.

Oscars for Eastwood and Gene Hackman (Little Bill Daggett) were only the beginning of the deluge of honors, and *Unforgiven's* success sent everyone in Hollywood scrambling to make Westerns. So many companies applied for permits to film in Monument Valley that the Utah Bureau of Land Management had trouble handling the rush.

The new interest in Indians as major characters spurred two film versions of the life of the Apache war chief, Geronimo, in 1993. The TNT Original, *Geronimo,* starring Joseph Running Fox as Geronimo, with Nick Ramus as Mangus Coloradus, actually came closer to telling the Apache's side of the story than Walter Hill's *Geronimo, An American Legend* (Columbia). Wes Studi (Magua in *The Last of the Mohicans*) played the Geronimo, but the screenplay made him something of an enigma; Jason Patric, Robert Duvall and Gene Hackman got top billing.

In 1993, the young Fox network introduced its first Western, "The Adventures of Brisco County, Jr.," a lighthearted adventure series star-

Clint Eastwood stars as outlaw William Munny with Gene Hackman in "Unforgiven" (1992 Warner Bros.)

Back row, l-r: Christian Clemenson, Julius Carry, John Astin, Bruce Campbell (as Brisco County, Jr.) and Comet; seated front: Kelly Rutherford of "The Adventures of Brisco County, Jr." (1993 Fox) (courtesy of Fox Broadcasting, photo: E.J. Camp)

ring B movie hero Bruce Campbell in the title role. Like "The Wild, Wild West," the series introduced fantastic and science-fictional elements into stories set at the turn of the century, but it did so with a wicked sense of humor. It also did homage to the B Western by hiring former Western TV stars for cameos and writing in respectful send-ups of old Western movies. Unfortunately, Fox canceled the series in 1994.

Even if the Western series can't survive on network television, the new cable medium seems ready to make room for the modern version of the B Western. Baby boomers who grew up with Duncan Renaldo's portrayal of O. Henry's Robin Hood of the Old West welcomed the TNT Original "The Cisco Kid" (1994), with Jimmy Smits and Cheech Marin as Cisco and Pancho. Richard Donner's new version of *Maverick* (1994 Warner Brothers), with Mel Gibson, Jodi Foster and James Garner, also demonstrated that the old barriers between the large and the small screens no longer apply. Advances in technology may have more impact on the Western than changes in tastes and attitudes.

In fact, Hollywood's attitude toward the Western has so changed that the two major Western films of 1994 dared to try a much-filmed subject — the gunfight at the O.K. Corral. *Tombstone* (Hollywood Pictures), which starred Kurt Russell as Wyatt Earp, Val Kilmer (who stole the show as Doc Holliday), Sam Elliot as Virgil, and Bill Paxton as Morgan, took the more conventional approach, sticking to the events leading up to the Wild West's most famous shoot-out and its aftermath. In *Wyatt Earp* (Warner Brothers), *Silverado* partners Lawrence Kasdan and Kevin Costner reunited to produce a three-hour epic version of the controversial lawman's life. They assembled a huge cast, which included Dennis Quaid, Gene Hackman, Michael Madsen, Isabella Rossellini, JoBeth Williams and Mare Winningham. Ten or twelve years ago, it would have been unthinkable to sink such an investment of money and talent into a Western.

The Western is back. Is it back to stay? A look at its history tells us that our interest in the Western runs in cycles — it has fallen out of favor before. The fictional Western faded in the '70s because, as it existed, it no longer fit changing cultural attitudes. It had grown stale. After almost a century of building on itself, copying itself and diluting itself, the old Western collapsed like a house of cards.

The core of the Western myth survives because it exists independent of fiction, which is after all only the medium in which we interpret it. It's made up of equal parts of fantasy, legend and history, a true source of dreams to which we may return when we tire of re-runs and copies. If we remember that, the Wild West will live forever in print, on big screens and small — and in our imaginations. ■

There Was an Old West

By Will Henry

Buffalo being herded (courtesy of National Buffalo Association)

WHEN ONE WHO HAS WORKED THROUGH THIRTY YEARS AND FIFTY books to protect and preserve it, then comes to that place wherein time bids him say godspeed to the Western Story, what is there for him to set down that will speak truly to the heart of the matter—the secret heart of it—as he has come to know and treasure it in his own lifetime? What canvas can be painted in a properly few brushstrokes that will reveal, by half, his love affair—man, boy, and now old man—with the American West? What poetry can describe with adequate *amourette* the romantic dalliance ensuing with the American Western, that so uniquely salt-cured native literature of our vanished frontier past?

And what, really, is this unwanted child of our American storytelling heritage? What is there about the Western that, long orphaned and roundly disdained by the world of letters, has allowed it to survive to become our only original literature?

As well, who are we, the vintners of its thousand myths and legends? We who have all toiled lovingly amid its arid cacti vines to bottle the rawhide wines of the Old West against the day when minstrels may no longer stroll, and the voice of the storyteller falls silent upon the land. What wondrous alchemy of the sagebrush Magi did Ned Buntline bring to his *reductio ad impossible* of the lore of the American frontier that it has spread 'round the world to universal popularity? Indeed, that it has since become the glass of critical fashion, the very mold of academic form. Why are respected full professors of English Literature and staid Doctors of American History suddenly mad for what the ruder populace has been acclaiming, *vox clamantis in deserto,* since Edward Z. C. Judson personally created the Wild West—created it whole, out of the entire cloth of his posturing heroes, vacuous heroines, verdigreed villains and, beyond all, his mythic land and time of their being that itself never existed?

Writers of the Western and the West have "come a far piece" from Judson's dreadful/marvelous dime novels.

The literature of the West has become a serious literature.

College courses are taught upon it and, as recruits from these classes

> "...but the loveliest myth of all America was the far West...a lost impossible province...where men were not dwarfs and where adventure truly was."
>
> BERNARD DE VOTO

go forth, more courses will be taught and more serious scholarship imposed upon the storytellers' original wares. Just here, let the keepers of the Western's watchfires beware. This riskful *abrazo* returns the matter to its positing: What is the Western and why has it survived these hundred-plus years as the people's choice, and now the brand-new pet of the tenured guardians of the Western World, on campus?

The West, friends. That is what the Western is all about.

In the beginning, the Western spelled hope. It held out the West to unnumbered emigrants as the American Hope for a new day and a better life. It is no different today. Through the medium of the American Western, in all its art forms, hope is held forth to any and all the of earth around who *must* believe there is a better day to come and that, if only man can be true to himself, there is nothing he cannot dream to conquer.

It is a message, pilgrims. To all people everywhere. Don't give up. Fight on. Live Clean. Be True. Be square. Be fair. You will always win in the end. You must; it is the Code of the Old West.

But we all know there never was an Old West.

Never could have been, really.

Still, something remains. Something poignant with yesteryears. Redolent of mountain red cedar and yellow aspen. Splashing with snow-cold water. Grand of raw blue sky. Cotton cloud. Woodsmoke adrift in the valley. Afar the metaled ringing of an ax. The bell of a cow. The alerting whicker of a pony, nostrils to the wind. The lowing mutter of the herd bull up on the bench beyond the fork. A woman's voice calling through the evening hush. A child's laughter, far away as heaven, near as the heartbeat it celebrates. Sunset cry of loon on mountain meadow marsh. Soughing of the pines, red with the downing sun. Man at musical chant driving cattle from the higher grass. *Whoo dogie, whoo dogie,* easy across the slide, *coo-ee, coo-ee,* we're home. The night is coming in and so are we. Safe off the mountain, *coo-ee, dogie, coo-ee.*

No Old West you say?

Listen to the cowbell. Smell the cedar incense on the wind. Hear the axblade sing. Hark to the rider talking down his cattle.

The Old West lives in an untold legion of human hearts and minds.

Let it stay there.

Don't ever change it. Cherish its myth, remember its legend, write down its folklore. Guard it, defend it, keep it safe, that you may pass it on in your own time as something you want your child to have and to know as you have had and known it, unspoiled and as a true believer.

Keep the faith, friends; we all know the real truth.

There was an Old West.

There *had* to be.

■